BOOKS BY

JAMES A. MICHENER

Tales of the South Pacific
The Fires of Spring
Return to Paradise
The Voice of Asia
The Bridges at Toko-Ri
Sayonara
The Floating World
The Bridge at Andau
Hawaii
Report of the County Chairman
Caravans
The Source
Iberia
Presidential Lottery
The Quality of Life
Kent State: What Happened and Why
The Drifters
A Michener Miscellany: 1950–1970
Centennial
Sports in America
Chesapeake
The Covenant
Space
Poland
Texas
Legacy
Alaska
Journey
Caribbean
The Eagle and the Raven
Pilgrimage
The Novel
The World Is My Home: A Memoir
James A. Michener's Writer's Handbook: Explorations in Writing and Publishing

with A. Grove Day
Rascals in Paradise

with John Kings
Six Days in Havana

JAMES A. MICHENER'S WRITER'S HANDBOOK

JAMES A. MICHENER'S

WRITER'S HANDBOOK

Explorations in Writing and Publishing

RANDOM HOUSE
NEW YORK

Published in the United States by Random House, Inc., New York and simultaneously in Canada by Random House of Canada Limited, Toronto.

Grateful acknowledgment is made to Random House, Inc., and McClelland & Stewart, Inc., for permission to reprint excerpts from *Journey* by James A. Michener.

ISBN 0-679-74126-7

Manufactured in the United States of America

Book design by Carole Lowenstein

Contents

A Word of Explanation

The writer who sits at her or his desk with an empty piece of paper staring back is like the explorer who stands at the edge of a new continent, uncertain of how to proceed. The basic process in writing a novel, a short story, or a play is one of constant exploration. Why does this defect in character lead to that behavior? Where do we go from here? How do you bridge the awful gap between a stirring start and a worthy conclusion?

This book provides visual proof of how inescapable this constant exploration is, how imprecisely it is sometimes pursued, and how it can lead to many false starts. Exploration is, as many adventurers in exotic lands have discovered, a process of trial and error, of selecting and rejecting a variety of courses before deciding on what is most profitable. Discovering the proper course of a narrative is like the charting of a new river as one follows its twists and turns.

The manuscript pages reproduced here show an exploring mind at work. Although the pages are rarely laid out in neat columns of tidy sentences, they do represent the search for exact procedure, the right name, and, sometimes, the deviation from the norm that would be more appropriate. They are offered as they came from my desk, and, obviously, each page was subsequently pored over and evaluated. More important, the pages that outline entire books, or substantial chapters within those books, depict ideas and choices caught in mid-flight while the writer was struggling for control.

I call this a workbook, for it shows in step-by-step fashion how the manuscript for a published book moves through a complex chain of operations from initial concept to finished book. It is therefore not a book on writing, for that's only one third of the job, nor is it a book on editing, because that comes late in the process. And it certainly isn't a book on the preparation of the finished manuscript for the printer, because that concluding part of the system is left in hands other than the writer's.

No, this is a portrait of exploration. A workbook that begins as close as possible to the moment when the idea for the book is first conceived, moves through the tentative early steps, looks at how the writer herself or himself edits his own work, then moves to the skilled editor, the uniquely gifted copy editor, the illustrator or cartographer, and finally to the provisional galleys, which signal that the work is truly in print and, with some polishing touches, is eligible for publication. Shown are the sweat and grime of these various steps—considered romantic exercises by those who have never performed them.

The virtue of this workbook is that it presents these steps as they apply to passages of such limited length that the reader can keep them in mind while turning the pages. By following individual sections, paragraphs, sentences, or even specific words, the reader can trace the writer's thought processes.

The subject matter has been chosen from two of my published books, the novel *Journey* and the nonfiction *The World Is My Home,* and it will be interesting to judge which of the two forms presented the more difficult problems. Actual pages are shown, often as they came directly from the typewriter or word processor. I use the former exclusively, my secretary the latter, for it requires a dexterity I do not have. Although all original editing was done by hand, it is the ease of the secretary's word processor that makes true editing possible.

My books have been praised—or condemned—as being 'easy to read.' The book that follows proves the truth of Nathaniel Hawthorne's growl: 'An easy read is a damned hard write.'

Because in my old-fashioned cut-and-paste kind of editing I use paper of different colors to keep track of what I'm doing, throughout this book to achieve differentiation and clarity, a mix of Bendays has been used. I invite the reader to check 'Bendays' in the dictionary, for it is one of the miracles of the printing profession and will be used here to good effect.

JOURNEY

A Canadian Novella

Salvaging a Canadian Manuscript

The genesis of my novel *Journey* was extraordinary. I had for some years worked on a long novel about Alaska, and whereas the main body of the manuscript hit those topics that would generally be of interest and might to some degree be familiar to the American reader, I was determined that anyone who read the book would be aware that Alaska had been in Russian hands longer than in American, and I planned some good chapters on that point. I would think that any sensible writer on Alaska would be obliged to dwell on that inescapable fact.

But I also had a highly personal agenda. I've always been an admirer of Canadian history, the Canadian landscape, and Canadians in general. However, my interest this time was not in Canada as such, but in the great Mackenzie River, perhaps the least known and appreciated of all the world's great rivers. I was determined to do the Mackenzie justice, and to let the world know that there had been a Canadian gold rush to parallel the well-known one through Seattle and Alaska.

With those motives impelling me, I fitted into my Alaska novel not a separate chapter about the Canadian gold rush through the little town of Edmonton in Alberta, but rather an extended episode within the long chapter about the gold rush in general. Selecting from the hundreds of 1897–1909 characters who filtered through Edmonton, I chose four upper-class Englishmen with their Irish servant and set the five loose from their London club, brought them across the Atlantic by a new type of ship and across Canada by the transcontinental railroad recently put together by Canadian and American geniuses.

Now they found themselves on a branch of the Mackenzie, and, perilously late in the autumn, they ventured north, intending to sail as far as they could before the great river froze and then, close to the Arctic Circle, to hunker down for the winter and wait for the spring thaws that would allow a speedy trip to the gold fields. Xenophobic to a ridiculous degree, Lord Luton, leader of the party, was determined to make his entire trip on what he called empire soil—that is, without touching the United States or its properties; this ill-conceived plan led to disaster and the death of three of his team.

When the manuscript was finished, my editor and I saw that this segment of the chapter on gold had grown so long that cuts were obligatory, and I acquiesced in eliminating the Mackenzie tale. *Alaska* was published without it and no one could have noticed the loss, for the episode had nothing to do with Alaska, since its characters never set foot in that territory, and its deletion in no way damaged the novel.

But I had spent so much research time and energy on the story of the splendid river that I could not easily surrender it, and after finding that not even the passing of years dimmed my enthusiasm, one day I had a friend call a Canadian publisher with a proposal: 'Jim Michener has a short novel about Canada half done and he wonders if you'd like to publish it.'

'We'll fly down to Florida and look it over' was the response. Thus the expanded novel outlined on the opposite page came to be written and later published. This workbook explains the steps whereby this unplanned relationship produced a book.

It has been my habit, when brooding over the possibility of writing a long manuscript on a specific subject, to reach a moment of decision and on that day to type out, in the upper-right-hand corner of a sheet of typewriter paper, a statement of what propelled me to this decision. The next day, in the opposite corner, I type out the basic ideas to be presented in the book. In the space below I write the probable chapters as I am able to devise them at the moment. This single page becomes my intellectual and artistic guide for the next three years.

17 April 1988

My interst in the Canadian novelette has not abated, and I'm about convinced to call Cana da and proposition them on taking the novel. If so, and if they accept, I have some stron g ideas as to how the relativelt short segme nt [illegible] be nurttured into a real novel with a tre[illegible]ndous impact. I see it in three sectio ns: I. Getting to Edmonton; II. Rafting dow n the Mackenzie and first winter in the Arct ic at some point near the Gravel, a riveette wh ch enchants me so much I'd like to spend a winter there; III. Disaster along the Peel and the hike across barren land to Dawson. I have much of the basic material in mind vut would need more data about crossing the Atla ntic by ship, across Canada by rail, and the fknal crossing of the wilderness. But this c ould be accomplished; also more about that w oman whose photo has always stayed with me.

15 April 1988

As I take my evening walks these days my mind lingers on the manuscript of the Canadian segment of *Alaska*, and I cannot dismiss it. I live with L rd L ton and think his relationship with Murphy, or whatever I was calling him in *Alaksa*, was quite solid, especially their work together to save themselves during the last leg of their terrible journey. Almost as if someone wanted to ignite my interest, a woman journalist call- ed me from Toronto for an kost intelligent chat, and I do think I shall call her back and commission her to find a publisher in Canada who might want to take a risk on this manuscript. That wou;d be a most improp er way to market a novel, but I can't involve anyone in New York. I think I'll have John call her in con- fidence; I'd be too embarrassed, and she might ne, too but something very good could come of this. I believe I'd call it, if this goes through, *Voyagers*, as they drift down the Mackenzie, a river of powerful signifi- cance for me. Could be quite good.

I. The trip to Edmonton

The news from Seattle
Assembling the team
Crossing the Atlantic
The Canadian Railway
Conjoy & Edmonton
How end?
Indians dancing at night
Buying the boat
More about woman
BOAT ON GREAT LAKES ??

III. From the Peel to Dawson

MURPHY
FINNERTY
FOGARTY

The big decision at the KAT - BELL - Porcupine
The Peel.
More detail at the 2ND Camp
Boots, hunting
MORE DETAIL on the land between rivers.
The 2 men in the wilderness
DAWSON AS IS
MOSQUITOS
CANS OF FOOD
IDEA OF HAN GOOD
3 GRAVES

WAPITI
STENCH

REFUSE TO CUT BOAT
ABANDON BOAT
DEATH OF H.C. AS IS

PEEL
ABANDON

SWAMP
MOSQ
HAN
GRAVES
FAREWELL
THEP AS IS

DAWSON
AS IS
SHIP
WOMAN
HUSB
AUSTR
HOW LONG
3 DEAD
PRAY
LL. GEORGE

II. The Mackenzie

They have their boat at start
The Rentor's boat (Indian?)
Follow them down the river
(always || to the Yukon)
STORM AT Great Bear Lake
LOSE SOMEONE?
CAMP AT GRAVE
DEATH OF PHILIP
TRIP TO NORMAN
REJECTION OF MAPS
INDIAN BACK TO BUILD CAMP
WRECK AT GREAT BEAR
They see the woman - KEPT

HERMEN LOST AT G.B.L

Mapping the Terrain

I am tempted to say that maps were more important to this novel than to any of the other writing I've done, but that would not be true, for the maps to both *The Source* and *Centennial* were crucial to their narratives. But *Journey* presented special problems because the great Mackenzie and its unique lakes had to be detailed but most important of all was that nest of little twisting rivers far north of the Arctic Circle where gold seekers made life-or-death decisions. The Bell, the Rat and the Porcupine, three little nothing rivers, intertwined in a remarkable way, for if one negotiated them properly, one found a low navigable pass across the top of the Rocky Mountains and the relative safety of the majestic Yukon. If one missed the cutoff through ignorance or arrogance, one found oneself in the dreadful Peel River and faced a very real risk of death through having to lay over an extra winter in the Arctic. Maps had to show this.

And when the party whose fortunes I was following did get frustrated by the Peel, I had to have maps of an area that had not been properly mapped. I had to draw my own, with each lettered spot a focus of terror.

NOTES FOR THE MAP MAKER

Top Map

The main purpose of this map is to show the relationship between the Bell and the Rat, with the Continental Divide intruding between their headwaters but providing a negotiable land portage. Anything to make this more intelligible to the reader will be appreciated. Show Porcupine, Bell, Rat, Mackenzie, Peel. Do not show Fort McPherson as that clutters. Label northern exit of the Porcupine 'To Fort Yukon'. Label south exit of Porcupine 'To near Dawson' but do not, of course, use quotation marks.

Bottom Map

The main purpose of this map is to help the reader follow the final leg of Lord Luton's expedition as it concludes its second winter in the Arctic. The camp where deaths occur must stand out on the left bank of Peel; their route in the half-boat west on the Peel; their turn south on the Peel to the point where they abandon the boat and set forth on foot. Dotted line should show the course they traversed with text showing the tundra, the mosquito attacks, and their lifesaving meeting with the Han Indians. The three graves should be shown, and the separation point where Luton and Fogarty climb into the mountains while the Han return to their home. Their course into Dawson should be shown and the manner in which the Klondike flows into the Yukon.

Note: The Continental Divide is giving me a lot of trouble. I am not skilled in depicting terrain, and have never mastered the symbolic representation of tall mountains. If you can correct this deficiency, I'd like to have you show the Continental Divide down the complete map or maps.

Note: The mouths of the Mackenzie provide the world's best visual depiction of how a drownedriver mouth degenerates into a swampy delta usful to no one except caribou. Please do your best. My best isn't so hot.

The Area of Confusion

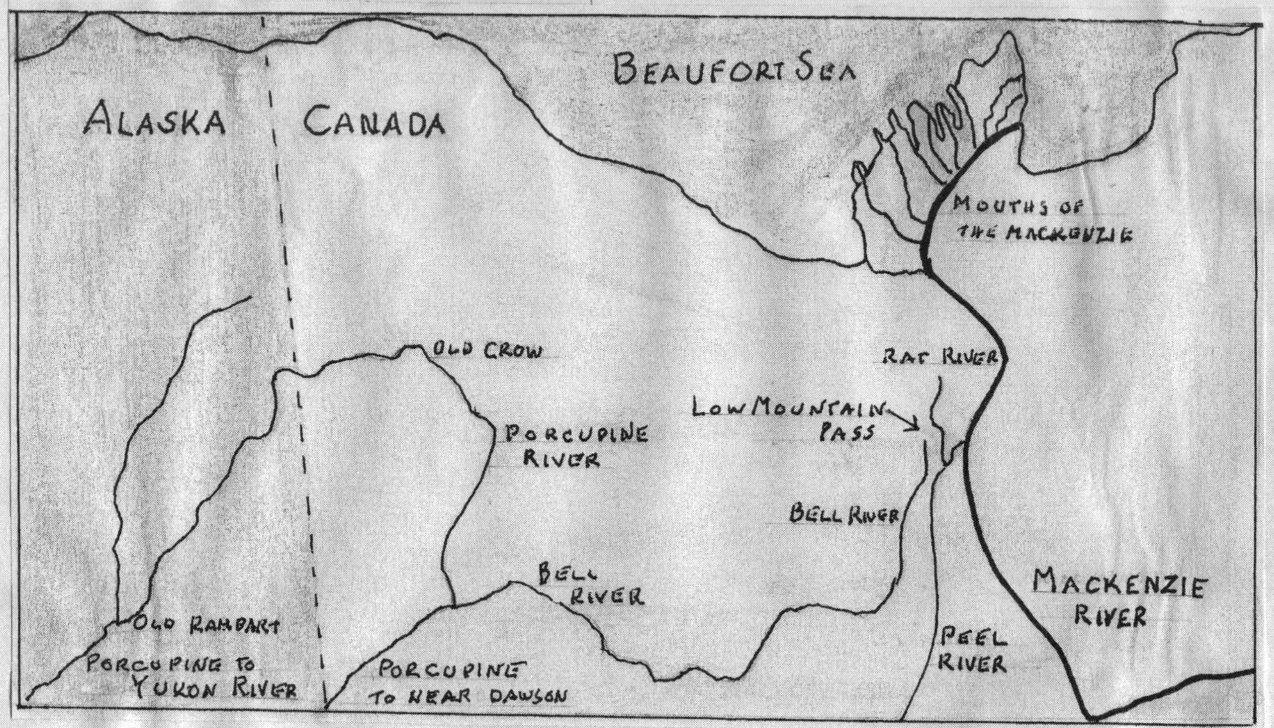

The Peel River Disaster

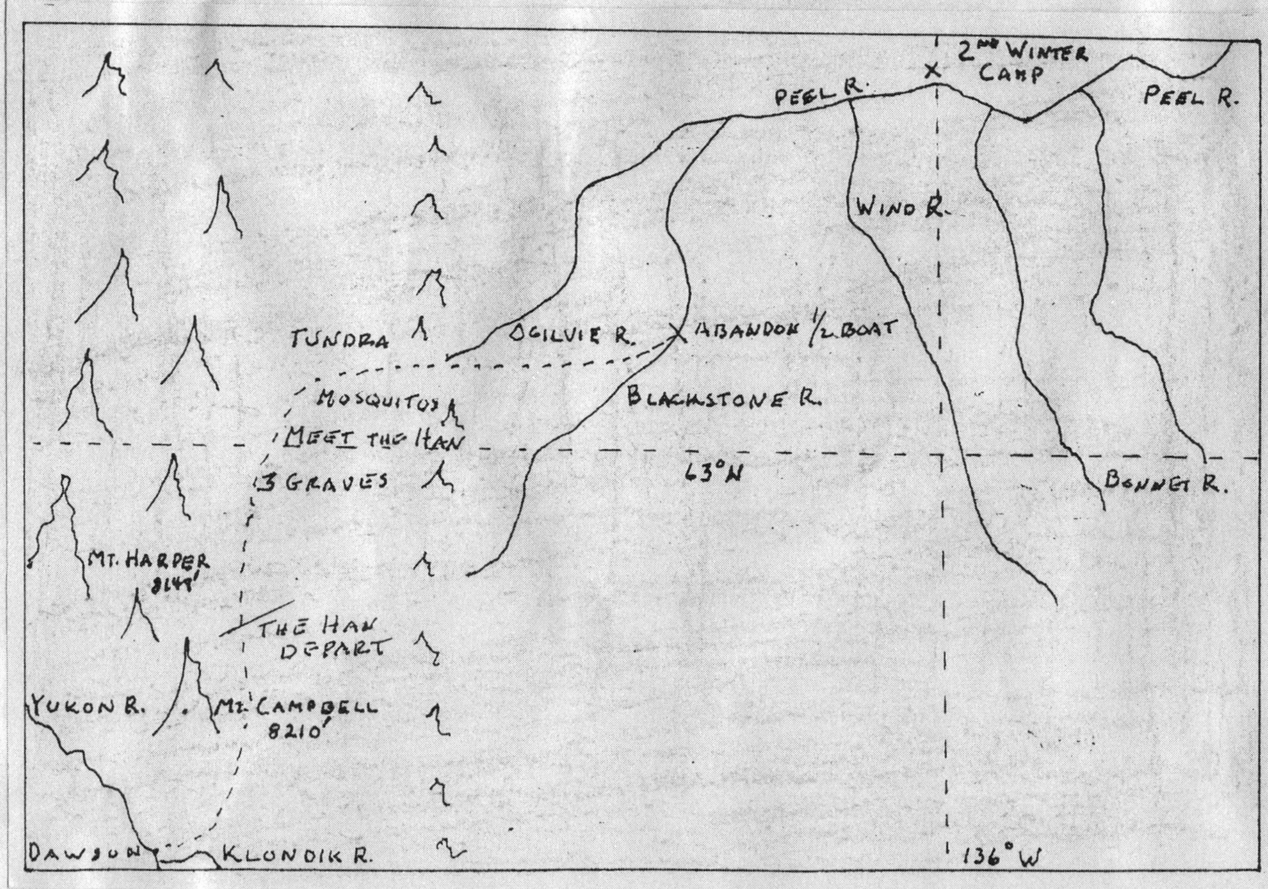

The Original Draft–Unedited Carbon Copy

If any aspect in this book warrants giving it the title 'Exploration,' it is this group of ten pages, which show exactly what comes from the typewriter as I try to steer my thoughts through a difficult problem. At the time I wrote this passage I was convinced it formed an exciting segment of a chapter in my Alaska novel. It focused on the little-known Canadian gold rush that occurred simultaneously with the great American rush to the Yukon. Since I had high hopes for this chapter, I wrote it with enthusiasm but with no firm direction.

If I seem to be fumbling around in these pages, you must remember that in the famed Alaskan gold rush of the late 1890s, the rush, that hideous torture of getting to the fields, did occur in American Alaska, but the gold itself was found only in the Canadian Klondike. Even that great wandering river, the Yukon, which was the scene of one of the most memorable episodes during the rush, was completely Canadian insofar as the gold mania was concerned; it did not enter Alaskan territory till a short distance beyond Dawson City. I hoped to make the American reader aware of these contradictions. As I worked I had no intimation that this material would ultimately be published as a Canadian book. It was part of my American novel, and a strong part.

Each of these provisional pages was typed slowly with two fingers on a heavy old-style manual typewriter. Because I like to cram the maximum number of words on a page, I use narrow margins and type right to the bottom of the page; this excuses me from frequent changes of pages and carbons. To print the maximum number of characters per line, I invariably use a machine with an elite typeface, as compact as is practical, and I go to great pains to find and nurture those old beauties.

When I decided to move to Alaska to try my hand at a novel about the state, I stipulated only one requirement: 'I must have an old elite manual typewriter.' When I reached Sitka, where I would live in a log cabin for much of three years, I found a very nice machine awaiting me, a huge heavy affair with the biggest pica type I'd ever seen. Look at the various pages from that first typing and you'll see what I mean. My margins are narrow, the last line scrapes the bottom of the page. So I am being conservative, but the type looks as big as a barn, necessitating the constant rolling in of new sheets of paper. I am not happy when I look at those carbons.

For use in this book they have had to be retyped on a word processor, which fortunately approximates closely the big type originally used. In all respects this is my original effort at writing a novel.

As I work I follow two rules: 'Search for the right name till you find it. And write as if you knew everything in the world.' In obedience to the first I do not hesitate to change the names of my characters even in the middle of a sentence if a better surfaces, and I am free to do this experimenting because when the page of typing is transferred to a word processor, it's a simple trick to tell that wizard machine: 'Throughout the manuscript, change the name *Herbert* to *Alistair*,' and in a short time the processor obeys. Resonant names are of major importance to me and I play around with them, thanks to the processor.

Because in this first draft I am struggling to outline a narrative progression, I do not interrupt my thought processes to check with almanacs, atlases, or encyclopedias to verify dates, spellings, or other data; I am aware as I type that I don't have the facts, but I am secure in the knowledge that I'll be able to find them when I go back to edit. So, for uncertainties I either leave a blank or type in what I guess to be the correct information adding immediately after the data a series of question marks: 'Magna Carta was granted by King John???? in 1215????,' with the intention of dealing with them later when I have my research books at hand. I advocate this strategy, because the forward motion of the narrative is all-important.

The other device I have used to good effect is to draw a big round penciled O in the left margin opposite any passage that I realize is not what I seek. I rarely stop typing to correct it then, for I react poorly to interruptions, but when the draft of the segment is completed, those big gaping O's stare at me until the marked passages are emended and improved.

But that was the last fresh meat the enjoyed before Christmas, and one night in early January, after Blythe had lost three more stainless teeth, the young man said: 'I doubt I shall see spring.'

'Now look here, Trevor,' Luton began to bluster, but the young fellow sai with the gentleness that had always marked him: 'Evelyn, will you please find my Palgrave?' and when the precious little book was found, the one that contained the lyrics and the odes which made English different from all other languages, Trevor asked: 'Will you read some of the short poems?' and in his strong baritone Luton read those wonderuully simple lines, those single thoughts which seemed to reprewent the best that England had ever offered the world: 'My heart ache ,and a drowsy numbness pains...' or 'She dwelt among the untrodden ways...' or 'Tell me where is Fancy bred...'

As this essence of love and beauty and the longings of youth filled the cabin, Blythe sighed and thereafter his breath was unevenly and he said: 'Evelyn, will you read me the Herrick?' but Luton could not find it, so Trevor in his trembling hands leafed through the pages and found the magical six lines:

'Whenas in silks my Juila goes
Then, then (methinks) how sweetly flows
That liquefaction of he clothes.

Next, when I cast mine eyes and see
That brave vibration each way free;
O how that glittering taketh me!'

Looking at Carpenter and not at Luton, he said: 'When I reached home I was to have married Julia Deland, your cousin. Will you tell her?' And in this ca in close to the Arctic Circle, with the temperature minus fifty-seven and with escape in any direction impossible, Trevor Blythe, twenty-three years old, die

SPACE

As before, February was the month of hell and ice, except that this year there was no spring-like break in the middle, and much of the misery it brought stemmed from the fact that the days were lengthening, visibly so, but the rate was so slow and the persistence of the cold so deadening that it seemed a perversion, a teasing of the spirit. Spring was coming but it did not come.

Camp routine continued as before. Lord Luton shaved, and tended his clothe , and mardhed erect rather than bent over as some did in order to keep whateve heat they had trapped in their belly. He ran three laps in this winter's version of a track and he goaded others into doing the same. He ate sparingly, preferring that others take the larger portions, and he did everything possibl to sustain the spirits of his two remaining partners. He was an impeccable leader, and barring that one dreadful night when he threatened to shoot Murphy he never lost his composure. His party had fallen upon rough times and he intended leading the survivors to safety.

Harry Carpenter was the regimental major. His clipped mustache had proliferated into a beard, but he kept it clipped, too, and when he sat in the cab in divested of the heavy clothes he had to wear when outside, he was a han some man, not so rugged as before and somewhat drawn about the face because of the scurvy which attacked him , but still a proper officer of relaxed bearing rather than stiff. Had he stayed in India and become the colonel of his regiment his men would have called him 'good old Harry,' and here in the wastes of northern Canada he was the same. He did not run every day; he couldn't, but when he felt that Luton was sioently chiding him he tried; but after one lap he would return to the cabin exhausted.

He was reading Great Expectations for the third time, not aloud this time for neither Luton or Murphy had cared much for the story the first time around and had more or less complained at the waste of time during the second reading. He was sorry that he had confided to Murphy his concern about his incipient scurvy, but now he wished he had someone with whom to discuss the matter; to do so with either Luton or Murphy seemed quite impossible and what was worse improper, He suffered his debilitating disease in silence, supposing that Murphy had informed Luton of the matter. Throughout the cabin, night and day, here was a conspiracy of silence regarding his affloction, and he even more than the others wanted it to be that way.

Murphy resembled his master in his stolid acceptance of conditions. He ran with Luton on most days. He sought vainly to find the meat that would ensure the safety of his team, and he maintained that stubborn cheerfulness which made and good Irish serving man a model of his calling. Though not called upon to wait on his companions, he found pleasure in heating Lord Luton's shaving water in the morning and in honing and stropping the razor. He helped Carpenter in a dozen ways and strove to maintain good spirits in the cramped quarters. He was appalled that they should be spending a second winter in such surroundings and he watched almost breathlessly for even the slightest promise of spring: 'Soon we'll be over the mountains, that I'm sure, and there will be the gold-fields.' He was the only one who ever mentioned gold; the other two had never been obsessed with it and were now concerned only with survival.

But as February, that cruel month, waned, so did Carpenter's reserves; each day he grew weaker until once toward the end of the month he was unable to get out of bed in the morning, which now showed a clear difference from night. When 'You joining us for a bit of running?' Luton asked he grinned and said: 'I shall sit this out in the tea tent,' as if they were participating in a cricket match.

On the last day of February Lord Luton lost his composure and, sick at heart over the weakening condition of his friend, he sat on Carpenter's bed and took him by the shoulders: Look here, Harry, this won't do. It won't do at all.' Harry, thinking that he had been rebuked for purposeless malingering and unable because of his illness to see that Luton was merely using the hale-and-hearty approach of the regimental messhall, took offense at his friend's chiding.

Hiding his intention, he rose on pitifully weakened legs whose sores had never healed but only worsened, put on his heaviest clothing, and said cheerfully: 'You're right, Evelyn. I'll take a but of jog,' and with that he stepped out into the bitter February cold.

The other two, seeing his head for the running track, agreed that spurring him to action had been a good idea, but they did not continue to watch as ran right past the track, slowed down from the gasping pain near his heart and, when he was out of sight, began to take off his outer garments one by one. Heavy parka, gone! Woolen jacket with double pockets, thrown aside! Inner jacket, also of wool, away! Now his good linen shirt came off and next his silk-and-wool undershirt, until he stumnled ahead, naked to the waist in cold that had fallen below thirty degrees minus.

There was no wind, so for a few minutes---perhaps a hundred and forty seconds---he could move forward, but then his scurvied legs refused to function and his lungs began to freeze. Grasping for the branches of a stunted tree, he held himself erect and in that naked position froze to death.

when his return was delayed, Lord Luton said to Murphy: 'Good, Harry's whipping himself bacl into shape,' but when the absence was prolonged, Luton said with obvious apprehension: 'Murphy, I think we'd better look into Harry's running,' and when from the cabin door they stared at the track they saw nothing.

'Whatever could have happened?' Luton asked, and Murphy had no reasonable surmise, but when they went tentatively toward the running oval neatly trampled in two feet of snow, Murphy spotted on beyond the red-and-gray parka lying on the ground and he rushed forward to retrieve it. As he did so, Luton, coming behind, spotted the woolen jacket, and then the inner jacket and not far beyond the erect corpse of Harry Carpenter, already frozen almost solid.

There was an additonal horror to his manly suicide. His two companions, not wishing to bring the corpse into the cabin but unable to dig at that moment a grave in the permafrost, collected his strewn garments and placed them like robes over the stiff body, which they laid in the snow. When they returned next day they discovered what food the ravens of the arctic fed upon.

SPACE

March was a difficult month for with the coming of the vernal equinox, when night and day were twelve hours long at all spots on the earth, they had visible reason for thinking that spring was already here, and they wanted the snow and ice to melt so that they could be on their way again. But this did not happen, for although the days grew noticeably warmer and those fearful, silent nights when the temperature dropped to minus sixty were gone, it still remained below freezing and no relaxation of winter came.

It was a time of irritation, and one day when Luton was beginning to fear the onset of scurvy in himself he railed at Murphy: 'You boasted that night last year that you were a poacher extraordinary. For God's sake, let's see you poach." and Murphy said merely: 'Yes, Milord'

Even in the closeness of the cabin, Lord Luton maintained the separation by caste. Murphy was a servant, an unlettered man who had been brought along to assist his betters, and never did either man forget that. During two winters each more than seven months long, Luton never touched Murphy, although Murphy sometimes touched him when performing a service, and it would have been unthinkable for Luton to have addressed him by a first name. As had Murphy referring to his lordship as Evelyn, the cabin would have trembled as if struck by an earthquake. From these strict rules, hammered out over the centuries, there was no deviation. If Murphy had to address Luton directly, it was Milord and nothing else; Luton even considered Sir too familiar.

And yet there was a mutual respect between these two. The Luton Party had started with five and only two had survived, and at times Luton had/entertained, but never voiced, the judgment that if in the end there was to be only one to reach Dawson, it would probably be this happy, moon-faced Irishman. 'Damme,' he muttered to himself one day as he watched Murphy running his laps on the track that was beginning to show mud, 'peasants have a capacity for survival. I suppose that's why there's so many of them.'

In fairness to Luton, he never demanded subservience of a demeaning kind. The original rule still prevailed: 'Murphy is the servant of the expedition, not of any individual member.' And in a dozen unspoken ways the lord let the manservant know that the latter's contibution was both essential and highly regarded. It was an arrangement which only two well intentioned men could have maintained through these difficult conditions, and/if they remained obedient to it, they had a fighting chance of reaching Dawson City.

They spent much time during the days after the equinox deciding how to proceed in the more fortunate days that were coming, but before they could make any of the important minor decisions as to whether they should keep or that during their final push, they had to determine one overriding matter: 'Shall we attempt to take one of the boats all the way to the headwaters of the Pelly, or shall we go/the rest of the way on foot?' They discussed this interminably, and they did so because Luton inwardly acknowledged that his earlier wrong decisions had probably caused the deaths of Blythe and Carpenter. He wanted to share responsibility this time, but he did not wish to say so.

Murphy would say: 'If we keep a boat with us, Milord, we can carry more stuff,' and Luton would respond: 'But if head out swiftly on foot with the simplest backpacks, we can certainly make it before another winter.'

On another occasion Murphy would defend the backpack and Luton the retention of the boat, and each calculated danger or emergency was anticipated. It was Luton who had the courage to voice one of the most persuasive of the possibilities: 'Murphy, we've seen men die...from causes they could not control. If only one of us survived, which way would be better?' and Murphy said without hesitation: 'If he lived and was alone, he'd have to leave the boat,' and that settled the matter. 'We're both going to live. We'll keep the boat till the last practical moment.'

The choice having been made, the two men spent much of April deciding in minute detail ~~xxxxxxxx~~ what would be ~~xxxxxxxxx~~ carried by boat to the headwaters and what articles would be taken forward in each of ~~xxxxxxxxxx~~ backpacks ~~xxxxx~~. They must take the tent, and the tools survival and all available food, which as not much. Looking at the dried bea and the other edibles which the body alive but allowed the extremities to die, Luton felt intimations of scurvy---a loosening tooth, a sensation of numbness in his toes---and when Murphy was gone he inspected both legs and saw with horror that when he pushed his forefinger into the flesh of his right leg, the indentation remained.

At this moment, in the twenty-first month of this doomed expedition, he almost lost heart, but when he heard the approch of Murphy he stiffened and presened his servant with the obligatory posture of a gentleman still in control. 'Murphy, we really must see if we can get outrselves some meat.' That was all he said, but the Irishmar knew that Lord Luton was not going to make it through the mountains unless he, Murphy, brought home some ~~xxxxx~~ game.

He thereupon started the most significant poaching journey of his life, traveling each day up and down the Peel River, looking for anything that movec and each night when he returned empty handed to the terrible disappointment of ~~xxxxxxxxx~~ his waiting companion, he could see the lord's shoulders not sag but stiffen with determination: 'Good try, Murphy. I'm sure you'll ~~xxxxx~~ get something yet.' But it was not Murphy who saved the expedition. On one of the last days durin which Luton would be strong enough to journey into the field beside the Irishman, they came upon ~~xxxxxxxxxxxx~~ marks which excited them to the trembling point. A herd of caribou moving north for the summer had crossed this way leaving signs which had not been present yesterday.

They could not be impossibly distant, both men agreed on that, so the cha began with the men following the signs with desperate intensity, but ~~xxx~~ when the silvery night fell the caribou had not yet been overtaken, and there was a temptation for the men to go back to their cabin, but Luton pointed with his finger to where they stood, and through the shortening ~~xxxx~~ night they stayed in positior each man striving to catch a little sleep to fortify him ~~xxx~~ against the demands of the coming day and it as fortunate that they remained where they were, for at dawn Luton ~~xxxx~~ whispered: 'I'm going to look over that hill. Stay here if I rouse anything.

When he had crept quetly to the crest of the hill stoll covered with spa snow, he broke into a sweat, for there below him stood a small herd of carib , their horns sharply etched in the luminous dawn. 'Should I try to call Murphy?' he asked himself, ~~xxx~~ rejecting that tactic ~~xxxx~~ immediately. He either go a caribou himself or he died along the Peel.

Moving like a ghost, which he nearly was, he closed upon the unsuspectin animals, prayed for composure, then raised his rifle slowly but without hesitation, and pulled the trigger. At the sound of his shot the ~~X~~ caribou ~~xxxxxxxxxxx~~ sped away, leaving one of good size dead on the graound.

As soon as Murphy saw the liefless beast he began gathering brush, and while Luton built a substantial fire, the Irishman slaughtered the beast. By unspoken agreement he rippdd out the liver, and that was the first portion of the meat they/roasted on sticks over the flames. Jamming it into their mouths half raw, they allowed the blood to trickle down the sides of their mouths, as before, they could almost feel the lifesaving juices running into their own livers and down the veins of their legs, which only a few minutes before had been doomed.

There as now no thought of hurried departure from their present camp; their job was to lug as much of the caribou to the banks of the Peel and there to gorge as much of its potent goodness as they could, and after many days Lord Luton said: "Murphy, I think we can make the try.' So the half-boat was loaded, the campsite was saluted, and a final farewell was said at the rude grave of Harry Carpenter. With no recriminations, no voiced regrets, the two men resumed their journey up the Peel, poling and pulling as before.

But now there were no rapids to be forced knee-deep in icy water, and in time they reached the headwaters beyind which they could not go. Their compass direction would/remain south-southwest until they intercepted soem west-flowing river, several of which had to lie beyond the mountains.

SPACE

It was providential that in the planning they did during the month of April they decided to take with them not only their own insect nets but also tho of the others, because in Harry Carpenter's reading about the Yukon he had several times/encountered reports of how feroxciously/the mosquitoes of the arctic could be when attacking people. Now, as they left the valley of the Peel, they were discover how voracious these powerful enemies were.

They were hiking along a swampy area, eyes on the compass to maintain a steady course, when a multitude, not merely a swarm, of mosquitos struc , insanely hungry for blood after the end of winter. Before Luton could unpack his net, they attacked him from all sides, thousands of them striking every centimeter of exposed skin. They did not issue warning buzzes; they simply engulfed an area, sinking their probobocises deep into the skin. Their sting/also carried what seemed to be an espcially potent irritant, for once they struck, a man had an almost uncontrollable desire to scractch, but if he did so, he usually exposed more skin which was immediately blackened by new hordes.

''My word, this is rather frightening,' Luton cried as he adjusted his net ting to kepp the little beast from his face and eyes, but Murphy expressed it better when he muttered as they attacked him in a score of different places: &Stand fast, Milord, or they'll fly off with you.'

Once the two men had their nets effectively in place, they found perverse delight in chronicling the perversity of their foe. Luton said: 'Look at this rivet on my glove. You'd not thihk even a gust of air couldforce its way in there, but they do.' Belatedly, Murphy found x the slightest possible tear in one of his nets; the mosquitos had spotted it in the first moments of their attack. No opening, no gap in clothing could be so insignificant but what the murderous creatures could exploit it. And they were murderous, for tadxition in the arctic was replete with stories of unprotected men who had been caught in summer and driven to suicide by the millions of mosquitoes who assaulted them without respite. There were many cases in which caribou or horses or the deer brought to Alsaska by Laplanders had been killed by overwhelming and relentess attacks.

For three weeks the two travelers battled these remorseless enemies, building smudge fires at ~~night~~ dusk and taking turns as to who would keep them burning through the night; if the caretaker fell asleep, the mosquitoes soon awakened both him and bis partner. /There was no comparison in all of nature with the arctic mosquito; mercifully it appeared only in latr sprin and summer, but when it did men shuddered and animals sought high ground where the movement of wind would keep the pests away.

33 lines

On a memorable day in June, the travelers forgot their endless battle with the insects and conducted a small celebratuon, for they had intercepted a small stream whi ran to the west, and as they hurried down it, certain that it must lead to either the Klondike River or the Yukon direct, they came upon a breathtaking sight. Below them, on a narrow ledge of land fronting a great river, lay/the tenxts and false fronts of Dawson City. Seeing it nailed down in reality, and not a chimera, the two men stood silent. They had completed their journey. They had survived trialsthat few had ever equaled and none surpassed. They had defeated scurvy and temperatures of minus seventy and rapids up which boats had to be hauled by bare hands, and they had reached their destination after twenty-two months and miles of hellish travel.

Neither of the men exulted or gave cries of victory, and neither revealed what prayers or thanks they gave, but Lord Luton, in this moment of extraordinary triumph knew what he must do. xx Instructing Murphy to pitch their tent on the eastern slope of the hill from which they had spied Dawson, he said: 'Murphy, we'll enter the city in dignity,' and he kept himself and the Irishman less than a mile from their destination for three days while they cleaned their gear, dusted their clothes, and made themselves genurally presentable.

They had a problem with Murphy's beard. 'It must come off,' Luton insisted. '~~Xmxhd~~ It would look improper for me to present myself clean-shaven while you had that wandering growth. Make it look as if I didn't care.'

'I'd like to keep it, Milord. It was most helpful with the mosquitoes.'

There was no reprieve, and during most of the second day, Murphy heated water, soaped his heavy beard, and hacked away at its edges, crying out when the pain became unbearable. Finally he threw down the razor: 'I cannot,' whereupon Luton retrieved the razor and cried: 'Well I jolly well can.' And for the first time during this long journey Lord Luton touched his manservant.

Perching him on a log and covering his heavy beard with as much lather as their last shreds of soap would produce, he grabbed Murphy by the head, pulled his face upward toward the warm June sun, and began almost pulling the hairs out by the root. It was a process so painful that finally Murphy broke loose, leaped to his feet and cried: 'I'll do it meself!' And the rest of that day with a tired old razor which he stropped at least fifty times, he fought the battle of the beard, exposing always a bit more clean Irish skin. At the close of day he looked quite presentable, a lean, capable, rosy-faced men who, as much as Lord Luton, had held this party together.

That night after they had put finishing touches to their gear, organizing it in trim backpacks and tucking in the edges of the canvas, they spent the last hours of sunset staring down at the amazing city they would be entering in th morning. From nothing in early June of 1896 it had grown within two years to a metropolis of more than thirty thousand. 'That was the target,' Luton said, and when they returned to their tent the two men consumed the last of the caribou that had saved their lives.

At eight in the morning of 21 June 1899 Lord Luton and his servant Matthe Murphy from London walked proudly, almost defiantly into Dawson City and when word flashed through thetown that a noble lord had arrived, several thousand people, having nothing better to do, for they were associated with no mines, gathered about to ask questions, which Luton answered with austrere proprety. Yes, the company had taken almost two years to come down the Mackenzie and over the mountains. Yes, the reports were correct. There had originally been five members but three had died, one by accident, two of scurvy. Yes, they had spent two winters near the arctic circle. Yes, he was the intended heir of the Marquess of Deal.

When Major Steele of the Mounties heard that Luton was in town, he hurrie to meet him, bringing several packets of mail and a list of inquiries from London. but Luton could express no interest in them. He was relieved, however, to know that Steele had received an ample deposit of fudns to be delivered to Lord Luton's party, should it ever arrive. The sender, Luton's father the Marquess, had expected Evelyn to reach Dawson in the summer of 1898; the boy was a year late.

When Steele asked: 'Will you be heading for the goldfields?' Luton starec at him in amazement and said nothing. Gold was not on his mind or even his consciousness; he could not recall that he had ever been interested in it, ar certainly it was no concern of his now. Later, when Steele related the story he said: 'He looked as if he had never heard the word. But then most of the people who reach Dawson from Edmonton never went to the gold fields. They

seemed content merely to have got her alive.' Steele's people compiled of summary of the Edmonton traffic:

> There left the town in the years 1897-1899 some two thousand persons. men and women alike, Canadians and foreigners with no distinction. More than half turned back without ever reaching the Klondike. At least seventy perished en route, and they among the stringest and best prepared of their societies. Of the less than a thousand who reached the goldffelds there is no record of anyone who found gold and only a few cases in which claims were actually staked, invariably on nonproductive streams. Most who did succeed in arriving here turned right around and went home without even trying to visit the fields which they knew had been preempted, the most notioiurs case being that of Lord Luton, heir to the Marquess of Deal.

Luton achieved local immortality by the boldness of his action. He arrived with his manservant at eight in the morning, received his accumulated mail with indifference, not even opening the letters, and at ten spotted the old sternwheeler Jos. Pemberton at the wharf. Inquiring as to its detination he learned that it was headed for the mouth of the Yukon and thence along the shore to St. Michael, where steamers to Seattle and San Francisco would be waiting.

Hesitating not a moment, he marched sedately to the ship, his manservant trailing behind, and asked if he could purchase a ticket to Seattle. When it was explained that that the Jos. Pemberton could supply passage only to St. Michael, but that many large ships would undoubtedly be waiting there on which passage could certainly be obtained, he bought his ticket, remained aboard until sailing time, and saw no more of Dawson City, or the Klondike.

Having paid his own fare, he then turned to Murphy and asked: 'Shall you be staying with me?' Murphy said: 'No, Milord. I came to get me a gold mine and I shall.'

So they parted, no more having been said on either side, but as the steadfast Irishman headed for the gangplank which take him forever from Lord Luton, Evelyn could not permit his faithful servant to depart without some recognition. Striding towrad the gangplank, he intercepted the Irishamn, and with his left hand he grasped Murphy's left shoulder, as if he were going to assault his neck, and in a hudhed voice, so that no passengers could hear, he said: 'Stout fellow, Murphy,' whereupon he turned on his heel and vanished.

Thoughtful biographers of the twelfth Marquess of Deal, as he bacme in 1909, judged that his disastrous expedition to the Klondike was not all loss not by any means:

> It was this prolonged and dreadul experience in which he lost three of his party, including his sister's only son, that put steel into the heart of the Marquess, so that when Lloyd George tapped him in 1916 to whip the British industrial effort into line so that Britain could muster its full strength against the Kaiser. he was as well prepared as man could be to discipline the private sector.

A blue-blooded nobleman and a man who in the privacy of his club had called Lloyd George 'that insufferable little Welshman, no

one of VIII-141

gentleman at all,' he rallied to his assignment, became/Lloyd George's most trusted accomplice, and performed wonders in helping to throw back the German might. In dealing with some refractory industiralists who came to him complaing that they simply could not accept the difficulties involv d in this proposed measure or that, he never referred to his two years in the arctic, but he did look the man in the eye, stare him down and ask: 'Di ficulties? Do you know what difficulty really is?' and always he got his way.

SPACE

(Here move on to VIII=201 but start on a new page.)

Editing the First Draft

Typing out the first draft of a manuscript is fierce work and often frustrating, for composition goes neither swiftly nor accurately and disappointments are many. But whipping this first amorphous mass into some kind of order and direction is one of the more pleasant experiences a writer can have. Now it becomes clear that the chapter is viable, that there are passages that can be improved, and in my case those big warning O's in the margin summon me to duty.

This close editing is so enjoyable and rewarding that I can scarcely wait to get to the typewriter in the morning and confront that day's tasks. I see a dozen spots where the narrative can be clarified or invigorated, and those dangerous passages that merely tell about the action without showing it. 'Let the people back into the scene,' I tell myself. 'Let's hear their voices.'

Now a peculiarity of my work habits imposes itself, not onerously but with clear demands. When I have been typing out my first draft I memorize the start and finish and look of each page, engraving its number in the upper-right-hand corner in my mind. For example, it is then and forever VIII-137 (its identification as Chapter VIII of the long Alaska novel remains inviolate). When I have to enlarge that page with an insert, I try to avoid numbering it VIII-137A, although sometimes I cannot evade it. I want it to remain VIII-137, and so I keep it, as if protecting its validity.

To kill a scene and rewrite it at greater length, I cut out the inadequate section with ruler and sharp Stanley palm-fitting knife, type its replacement, and with a small plastic bottle of self-dispensing Elmer's glue paste in the new material. Obviously, this results in some pages that are markedly longer than the normal eleven inches of standard typewriter paper. Occasionally, the revised pages reach double or even triple length, but the integrity of the manuscript's pagination has been retained. And the long pages can be doubled back on themselves to allow normal filing.

I do not recommend this peculiar habit to others. I mention it only because it works for me. Besides, with the new word processors, the ancient art of cutting and pasting, dating back to the 1450s and Gutenberg, is no longer necessary. With enviable skill and speed, the writer using the new machines can do with the flick of a finger what I laboriously do with ruler, knife and pastepot. Of course, in using the processor the record of the brainwork entailed in drafting revisions is lost, so that memories of how the writer worked, what he did with material of poor quality, and the steps he took to correct it are gone. Today writing is more swiftly accomplished, but the thought processes involved in rewriting are not preserved. Of course, it would be technically possible to record and save the portions of a manuscript thrown away, but this would require so much detailed work that no one I know deems it practical.

Some of the more interesting pages of this book would not have been possible had I used a word processor with the speed and facility that experts can manage; the handwritten notes would have been lost. On the other hand, when I started assembling once-printed pages to illustrate various points, the meticulous printouts of the various stages were on file in the computer and it was easy to reprint them. I might ask for a fifty-page printout of a long-vanished state of the manuscript, and within a few minutes there it was on my desk.

The facing illustration shows how a pair of my pages from the original copy look after I have inserted so many changes that each has become ridiculously elongated. The various additions are highlighted. Three additional pages of normal length on which I did extensive work follow.

VIII-140

seemed content merely to have got here alive.' Steele's people compiled a summary of the Edmonton traffic:

> There left that town in the years 1897-1899 some Fifteen Hundred persons, men and women alike, Canadians and foreigners with no distinction. More than half turned back without ever reaching the Klondike. At least seventy perished en route, and they among the strongest and best prepared of their societies. Of the less than a thousand who reached the goldfields there is no record of anyone who found gold and only a few cases in which claims were actually staked, invariably on nonproductive streams. Most who did succeed in arriving here turned right around and went home without even trying to visit the fields which they knew had been preempted, the most notoriours case being that of Lord Luton, heir to the Marquess of Deal.

Luton achieved local immortality by the boldness of his action when he reached Dawson. He arrived with his manservant at eight in the morning, received his accumulated mail with indifference, not even opening the letters, and at ten spotted the old sternwheeler Jos. Parker anchored at the waterfront. Inquiring as to its destination, he was told: 'The young feller at Ross & Haglan can explain.'

Hesitating not a moment, he marched to the store and demanded passage to Seattle. A bright young clerk said: 'Boats from here have to be shallow draft. That one goes only to St. Michael.'

'What do I do then?' Luton asked severely, and the clerk replied: 'Oh, sir, one of our R&R steamers bound for Seattle will be waiting to transfer you the moment you arrive.'

As Luton signed his name to the manifest, the young man said: 'Evelyn, that's a funny name for a man,' and the noble lord stared down at him as if from a great height. As he started to leave he grumbled to himself: 'I came through Edmonton to avoid America. Now I'm heading into the heart of the damned place.' He shook his head: 'Of course, I could return the way I came, but anyone who used that route, going or coming, would be insane.'

Having paid his fare, he turned to Murphy: 'Shall you be coming with me?' and the servant replied: 'No, Milord, I came to find me a gold mine and I shall.'

So they parted, but as the steadfast Irishman carried the luggage to the gangplank which would separate him forever from his master, Luton could not in decency permit this faithful man to depart without some gesture of appreciation. Reaching out with his lean left arm, he grasped Murphy's left shoulder and said in voice so low that no passengers could hear: 'Stout fellow, Murphy.' Turning on his heel, he vanished.

Thoughtful biographers of the ninth Marquess of Deal, which he became in 1909, judged that his disastrous expedition to the Klondike had not been all loss:

> He spent twenty-two months getting to Dawson and remained exactly three hours, but it was this prolonged and dreadful experience, in which he lost three of his party, including his sister's only son, that put steel into the heart of the Marquess, when Lloyd George tapped him in 1916 to whip the British industrial effort into line so that Britain could muster its full strength against the Kaiser, he was as well prepared as a man could be to discipline the private sector.
>
> A blue-blooded nobleman and a man who in the privacy of his club had called Lloyd George 'that insufferable little Welshman, no gentleman at all,' he rallied to his assignment, became Lloyd George's most trusted accomplice, and performed wonders in helping to throw back the German might. In dealing with refractory industrialists who came to him complaing that they simply could not accept the difficulties involved in this measure or that, he never referred to his two years in the arctic, but he did look the man in the eye, stare him down and ask: 'Difficulties? Do you know what difficulty really is?' and because everyone knew of his arctic actions, he got his way.

SPACE

(Here move on to VIII-201 but start on a new page.)

VIII-137

It would be popular to say that in this time of Lord Luton's near collapse his valiant manservant leaped into the breach and saved the expedition, but that did not happen, for Luton, realizing in the warmth of the cabin how close he had been to surrender, pulled himself together, prepared their evening meal himself and in the morning shaved as usual. Then, dressing in his usual meticulous way, he took down his gun and said: 'Time comes, Murphy, when a man must find his own caribou,' and off he marched, thinking as he went: This may be the final effort. My legs. My damned legs.

Murphy, of course, trailed behind, and during that long cold day when even he tired of climbing the snowy hummocks, he knew that this was for Luton the do-or-die effort, and he had not the heart to stop the nobleman. It was good that he didn't, for toward evening they came upon marks which exicted them to the trembling point. A collection of moose moving north for the summer had crossed this way leaving signs which had not been present yesterday.

The animals could not be impossibly distant, both men agreed on that, so the chase began, the men following the signs with desperate intensity, but when the silvery night fell the moose had not yet been overtaken. There had to be a great temptation for the men to go back to the safety of their cabin, but without speaking Luton pointed to the spot where they stood, and through the early hours of the shortening night they remained in position, each man striving to catch a little rest against the demands of the coming day which. It was fortunate that they did, for at midnight, when the waning moon stood high, Luton thought he heard a movement to the east: 'I'm going to scout over that hill. Watch sharp if I rouse anything and it comes this way.'

When he had crept quietly to the crest of the hill still covered with sparse snow, he broke into a sweat for below him in a cleared space grazed five moose, incredibly beautiful, and big, their huge horns gleaming in the moonlight. 'Should I try to call Murphy?' he asked himself. Rejecting that idea lest the animals be alerted, he tried to control his shaking wrists and mumbled: 'I do it myself or I die along this cursed river.'

Moving like a ghost, for he was nearly that, he closed upon the unsuspecting animals, saw once more how glorious they were, then raised his rifle slowly and pulled the trigger. Murphy, hearing the shot from behind the hill, cried: 'Good God! He went off to shoot himself!' And when he clambered up hill, he saw four or five moose running free across the tundra, and a dreadful panic gripped him. But then he also saw Lord Luton leaning on his gun over the body of a dead animal whose great horns shone in the moonlight.

When Murphy rushed up to the lifeless beast, he nodded deferentially to Luton, who nodded back. Both men then began gathering brush, and after Murphy had built a substantial fire, he slaughtered the moose. By unspoken agreement he ripped out the liver, and that was the first portion of the meat they roasted on sticks over the flames. Jamming it into their mouths half raw, they allowed the blood to trickle down their chins, and they could almost feel the lifesaving juices running into their own livers and down the veins of their legs, which only a few minutes before had been doomed. VIII-137

There was now no thought of hurried departure from their present camp; their job was to lug as much of the caribou to the banks of the Peel and there to gorge as much of its potent goodness as they could, and after many days Lord Luton said: 'Murphy, I think we're strong enough to make the try.' So the half-boat was loaded, the campsite was saluted, and a final farewell was said at the rude grave of Harry Carpenter. With no recriminations, no voiced regrets, the two men resumed their journey up the Peel, poling and pulling as before.

But now there were no rapids to be forced knee-deep in icy water, and in time they reached the headwaters beyond which they could not go. Their compass direction would remain south-southwest until they intercepted some west-flowing river, several of which had to lie beyond the mountains.

SPACE

It was providential that in the planning they during April they remembered how vicious the mosquitoes had been the spring before, for this cautioned them to take not only their own insect nets but also those of their dead companions. They were now about to learn how voracious the arctic mosquito could be when it found a walking target bearing blood.

It was providential that in the planning they did for the final push they remembered how vicious the mosquitoes had been the spring before, for this prodded them to take not only their own insect nets but also those of their dead companions. This was a prudent move, because in these final [illegible] miles they were about to learn how really vicious the arctic mosquito could be when it swarmed down upon a walking target bearing blood.

They were hiking along a swampy area, eyes on the compass to maintain a steady course, when a multitude, not merely a swarm, of mosquitos struck, insanely hungry for blood after the end of winter. Before Luton could unpack his net, they attacked him from all sides, thousands of them striking every centimeter of exposed skin. They did not issue warning buzzes; they simply engulfed an area, sinking their probobocises deep into the skin. Their sting also carried what seemed to be an espcially potent irritant, for once they struck, a man had an almost uncontrollable desire to scratch, but if he did so, he usually exposed more skin which was immediately blackened by new hordes.

'My word, this is rather frightening,' Luton cried as he adjusted his netting to keep the little beasts from his face and eyes, but Murphy expressed it better when he muttered as they attacked him in a score of different places: 'Fast and fast, Milord, or they'll fly off with you.'

Above: Page 140 with five inserts. Right: Page 137 with five. Areas marked in red identify passages carried over from the rough draft. Notice the pencil circles in the left margins, indicating material to be studied further. This work was done when these pages were still intended for *Alaska*. Conversion into a novella had not yet been considered, nor had any editor seen this material.

But that was the last fresh meat they enjoyed before Christmas, and one night in early January, after Blythe had lost three more stainless teeth, the young man said: 'I doubt I shall see spring.'

'Now look here, Trevor,' Luton began to bluster, but the young fellow said with the gentleness that had always marked him: 'Evelyn, will you please find my Palgrave?' and when the precious little book was found, ~~the one that contained the lyrics and the odes which made English different from all other languages,~~ Trevor asked: 'Will you read some of the short poems?' and in his strong baritone Luton read those wonderdully simple lines, those ~~single~~ thoughts which seemed to represent the best that England had ever offered the world: 'My heart aches, and a drowsy numbness pains...' or ~~[illegible]~~ 'She dwelt among the untrodden ways...' or 'Tell me where is Fancy bred...'

As this essence of love and beauty and the longings of youth filled the cabin, Blythe sighed and thereafter his breath was unevenly and he said: 'Evelyn, will you read me the Herrick?' but Luton could not find it, so Trevor in his trembling hands leafed through the pages for number 93 and found the magical six lines:

30 'Whenas in silks my Juila goes
Then, then (methinks) how sweetly flows
That liquefaction of her clothes.

Next, when I cast mine eyes and see
That brave vibration each way free;
O how that glittering taketh me!'

Reaching for Carpenter's hand he said: 'When we ~~reached~~ turned home I was to have married your cousin, Julia Deland. Will you ~~tell~~ speak to her?' Then he turned his ~~tired~~ wearied body toward Lord Luton, saying in a voice so low and wavering that it could scarcely be heard: 'Oh, Evelyn. I'm so sorry. I've let you down.' Tears came to his eyes, and in shame he turned his face to the cabin wall, and with the temperature at minus fifty-seven and escape in any direction impossible, this compassionate young man, his poems ~~unfinished~~ unwritten, died.

SPACE

As before, February was the month of hell and ice, except that this year there was no spring-like break in the middle, and much of the misery it brought stemmed from the fact that the days were lengthening, visibly so, but the rate was so slow and the persistence of the cold so deadening that it seemed a perversion, a teasing of the spirit. Spring was coming but it did not come.

Camp routine continued as before. Lord Luton shaved, and tended his clothes, and marched erect rather than bent over as ~~some~~ the others did in order to keep whatever heat they had trapped in their belly. He ran three laps in this winter's version of a track and he goaded others into doing the same. He ate sparingly, preferring that others take the larger portions, and he did everything possible to sustain the spirits of his two remaining partners. He was an impeccable leader, and barring that one dreadful night when he threatened to shoot Murphy, he never lost his composure. His party had fallen upon rough times and he intended leading the survivors to safety.

boat till the last practical moment.'

The choice having been made, the two men spent much of April deciding in

136 minute detail what would be carried by boat to the headwaters and/backpacks. They must take the tent, and the tools of

FOR survival and all available food, which was not much. Looking at the dried beans and the other edibles which kept the body alive but allowed the extremities to die, Luton felt intimations of scurvy---a loosening tooth, a sensation of numbness in his toes---and when Murphy was absent he inspected both legs and saw with horror that when he pushed his forefinger into the flesh of his right leg, the indentation remained.

At this moment, in the twenty-first month of this doomed expedition, he almost lost heart, but when he heard the approch of Murphy he stiffened and presented his servant with the obligatory posture of a gentleman still in control: 'Murphy, we really must see if we can get outrselves some meat.' That was all he said, but the Irishman knew that Lord Luton was not going to make it through the mountains unless he, Murphy, brought home some game.

He thereupon started the most significant poaching journey of his life, traveling each day up and down the Peel River, looking for anything that moved, and each night when he returned empty handed to the terrible disappintment of his waiting companion, he could see the lord's shoulders not sag but stiffen with determination: 'Good try, Murphy. I'm sure you'll get something yet.'

His journal now lacked the easy flow and broad philosophical base which characterized it the preceding winter, when five able men were really exploring life in a cramped cabin in the arctic. One night, after Murphy had returned empty-handed, he wrote in disjointed, trembling phrases:

> Again no meat. Pushed right forefinger in leg, mark remained hours. Am slipping. If I must die terrible isolation pray God able to do it with grace of Trevor Blythe, courage of Harry Carpenter. Right now pray Murphy find caribou.

137 Shortly after this confession of despair, Luton left the cabin and tried on weakening legs to run his customary laps, but as the used the oval which Harry Carpenter had tramped into the snow, he began to see images of that good man whom he had sent to his death, and of Philip lost in the Mackenzie, and of the poet Trevor Blythe, perhaps the greatest loss of all, and he began to stagger and duel with phantoms, so that Murphy, having learned from Carpenter's suicide, now watched from the cabin, knew that his master was in difficulty.

Running to help, he heard Luton cry to the phabtoms: 'I am strangled! I am cursed with grief! Oh God, that I should have done this to these men through my ineptitude!'

The Irishman, who was not supposdd to hear this confession, jogged methodically behind Lord Luton, overtaking him on a turn, where he said in his best matter-of-fact voice:

out by the root. It was a process so painful that finally Murphy broke loose, leaped to his feet and cried: 'I'll do it meself!' And the rest of that day with a tired old razor which he stropped at least fifty times, he fought the battle of the beard, exposing always a bit more clean Irish skin. At the close of day he looked quite presentable, a lean, capable, rosy-faced men who, as much as Lord Luton, had held this party together. VIII-139

The real trouble came at sunset when Murphy wanted to discard the now useless gear they had lugged so far and so laboriously. 'We'll throw this rot to the ravens,' he said, preparing to rid himself of the dried remnants of the moose and the heavier tools, but Luton restrainied him.

'No, we must march into Dawson as men who are undefeated,' and he insisted that Murphy follow him in arranging his backpack as meticulously as possible and then squaring the ends.

This nonsense Murphy refused to copy, and he started throwing things into a ravine until Luton roared at him in a voice demanding respect: 'Murphy! For God's sake let us finish our march like men. Let us go into that sprawling mess down there as if we were prepared to go another hundred miles.'

p.143 At the mention of such an additional distance under such conditions, Murphy shivered, but he did comply, and as the sun stayed high on this longest night of the year the two travelers looked down upon the target which had eluded them for twenty-two tortured months. 'We made it,' Luton said and most of that night he remained outside the tent, staring at the river and its ugly town.

At eight in the morning of 21 June 1899 Lord Luton and his servant Matthew Murphy walked proudly, almost defiantly into Dawson City and when word flashed through the town that a noble lord had arrived, several thousand people, having nothing better to do, for they were associated with no mines, gathered about to ask questions, which Luton answered with austrere propriety. Yes, the company had taken almost two years to come down the Mackenzie and over the mountains. Yes, the reports were correct. There had originally been five members but three had died, one by accident, two of scurvy. They had spent two winters near the arctic circle. Yes, he was the intended heir of the Marquess of Deal.

When Major Steele of the Mounties heard that Luton was in town, he hurried to meet him, bringing several packets of mail and a list of inquiries from London, but Luton could express no interest in such things. He was relieved, however, to know that Steele had received an ample deposit of fudns to be delivered to Lord Luton's party, should it ever arrive. The sender, Luton's father, had expected Evelyn to reach Dawson in the summer of 1898; his son was a year late.

When Steele asked: 'Will you be heading for the goldfields?' Luton stared
.144 at him in amazement and said nothing. Gold was not on his mind or even his consciousness; he could not recall that he had ever been interested in it, and certainly it was no concern of his now. Later, when Steele related the story he said: 'He looked as if he had never heard the word. But then most of

The Printout of the Revised Version

When the original draft has been edited, revisions have been made and new scenes added—all done by me with two fingers on my old typewriter and often printed by hand with pen and ink because my handwriting is abominable—the collection of cut-and-paste sheets goes to my secretary and her word processor. There the disorderly mass is converted into clean, crisp pages with ample margins and space at the bottom.

The typeface of the processor will obviously differ from that of my old typewriter, and this alone imparts to the printout the impression of being a real manuscript. But the difference is not only in appearance; the entire segment has been tightened, refocused, and in a curious sense purified. It can now be taken seriously.

Since it would not be profitable to reprint my entire edited copy, I have chosen five brief sections that illustrate how new material, unmarked, has been fitted in with the original material identified with Bendays. The original material will also be highlighted by Bendays on the published book pages reproduced later. It may be instructive to see how many of the words, phrases, and sentences of the first attempt survive, for although I'm not a good writer, I'm a masterly rewriter.

All editing on the pages following has been done by me alone, and I do not consider it to be in polished form because the moment it comes clean and neat from the processor, a score of people will begin to attack it: agents, editors, copy editors, and, above all, the writer himself. Often entire passages, sometimes of considerable length, will be eliminated. Others will be added, and line corrections of the most minute changes will be made.

When I handed this corrected manuscript of a segment to the publisher of *Alaska* I liked it as a glancing view of the Canadian contribution, but since the complete manuscript for the entire book was overlong, something had to be cut, and my salute to Canada was jettisoned.

It is interesting to note what happened to this relatively brief segment of my Alaska novel: in the first carbon, 5,000 words; this heavily edited copy when still part of that novel, 8,000 words; the final version when part of the Canadian novel, 18,000 words. In another manuscript the numbers could well be in reverse: the writer's first output is 18,000 words; his own editing cuts this to 8,000 words; professional editing cuts that back to a tight 5,000 words. That is what intensive editing is all about.

DEATH OF A HERO

he realized the true significance of death: `It means that messages of love will not be delivered.'

That night Lord Luton, seeing the desolation of spirit which had attacked the chief lieutenant, cried brightly: `I say men! Isn't it time we attacked another can of our Norman Wells supply,' and as before, Fogarty chopped the can open and brought out the saucepan. This time he was able to throw in a small collection of arctic roots he had grubbed from far beneath the frozen soil, and when stew was rationed out, it was twice as tasty as before and the three diners leaned back and smacked their lips, remarking upon what civilizing effect a substantial hot meal could have upon a hungry man.

But Carpenter was so debilitated that his high spirits did not last the night, and in the morning Luton lost his composure and, sick at heart over the weakening condition of his friend, sat at Carpenter's bed and took him by the shoulders: 'Look here, Harry, this won't do. It won't do at all.' Harry, thinking he had been been rebuked for purposely malingering and unable because of his illness to see that Luton was merely using the hale-and-hearty approach of the regimental marshall, took offense at his friend's chiding.

Hiding his intention, he rose on pitifully weakened legs whose sores had never healed but only worsened, put on his heaviest clothing, and said cheerfully: 'You're right, Evelyn. I could do with a bit of a jog,' and with that he stepped out into the bitter February cold.

The other two, seeing him head for the running track, agreed that spurring him to action had been salutary, but since they did not continue to monitor him as he ran right past the track, they did not see him slow down because of gasping pain near his heart

REACHING A VITAL DECISION

circumstance and the necessity for decisions of great moment, the two men seemed to reach a status of equality, each complementing the other, and necessary to the partnership. This was never better exemplified than during the days following the equinox when they had to make up their minds as to how they would operate in the more fortunate weeks they could be sure were coming when summer returned and all depended upon one crucial decision: 'Since we're through the gorges, shall we put the half-boat back in the water and pole our way to the headwaters and then hike over the mountains, or shall we abandon the boat here and start walking immediately?' They whipped this back and forth, with Luton always asking Fogarty for his opinion, because at long last the noble lord was beginning to acknowledge inwardly that his earlier obstinate decisions had been largely to blame for the deaths of Blythe and Carpenter.

Pleased that finally Luton wanted his advice, Fogarty would propose: 'Let's keep the boat, Milord, because with it, we can carry more stuff,' and Luton would respond: 'But if we head out swiftly on foot with the simplest backpacks, we can certainly make it before another winter.'

At the next discussion, Fogarty would defend the backpack and Luton the retention of the boat, and in this way each calculated danger or emergency was voiced and assessed. It was Luton who had the courage to investigate one of the most painful situations: 'Fogarty, we've seen men die...from causes they could not control. If only one of us survived, which way would be better?' and Fogarty said without hesitation: 'If he lived and was alone, he'd have to leave the boat, otherwise...' and that settled the matter: 'Since we're both going to live, we'll keep the boat until the last practical moment.'

VICTORY!

Then on a memorable day in June, Fogarty in the lead position went around a bend and shouted: 'Milord, there it is!' and when Luton hurried up he felt dizzy and had to shake his head to clear his eyes, for below him, on a narrow ledge of land fronting a great river stood the tents and false fronts of what had to be

Dawson City. Seeing it nailed down in reality, and not a chimera, the two men stood silent. They had defeated scurvy and temperatures of minus sixty and rapids up which boats had to be hauled by bare hands, and murderous mosquitoes and they had reached their destination after twenty-three months and nearly twenty-one hundred miles of hellish travel.

Neither of the men exulted or gave cries of victory, and neither revealed what prayers or thanks he did give, but Lord Luton, in this moment of extraordinary triumph, knew what any gentlemen must do. Instructing Fogarty to pitch their tent on the eastern slope of the hill, lest anyone down in Dawson see them before they were prepared, he said: 'Fogarty, we'll enter in style,' and he kept himself and the Irishman less than a mile from their destination for two days while they cleaned their gear, dusted their clothes, and made themselves generally presentable. From a tiny military kit which he carried, Luton produced a needle and thread, and for much of the second day he perched on a rock mending the tears in his jacket. Fogarty's beard presented a problem: 'It must come off,' Luton insisted. 'It would look improper for me to present myself clean-shaven while I allowed you that wandering growth. Would look as if I didn't care.'

'I'd like to keep it, Milord. It was most helpful with the mosquitoes.' There was no reprieve, and during most of the second afternoon, Fogarty heated water, soaped his heavy beard, and hacked away at its edges, wincing when the pain became unbearable. Finally he threw down the razor: 'I cannot,' whereupon Luton retrieved the razor and cried: 'Well I jolly

march into Dawson as men of honor who remain undefeated,' and to Fogarty's bewilderment he spread their gear on blankets and gave a demonstration of how it should be properly packed, with the four corners neatly squared.

When all was in readiness, Luton supervised the placement of Fogarty's pack on his back and then inspected the Irishman's clothes, brushing them here and there: 'Let us enter that sprawling mess down there as if we were prepared to march another hundred miles,' and when Fogarty said truthfully: 'Milord, I could not go another hundred,' Luton said: 'I could.'

At eight in the morning of 21 June 1899 Lord Luton, tall, trim and neatly shaven, led his servant Tim Fogarty into Dawson City as if they were conquerors, and when Superintendent Steele of the Mounties heard that Luton had arrived, he hurried to meet him, bringing several packets of mail and a list of inquiries from London, but Luton could express no interest in such things; his only concern was to dispatch immediate telegrams to the families of his three dead companions. Each message said: 'His death was due to an Act of God and to human miscalculations. He died heroically, surrounded by his friends.' He was relieved, however, when Steele informed him that a generous supply of funds had been received from London 'to be delivered to Lord Luton's party, should it ever arrive.' The sender, the Marquess of Deal, had expected his son to reach Dawson in the summer of 1898; he was a year late.

When Steele asked: 'Will you be heading for the goldfields?' Luton stared at him in amazement and said nothing. Gold was not on his mind or even in his consciousness; he could not recall how he had ever been interested in it, and certainly it was of no concern of his now. Later, when Steele related the story he said: 'He looked as if he had never heard the word. But then most of the people who reached Dawson from Edmonton never went to the goldfields. They seemed content merely to have got here alive.' Steele's people compiled a summary of the Edmonton traffic:

> There left that town in the years 1987-1899 some fifteen hundred persons, men and women alike, Canadians and foreigners with no distinction. More than half turned back without ever reaching the Klondike. At least seventy perished enroute, and they among the strongest and best prepared of their societies. Of the less than a thousand who reached the goldfields there is no record of anyone who found gold and only a few cases in which claims were actually staked, invariably on nonproductive streams. Most who did succeed in arriving here turned right around and went home without trying to visit the fields which they knew had been preempted, the most famous case being that of Lord Luton, the Marquess of Deal.

Luton achieved local immortality by the boldness of his actions when he reached Dawson. He arrived with Fogarty at eight in the morning, received his accumulated mail with indifference, not even opening the letters, and at ten, after having given depositions concerning the deaths of three members of his party, spotted the old sternwheeler Jos. Parker anchored at the waterfront. Inquiring as to its destination, he was told: 'The young feller at Ross & Raglan can explain.'

Hesitating not a moment, he marched to the store and demanded two passages to Seattle. A bright young clerk said:

one containing the new clothes he had purchased in Dawson, the other the backpack he had carried so far and with such uncomplaining determination. "no,' Luton said, returning the backpack, 'this is for you. To help you on the goldfields,' and he strode on ahead as was his custom.

But as he boarded the steamer he knew that he could not in decency part from this faithful helper without some gesture of appreciation. Reaching out with his lean left arm, he grasped Fogarty's left shoulder and said in a voice so low that no passengers could hear: 'Stout fellow, Fogarty,' and started onto the boat, indicating that the Irishman had been dismissed.

But Fogarty, as if already imbibing the spirit of raucous freedom that animated Dawson, reached out and grabbed Luton's arm, swinging him about: 'I have a name, Milord. Me friends call me Tim. And I have a little something for you.' Rummaging in the backpack Luton had just given him, he produced the treasured final can of meat and with proper deference handed it to Evelyn: 'You guarded this faithfully during our long trip. I'm sure you'll want it for remembrance.'

Luton, neither flinching nor showing color at this forwardness of his erstwhile gamekeeper, accepted the can with a slight bowing of his head as if expressing gratitude, then said evenly: 'It served its purpose, Fogarty. It got us safely here. And now, as you expressed it so eloquently, 'let us toss it in the ditch,"' and with an easy swing of his arm, as if he were once more bowling in country cricket, he tossed it far out into the waters of the Yukon. Then, turning on his heel without a gesture of any kind, he stalked onto the waiting ship.

Thoughtful biographers of the ninth Marquess of Deal to which title he was elevated in 1909, judged that his disastrous expedition to the Klondike had not been all loss:

> He spent twenty-three months covering the two-thousand and forty-three miles getting to Dawson and remained three hours, but more than it was this prolonged and dreadful experience, in which he lost three of his party, including his sister's only son, that put steel into the heart of the Marquess. When Lloyd George tapped him in 1916 to whip the British industrial effort into line so that Britain could muster its full strength against the Kaiser, he was as well prepared as a man could be to discipline the private sector.
>
> A blue-blooded nobleman and a man who in the privacy of his club had dismissed Lloyd George as 'that insufferable little Welshman, no gentleman at all,' he rallied to his assignment, became one of Lloyd George's most trusted adherents, and performed wonders in helping to throw back the German might. In dealing with refractory industrialists who came to him complaining that they simply could not accept the difficulties involved in this wartime measure or that, he never referred to his two years in the arctic, but he did look the man in the eyes, stare him down and ask: 'Difficulties? Do you know what difficulty really is?'and because everyone knew of his experiences in the arctic, he got his way.
>
> But that was not the characteristic which enabled him to become one of the most effective ministers of war, for as Lloyd George remarked in one of his cabinet summaries: 'The Marquess of Deal could reach a decision quicker than any man I ever knew, defend it with brilliant logic and ram it down the throats of all who opposed. But if his opponent marshalled relevant facts to support his case, Deal was prepared to listen and even reverse himself, acknowledging with disarming grace: 'I could have been wrong.' I asked him once: 'Deal, how in God's name can you be so overpowering when you first thunder out your decision, then be so attentive when the other fellow argues his case? And how did you school yourself to surrender so graciously if his arguments prove superior to yours?' and he gave a cryptic answer: 'Because I learned in the arctic that there is no sense in bulling your way ahead if you suspect in your heart you're wrong.' I do believe his willingness to listen to others, to bend his will to theirs, anything to keep production humming, helped us win our war against the Boche.'

Editorial Counsel

Having committed myself to publishing the Canadian material as a separate book, I tried to estimate the complexity of the task I faced: In their present condition these pages could not possibly stand by themselves. Too brief. Not enough fleshing out of the five main characters. No women. And the physical setting in the last part has been scanted. In their original setting within the novel these pages were just about right. I had wanted to speed through the Canadian diversion from the main story, I needed to rush back to the Alaskan portion. So on purpose I had adopted a highly compressed form. In that setting it worked, but now the rules changed.

In the process of some disciplined thinking, I made a list of things that would have to be done to achieve the conversion, and I caught most of the obvious lacks that others will note in the next few pages. Had I relied solely on my ideas, the elaboration might have been satisfactory, but now a radically new factor intruded and I would have been stupid not to welcome the insights it provided. I would be edited by two brilliant young women with wide publishing experience, Dinah Forbes in Toronto and Joni Evans in New York, neither of whom I knew personally but both of whom had strong publishing credentials.

Ms. Evans had recently joined Random House, my longtime publisher, after a meteoric career at Simon and Schuster. She is an extremely bright young woman with an uncanny grasp of the strengths and weaknesses of any publishing venture, and a sharp sense of how to capitalize on the former and eliminate the latter. Her first letter to me, printed below, shows that she fully understood our peculiar problem—how to convert a long short story into a full-fledged novella—and her advice centers on that exclusively. Obviously she touched on many points I'd already considered, but the acuity of her comment was so sharp and delivered with such force that she nailed down ideas that I might have been considering only tentatively. There was nothing tentative about Joni Evans, and her strong opinions helped.

Dinah Forbes, with the Canadian house of McClelland & Stewart, focused primarily on the closing portions of the narrative in which conditions in the Canadian Arctic dominated the story. An expert in Canadian studies on the far north, on the Indian tribes that live there, and especially on the character of the bleak landscape, she brought to my attention research sources that could not have been discovered by myself. The letter in which she summarized her recommendations is a gem of editorial counseling in that it identifies and proposes possible solutions to crucial problems.

The value of her work is shown in this comparison. In my original manuscript the segment dealing with the Canadian Arctic comprised only 33 lines. When I finished absorbing the new material she had brought to my attention, I felt compelled to add passages that brought the total to 559 lines. The assistance she provided was invaluable.

I must stress that in sharing the excerpts from the two letters, I have chosen mainly those passages that deal with the closing scenes of the novel. In their comments on the preceding portions—the ship voyage from England, the train ride across Canada, the long boat ride down the Mackenzie River—both editors were equally perspicacious. They gave advice that was substantial.

Other writers may properly ask: 'Do all editors provide so much help to their writers?' I cannot answer that question, for I do not know the habits of editors, nor whether other writers would be as receptive to counsel as I am. Also, in the case of *Journey*, mine was a unique situation: expanding a portion of a chapter into a novel while working with two different publishers in two different countries. If Ms. Forbes in Toronto and Ms. Evans in New York had not been understanding and cooperative, I could never have completed the project. I thank them for having set high standards in the editing profession.

The last two pages of this section illustrate the notes I made for myself while awaiting recommendations from the two women. Because I was absent from my desk I had to work in longhand, for me a most difficult task. A look at my cursive handwriting will explain why in my notes to my editors and secretaries I laboriously print everything.

Ms. Evans's Recommendations on the Manuscript

What we have here is a marvelous adventure story -- truly gripping at times -- that is not quite cooked yet. It doesn't feel developed or rich enough or rationalized enough in its present draft. The skeleton needs more flesh in the areas of character, scenery and fullness/motivation of story to capitalize on what is a stunning episode in history.

Perhaps most crucial is to make Luton more sympathetic in every way. I fully appreciate him as a hero with a tragic flaw of blinding pride and determination. But our credibility is stretched too far in this draft. His motive to stay off American soil needs to be grounded in some sort of concrete. He needs to suffer, if only privately, in the responsibility for the loss of three lives (now evidenced in a few paragraphs of remorse on page 180) and suffer at the same time each fatal strike fells his team. He is too cold, remote, and the reader is constantly resisting him, sometimes angry with him for his thoughtlessness (a mere telegram "satisfies his obligations" to the families of the dead -- indeed, one of those victims is his sister's son!). Couldn't we flash back to one of his expeditions in the Congo or the Amazon to get to know him better? Couldn't we learn why he is so extremely anti-American by some more vivid and direct story? While we admire much of this man (especially on his lonely trek to the Fort), we must learn to care about him, believe in him, grieve for him and finally salute him.

The other characters, too are terribly sketchy. Harry Carpenter, particularly, a fascinating character, is come and gone too efficiently. Philip, while we know him the best, seems to have no thoughts of his own and the tragedy that takes his life seems so quick that the reader is not sufficiently moved. Trevor Blythe never seems to have the mettle to undergo an expedition like this in the first place. There are many ways to develope these characters. Perhaps, for example, on the eve of departure, page 48, we could spend some time with each of them as they are saying goodbye to their respective families, giving us the opportunity to know them and their true hopes, dreams, fears of this trip. Only Fogarty satisfied me and I love the way he and Luton finally come whole, but I wish I could see Fogarty get some payoff (gold?) in this volume at the end of such an ordeal. (In fact, it struck me as odd that not one of the team is really looking for gold -- surely Philip could be, and that this entire adventure -- two years in the making -- should have some payoff for someone?)

The five men, through two long winters, valiance and pride aside, never show any inkling of cabin fever, of missing family, friends, women. A little tension between them would certainly add to the overall tension. Surely, when Harry dies, not only Luton, but Fogarty, too, just seem to get on with it. If the explanation for that is exhaustion, then we must see that exhaustion, feel it.

While Alaska's cup runneth over in richness of detail, scenery, trappings, etc., not enough can be visualized here. Where you may very well say it is all in Alaska, surely a book, any book, not to mention one as dependent on nature as this one, must stand gloriously on its own? I can't visualize the newly sprung towns of Edmonton or Dawson. The terrain never comes alive and the opportunity to make the environment a character (one of your specialties), as you do from time to time with the icy river, is not here. I could never visualize what the Sweet Afton looked like. Its weight. Color. Size. Shape. Does it have a cabin? What is it equipped with (we eventually realize they are sleeping in sleeping bags, but I can't see the baggage -- the guns, the warm clothes, the tools, etc., etc.)? Too, I never fully understood, and am not sure I do now, that once the boat was cut in half, they'd be walking through the water and that the boat was going to carry only the supplies. But then, I wondered, how do you dry wet clothes in freezing weather? Where is the intense discomfort? What does the sky look like? The mountains? What is the temperature before winter comes? Is there any green in July? There is not enough sense of the period, the wildlife, the birds -- and shouldn't we have more episodes of trapping, stalking and the victory of a fresh kill?

As for structure, there is a tremendous buildup to the events of the river journey and the Rockie crossing, yet when the moment is actually upon us, the denouement seems to occur in a flash. Where are the rapids we were so fearful of? The treacherous mountain passes? The reader is crying: More! More! And, again, after twenty-three months of hardship, are we to believe that they have arrived one year too late for the gold? What a terrible disappointment, but if that is indeed the truth, shouldn't that cruel irony be made into the point?

Perhaps I am being presumptious and you have already dealt with the points I raise, or disagree with them. Forgive me for suggesting my thoughts to the writer I most admire in the world, but I'm hoping these general suggestions will be of help in some way. Whenever you have the time or inclination, I'd be happy to talk in detail, or write in detail. At your service, as they say.

I do believe Journey can be a stunning success and will do everything possible to make it so.

Ms. Forbes's Recommendations on the Final Pages

(4) The final journey from the headwaters of the Peel to Dawson. I think this account needs substantial expansion. Currently there are only three and a half pages on this, possibly the most difficult part of the entire journey, and these pages focus on the food and on the shift of authority from Luton to Fogarty. My concern is that by squeezing it to its essentials, the length and difficulty of this part of the journey are much too understated. I have also found out what likely would have happened to them on this section.

I have just talked at length with a Parks Canada representative up in Dawson City, who has given me the best description of the land between Dawson and the Peel that I have yet found. What follows is a summary of the points he stressed:

The most important fact he gave is that an Indian tribe, the Han, had a large settlement on this route. They traveled the route frequently between the Wind River (a source of the Peel) and the Blackstone River, which flows down the west flank of the Ogilvie Range into the Yukon River. In this man's opinion, any party travelling from the Peel to Dawson in the 1890s would have encountered the Han, and, in his words, if they had any smarts at all they would have hired one of the Han to guide them through the Mackenzie Range across the plateau between the two ranges, through the Sila Pass in the Ogilvie Range and down to the Yukon about 20 miles south of Dawson. The Parks Canada man stressed that if Luton's party had not hired a guide from the Han, they likely would have perished on the trail as, once through the Mackenzie Range, they would have had no idea of where to cross the Ogilvie Range. There is evidence that some who tried the trail without help from the Han did perish en route.

Given this startling information, I think a new section needs to be written in which Luton and Fogarty both despair of ever making it to Dawson; they encounter a Han Indian after some days of aimless wandering; and perhaps Fogarty should be shown to be in command enough to hire the services of a Han Indian over Luton's objections, or perhaps Luton would make this decision himself. In this passage, I see Luton as already a broken man, not only dependent on Fogarty but now also dependent on an Indian. There is nothing British anymore about this journey, there is no adventure left, it's down to a desperate haul through an utterly foreign and forbidding land.

I have been able to find out the following about this area to assist you in writing any physical description of the landscape needed to account for Luton's loss of control of the expedition. I see the desolation of the landscape as a metaphor for his private desolation at his responsibility for the death of his friends.

The Mackenzie Range has been heavily glaciated, which means its peaks are quite rounded. Between it and the Ogilvie Range there is a wide, flat plateau broken by low ridges. The Ogilvie Range was more recently formed, and has not been glaciated, so its peaks are very jagged. Neither range is high enough for any climber to experience lack of oxygen (this occurs at about 10,000 feet, and the highest peak in the Ogilvie Range is only approx. 6,500 feet, and the Sila Pass through it is much lower). Both ranges and the plateau between them are technically below the tree line, and the creeks and riverbeds are treed. However, the land beyond the rivers is barren rock, loose scree and gravel, with marsh on top of permafrost in the low-lying land of the plateau and foothills, which would have been extremely difficult to walk over. The mosquitoes would have been intolerable. The land is bald, barren, and definitely would have struck Luton and Fogarty as a vile land, forbidding and desolate; they would almost certainly have abandoned their attempt to reach Dawson here if they had not met the Han. The Parks Canada representative thought that journeying across it would have been a terrifying and traumatic experience for anyone from England.

It would have been a difficult walk all the way because of the loose scree and the marshy areas, as much as for the heights they would have scaled. The land at the source of the Peel River (correctly: at the source of the Wind) is barren gravel and scree. The Mackenzie Range is not precipitous, but still would have been an arduous climb because of the scree. They might have met the Han after they crossed the Mackenzie and saw the plateau in front of them stretching hopelessly into the distance without any indication of the right way forward. I imagine the Han would have guided them across the plateau through the Sila Pass in the Ogilvies which apparently slopes gradually on its eastern side. The eastern flank of the Ogilvie Range undulates, but is still barren. The western flank, however, is heavily treed. I am enclosing a stat of a photograph of the western flank I've discovered in one of our books. So it's safe to say that from the Peel to the Sila Pass would have been frightening and desolate and from the Sila Pass into Dawson "breathtakingly beautiful" (not that Luton or Fogarty would have cared, except perhaps for a curious sense of relief to be in the Canadian forest again, or at least among trees again).

It's too late now for me to hunt out any more information for you, but I have been told that a book titled The Lost Patrol, by Dick North, describes exactly this route, taken one winter about ten years after Journey by an RCMP party in search of a missing patrol (who had perished on the route). I wonder if the college might have a copy of this book?

I am sorry to spring such an important and startling account of the land between the Peel and Dawson on you at this late date. I do feel your manuscript begs and deserves a fuller description of this part of the journey, and I also think the introduction of encounters with Indians at Athabasca Landing and on the Mackenzie will be an effective way of foreshadowing what amounts to the rescue of Luton and Fogarty by the Han. I like the subtheme of their eventual dependence on what was most foreign to them in this country -- the Indians. I hope you agree that these additional passages will only enhance the story...

...My reason for asking for more detail about the building of the cabin is that this is the first time on this journey these men have to do hard, drudge labour for themselves (other than fighting the storm on Great Slave Lake). I would be most interested to read here what the division of labour between them was: who directed the selection of the logs? to whose specifications was it built? who did the brute work of chopping -- Fogarty alone or all of them in turn, Fogarty being the most able? who gathered the moss and mud for chinking? how did the act of building affect the order of authority between Luton and Carpenter, between the younger and the older men, between the aristocrats and Fogarty? (I suspect Harry and Fogarty know more about building a cabin than any of the others); what were their personal reactions to this heavy labour?

JAM NOTES INSERT # (17) PAGE III - 185 LINE 3

.......---UP THE REMAINING MILES OF THE PEEL THEY REACHED THE UPLAND WHERE THE FINAL TRIBUTARY OF THAT RIVER HAD SO LITTLE WATER THAT ---- (JUMP AHEAD TO III-187, LINE 4)

INSERT # (18) PAGE III-187 LINE 13

.... ~~of~~ TO TACKLE THE ROCKIES.

FOR TWO DAYS THEY STRUGGLED ADJUSTING TO THE NEW EXPER. OF CARRYING EVERYTHING ON THEIR BACKS, AND MANY INGENIOUS STRATAGEMS WERE EMPLOYED, PACKING AND REPACKING, CONCENTR. THE BURDEN NOW HERE NOW THERE UNTIL EACH MAN FOUND ~~THE~~ ADJUST— WHICH SUITED HIM BEST.

THEIR GEAR WAS DIVIDED INTO 4 UNITS: TWO FORTY-POUND BACKPACKS, ON FOR EACH MAN, AND TWO MUCH SMALLER BUNDLES WHICH —

1. LUTON METICULOUS
2. FOGARTY SLYLY

IN THIS PART OF CANADA THE ~~ROCKIES~~ MNTNS WERE DIVIDED INTO TWO DISTINCT RANGES, WELL SEPARATED EASTERN FROM WESTERN.

1. ~~[illegible]~~ VERY OLD-GLACIATION - SMOOTHED DOWN
2. VALE, EXTENDED
3. VERY NEW, JAGGED

(THEY CLIMB THE EASTERN)

1. RELIEF AT REACHING CRSCENT
2. DESCENT INTO GROWING DESPAIR
3. ~~[illegible]~~ VAST, EMPTY PLATEAU
4. BALD AND BARREN
5. LOST, LOST

MOSQUITOES ~~ARRIVE~~ FOR THEY WERE ABOUT TO BE ASSAULTED

(PAGE III - 185 LINE 5) --- KEEP THE PESTS AWAY (THIS FOUND PAGE III-187, LINE 1)

LUTON AND FOGARTY, DRIVEN TO NEAR MADNESS

1. CLAWING AT HIS FACE - DESPAIR
2. FOGARTY
3. TWO HAN INDIANS
4. HIGHER GROUND TO ESCAPE
5. THE TRIP, THE FOOD

AT LAST, THROUGH THE MIRACLE OF HAVING STUMBLED UPON THE HAN,

1. FORK IN PATH UP THE OGILVIES
   RIGHT - YUKON - AM SHIP
   LEFT - DAWSON - IF OLD CHARON HIMSELF WAS ROWING HIS THE FERRYBOAT....
   DECISION-
2. NOW CAME THE... FINAL CHALLENGE... THEY BEGAN ALMOST QUIETLY, ALMOST
3. ~~(PICK UP PAGE III-187, LINE 13 8A) NOW CAME~~

Mtns

As he left the hut on the way to the trade he paused just a moment to whisper to Harry Carpenter, but what he said ~~[illegible]~~ L.L. could not

When they returned to the hut, a DISTRAUGHT Ensley could not dismiss the death of his friend and, tackling Fogarty he demanded: 'What did he whisper to you as he left?' and the Irishman equivocated: 'He praised you, sir.'

'What did he say?' Lutoo roared and Fogarty, shaken, whispered: 'He told me "Keep him strong for crossing the mountains."'

Mtns

With an almost satanic determination to ~~[illegible]~~ throw his team into deepest jeopardy, Ensley Lord Luton headed BOLDLY up the narrow trail that a handful of previous travellers had half-marked through the clustered boulders. It was a murderous climb from the ~~[illegible]~~ hidden crevices where the new-born Peel River starts its ~~descend~~ ascent from the Rockies. ~~When~~ AS Luton ~~left~~ was leaving the [illegible] tiers of that fabric river he kicked pebbles into it and told Fogarty: "It means a hard course to the Mackenzie ... a very hard course."

← Having bade farewell to his minions he adjusted his heavy pack & led the way up the Rockies.

The angle of the upward climb was steeper than any Luton had ever before attempted in ~~previous~~ PREVIOUS

Specific Queries

During every stage of editing, including even the moments before handing the manuscript to the typesetter, anyone involved in the project is free to point out places in the narrative that can be improved. Editor, copy editor, house lawyers and especially the author review the manuscript to catch last-minute errors. In the notes that follow, suggestions from four different readers have been melded into one report, and, finally, page 185-A is representative of the work done. I said earlier that I kept inviolate the original page numbers without using the device of 185-A, B, C, yet here that firm rule seems to have been ignored. The reason? The transformation of a chapter segment into a full-length book required inserts of such length that the system broke down. To help my secretary keep track, I cut the new material into page-size lengths and mailed them off to her; I was working in Maine, she in Miami.

Pg. 151, insert #21, line 8: "Mourned incessantly for Phillip" does not ring totally true although we need a phrase along these lines. Perhaps something such as "mourned privately so as not to distress the others"?

Pg. 153, insert. I too want to get the scurvy problem securely nailed down. The men would have heard about the curative power of root muices, grass distillations and even bark brewing. Carpenter would initiate the search for roots, but during the long drag, Fogarty would do the grubbing through the ice layer.

Pg. 154A. I think "canyon" might be a better noun than "gorge" as it suggests a greater difficulty. Also, in the description of the Mackenzie's tributaries which I sent to Sitka there was specific mention of a canyon and a waterfall either on the Peel or on its tributary, the Wind.

Pg. 156. I changed "tent" to "camp" only to include the idea of a fire as well as a tent.

Pg. 157, after the first paragraph: We could insert something easily about how they deal with their wet clothes. Perhaps this is a fixation on our part, but I guess we are curious.

Pg. 165. The water in the river would be very deep in places. I added this clause to suggest it was more than the boulders underfoot that caused problems,

Pg. 166: How do they bury Trevor? I worry the ground is too frozen. This holds true especially because it is well discussed later when Carpenter dies.

Pg. 167: Luton "never blamed himself for growing disaster" -- but he did indeed show some doubts earlier around page 150.

Pg. 181. Changed from moose to wapiti merely to add some variety to the animals they hunted. Wapiti would have been throughout this area, as would moose and caribou.

Pg. 183. Digging for roots marked the remainder of the journey, or the remainder of their encampment on the bank of the Peel? The answer depends to some extent on whether the new segment on their climb through the mountains will be written, and on how the issue of food is treated in that segment.

Pg. 185-B. In place of the description of the land between the two ranges, which is good as it stands, I propose a passage inspired by the research materials: 'The land they were entering sloped upward to a range of low, rounded mountains from which in some ancient time loose boulders and scree had tumbled in vast drifts. As they scrambled up in places skidding back in one minute what ground it had taken ten to gain, Luton said: 'Mark it, Fogarty. These mountains are very old,'

Pg. 185-B, carries a penciled rewriting of a suggested five lines about the mountains from Dinah, and I want to study this. Looks like a good idea. I like her word scree.

Pg. 187, I have always wanted the Luton party to say farewell to their Sweet Afton, but when they dwindled to only two I forgot. I will repair this deficiency.

Pg. 188 I believe that "backpack" is a relatively modern and an American term. A Brit more likely would have called it a knapsack, or rucksack, or haversack.

Pg. 188-K: I can't really see the climb here -- are they using ropes? Is it exhausting? I think we could use a little more description of the terrain.

Pg. 189. Here is where the new passage on crossing the mountains -- if it is to be written -- should be inserted. Perhaps it could begin with their despair on finding that the mountains they had climbed gave way, not to the Yukon valley, but to a barren and trackless plain, with a second mountain range discernible in the distance.

Pg. 190. There are twenty miles between where they would have emerged from the mountains and Dawson City. I added this and the sentence at the end of the page for the sake of accuracy only.

Pg. 194, insert. As mention is made of Nigel's death on page 195, I thought it likely that Luton would have received word in Dawson (unless the death happened later). The problem is that this passage gives a different complexion to Luton's decision to leave Dawson as fast as possible.

EVEN THOUGH HE HAD RECOVERED FROM HIS

III-185 A

that he received the heavier of the pairs, and it was always he who stepped out most boldly when the day's jorney began, but Fogarty, trailing behind, MONITORED watched him carefully and during the course of the day he would wait for a halt, after which he would slyly appropriate to himself the heavier burdens, and in this manner they approached the mountains that separated them from the goldfields. Luton, of course, realized what his ghillie was doing, and normally/ as a gentlemen and head of the expedition, abbreviated though it was he would have protested, but the attack of scurvy HE WAS so debilitated that he needed the assistance that Fogarty provided and was grateful for it! But each morning of course, when they set out afresh, Luton would heft his own rucksacks and cry as before: 'Let's get on with it Fogarty!' and he would forge ahead in full vigor. HEIST HIS OWN HEAVY PACKS AND RUNNING

The mountains they were entering consisted of two parallel ranges, roughly north to

south, with a broad upland plateau separating them. At the spot/ Luton guessed might be the one that would carry them the high mountains, milord to said: 'Mark it, Fogarty. / You can see that these mountains are very old,' and the Fogarty puffed: 'How can I see that?' Luton explained: 'Erosion , snow in winter, wind in summer, has worn their jagged tops away,' and the Irishman grumped: 'Then the map should call them hills, not mountains.' and Luton/ ,wishing to avoid an argument, conceded: 'You have a point, Fogarty. When we enter that range over there, we'll see real mountains New ones. All the peaks/ craggy and pointed. In those mountains climbing becomes a/ test.'

They would not/ have to wait for the more rugged mountains of the western range TO TEST THEM because as they descended the gentler eastern ridges they/ caught their first glimpse of a vast plateau so forbidding that each man shuddered to think that they must spend days trying to cross this bleak , unforgiving Arctic tundra, this desert really, without a tree or/ any stand of shrubs to alleviate the barrn stretches. This was desolation, as alien as any land Luton had seen in his many travels, a land without a single redeeming feature or even the slightest sign of hope.

In those first moments of inspecting the intermontane wilderness, Luton saw two aspects which terrified him: there was no/ defined path through the WASTELAND nor even the/ A CONTINUATION OF fragmentary trail which had led them from the Peel to the mountains, and the BLEAK AREA was speckled with a plethora of little lakes indicating that boggy swampland probably lay between, linking them together. The prospect was so forbidding that he halted on the rocky trail that would soon end to assess the chances of ever/ reaching the opposite mountains where the trail would presumably resume, and as he surveyed the terrain he and Fogarty must now try to cross. he brought the

9

What Finally Goes to the Typesetter

Since many of the words in the original segment intended for a minor place in the novel *Alaska* had already been carefully researched and edited, they could be retained as the basic structure of the proposed novella. It would not be instructive to reprint the entire intermediary version of the manuscript because it would be redundant. However, a few selected pages of the reworked copy will illustrate how the geography was more carefully explained, how characters were more fully described and, especially, how scenes containing dialogue were either introduced or expanded. One pair of facing pages shows how inserts replace cut passages.

(5)

Insert # 10, Page III-172 Line 12*

INTO THE BITTER FEBRUARY COLD......

As he WALKED UNSTEADILY TOWARD THE running track he paused one fleeting moment to whisper to Fogarty, but what he said, Lord Luton could not hear.

THE TWO MEN IN THE HUT AGREED THAT ----

Insert # 11, Page III-173 Line 8*

When they returned to the shack, a distraught Evelyn could not dismiss the death of his friend as MERELY the kind of accident one could anticipate during a protracted adventure. In a voice trembling with anguish and self-doubt he asked: 'What did he whisper to you, Fogarty?' and the Irishman replied: 'He praised you, Sir.'

'What did he say?' Luton cried, his voice an agitated DEMAND, and Fogarty whispered: 'He told me "Keep Evelyn strong for crossing the mountains."'

'Why would he have said that?' in higher voice.

'Because he knew we were trapped...by those mountains Trevor wrote about.'

The two survivors were to experience one additonal horror in Harry's manly suicide. Not wishing to bring his corpse into......
(Page III173, Line 8*)

Insert # 12, Page III-183, Line 12*

and in an effort to capitalize upon this temporary improvement, the Irishman adopted as his credo Harry Carpenter's final instructions (Commission? ?): 'Keep Evelyn strong for crossing the mountains' and he directed his efforts toward that seemingly impossible goal.

Adopting a routine he would he would adhere to throughout the remainder of this devsatating journey, he went out three or four times each day with a spade..... (Page III-183, Line 9*)

Dinah – these are FYI to show the parts he deleted from orig ms. + inserts of last week (June 14) – call me if you have questions. Theresa

III-185

test.'

(KEEP THIS, PERHAPS?)

BEHIND WHICH DAWSON LAY

~~They would not have to wait for the more rugged mountains of the western range to test them, because~~ as they descended the gentler eastern ridges they caught (and) their first glimpse of ~~a vast~~ the splintered, craggy mountains through which they must find ~~plateau so forbidding that each man shuddered to think that he~~ a pass. But between where they stood and that stern jumble of ~~must spend days trying to cross this bleak, unforgiving Arctic~~ peaks and ragged troughs lay a wide valley so bleak that each man ~~tundra, this desert really, without a trek or any stand of shrubs~~ shuddered to think that he must first cross this unforgiving Arctic tundra. ~~to alleviate the barren stretches.~~ This was desolation, as alien as any land Luton had seen in his many travels, a land without ~~a single redeeming feature or~~ even the slightest sign of hope.

In those first moments of inspecting the intermontane wilderness and the mountains beyond, Luton saw ~~two~~ three aspects ~~which~~ that terrified him: there was no defined path through the wasteland nor even a continuation of the fragmentary trail ~~which~~ that had led them from the Peel to the mountains; ~~and~~ the bleak area was speckled with a plethora of little lakes indicating that boggy swampland probably lay between, linking them together; mountains they faced gave no hint of any pass through them. The prospect was so forbidding that he halted ~~on the rocky trail that would soon end~~ to assess the chances of ever reaching the opposite mountains. ~~where the trail would probably resume, and~~ The clear path they had followed up the Mackenzie River and along the gloomy Peel had deserted them. As he surveyed the terrain he and Fogarty must now try to cross, ~~he~~ Luton brought the Irishman to his

Insert to Insert #17 at Page 185~~B~~ C

'~~We must~~ Our job is to cross this wretched vale and climb ~~those~~ the stern mountains,' but Fogarty ~~replied~~ cautioned: 'Milord they are too sheer. We cannot cross them ~~until~~ unless we happen upon a low pass to take us through, and I can see no pass. We must follow the valley westward until we

lower III-185 D

without it would have been suicidal ~~xx~~ along the/Mackenzie---they were blackened with the little warriors, and the stinging was so incessant and painful that had they not found protection under their nets they might well have been stung to death by hightfall, so tenacious

ingecpious PAINFUL

and/~~dangerous~~ was the stiging. But when the two men arranged proper protection under the green netting, they were able to survive, even though thousands of the insects swarmed over them, battling to find even one opening in the men's clothing through wiich they mig gain entance to the target below.

Within minutes of the opening attack the ankles of the two men were a mass of inflambed bites and not until Luton showed FOGARTY ~~Murphy~~ how to ties cords about his pant legs were the terrifying ~~pests~~ beasts kept away. It was a long and terrible day, that first one when the mosquitoes struck, and the men were/so busy protecting themselves that any thought of marching ~~any~~ farther toward the western MOUNTAINS ~~mythical~~, wherever they might be, was preposterous. When night finally came and smudge fires were lit to keep the insects at bay, Luton and Fogarty had to sleep side by side to share and tend the fire, and before they fell asleep Luton said: This was NOT a good day, Fogarty. A frew more of these....'

OBS

'I'm sure I CAN STILL ~~could~~ find the Peel....' AT THE MENTION OF THAT REPUGNANT RIVER LUTON SHUDDERED AND SAID

'We are engaged in a challenge, Fogarty, and the more hidepus it becomes....' The Irishman,/formulating his own/to finish the sentence, thought: He intends to move forward until we perish. Making the sign of the corss, he vowed: And I SHALL stay with him till he does. BUT ~~But~~ Then he added: The minute his eyes close for the last time, back to the Peel and Fort Norman.

The next day was thw worst the two men would know, for with the coming of dawn and the dying down of the smudge fire, the hordes struck with reneweed fury, attacking any ~~xxxx~~ centimeter of exposed skin.

~~spoke too soon,~~ for they were about to be assaulted by one of the most tormenting trials of arctic travel.

During the PRIOR spring season ~~the year before~~ they had encountered mosquitoes, but the steady winds WHICH THEN HAD BLOWN ~~that blew~~ down the Mackenzie, plus the lively breeze along the Gravel, had kept the little pests more or less under control; they had been irritating but not devastating. Now, however, the two men were TRUDGING ~~poling their Sweet Afton~~ through areas so swampy that THEY ~~it~~ seemed created for the breeding of huge mosquitoes in swarms that sometimes darkened the sky. They were of a fierceness never before encountered and about which they had not been warned. It began one morning when

III-185 12

they insisted that the two strangers leave the path, which Luton was reluctant to do, and visit a site on a little rise beside a clear lake. There Luton and Fogarty found three mounds, each the size of a grave, and where ~~the~~ headstones might properly have ~~been~~ rested, THERE ROSE three small piles of stone.

'Who?' Fogarty asked in sign language, and so clearly that it could not be mistaken, the little Han woman indicated that the three corpses had been white men like himself, that they too had become lost ~~in their wilderness~~, and that they had perished from mosquito bites and madness and starvation. To indicate madness she rotated her forefingers about her ears, CROSSED HER EYES and staggered to her imaginary death.

Luton, ~~was~~ tremendously affected by ~~this account:~~ HER PERFORMANCE, MUMBLED: 'Damn me, we've got to give the poor souls a Christian burial,' and to Fogarty's astonishment ~~Milord~~ Luton stood bareheaded facing the graves and recited long passages from the Book of Common Prayer, ~~(????),~~ saying at the close: 'Heavenly Father, accept belatedly the souls of these good men who perished in their wilderness of Gibeon.'

Nota bene: Three times I've written Gibeon and three times it's been changed to Gideon. Let's check Joshua ix. 3-27, and leave it Gibeon, a name Luton would have known. OR 2 SAMUEL, ii.24.

It required ~~five~~ three days for the Han couple to lead their guests across the ~~great~~ wilderness and up the first rises of the jagged mountains, and when they had deposited them safely, ~~on the far side, right at the feet of the western range,~~ they indicated that from this spot two ~~well-marked footpaths~~ visible tracks led to Dawson; They would accompany the men no further, ~~so~~ that evening as the four travelers shared their last frugal meal, Lord Luton addressed his saviors in flowing and gracious words they could not possibly have understood: 'Beloved friends, guides and helpers, when I first saw your people engulfed in the strangeness of Edmonton, I saw you as savages. When ~~I encountered you~~ you helped us find the again ~~along the great Mackenzie~~ mouth of the Peel I chuckled at your confusion about the

13

could return the way I came, but anyone who used that route, going or coming, would be insane.'

Having paid his fare he turned to Fogarty: 'Shall you be coming with me?' and the servant replied: 'No, Milord, I came to find me a gold mine and I shall.'

So they parted, but as the steadfast Irishman carried the luggage to the gangplank which would separate him forever from his master, Luton could not in decenty permit this faithful man to depart without some gesture of appreciation. Reaching out with his lean left arm, he grasped Fogarty's left shoulder and said in a voice so low that no passengers could hear: 'Stout fellow, Fogarty,' and started onto the boat, indicating that the Irishman had been dismissed.

But Fogarty, as if already imbibing the spirit of raucous freedom that animated Dawson, reached out and grabbed Luton's arm, swinging him about: 'I have a name, Milord. Me friends call me Tim. And I have a little something for you.' Taking from his pack the last two cans of meat, he handed them graciously to Luton, who did not flinch or even show color at this effrontery from his servant.

Accepting the cans, he said evenly: 'They served their purpose. They got us here. And as you so elegantly phrased it, we shall "toss them in the ditch." ' And with an easy swing of his arm, as if he were bowling in cricket, he threw first one, then the other far out into the waters of the Yukon. Then, turning on his heel without a gesture of any kind, he stalked

Inseert # 3, Page III-161, Line 3

...would be judged insane.

Turning to Fogarty, he held out a ticket for the little steamer, but he did with a gesture so impersonal and demeaning as if to say: 'Here it is, come aboard if you wish' that the gamekeeper ignored it, and to Luton's surprise said rather blithely: 'No, Milord, I came to find me a gold mine and I shall.'

'You mean...' Luton fumbled, 'you're not coming?'

'No,Milord,' Fogarty said brightly, 'we've come to a free land and I aim to run own gold mine...me own way.'

There was no rancor in what he said or how he said it, and when the flustered nobleman started for the gangplank which would separate him forever from Foga the Irishman for Luton's two small pieces of luggage, one containing the new clothes he had purchased in Dawson, the other the ack had carried and with such uncomplaining determination. 'No,' Luton said, k the ack, 'this is for you. To help you on the goldields,' and he strode on ahead as was his cu

But as he boarded the steamer he knew that he could not in decency this faithful helper without some gesture of appreciation....

Insert # 4, Page III-XX 161, Line 10*

....something for you.' Rummaging in the backpack Luton had just given him, he produced the treasured final can of meat and with proper deference handed it to Evelyn: 'You guarded this faithfully during our trip. I'm sure you'll want it for remembrance.'

Luton, neither flinching nor showing color at this forwardness of his erstwhile gamekeeper, accepted the can with a slight bowing of his head as if expressing gratitude, then said evenly: 'It served its purpose, Fogarty. It got us safely here. And no as you expressed it so eloquently, "let us toss it in the ditch,"' and with an easy swi

xxxxxxxx your team and mine did. He sat the winter out in a warm boarding house in Edmonton . He came to our restaurant for his meals and what with one thing and another we got married. That's him, standing over there. He jokes that he's the only man in Alaska with no neck, but he is fierce in a fight.' Then she added one of those extraordinary touches which distinguished her, amusing, revealing and just a bit self-deprecatory: 'An unmarried woman in Edmonton, especially a widow with no children, xxxxxxxxxxxxxxxx working in a public place like a reastaurant, I do believe I received six proposals of marriage a week, and Vernor had three big fights before he drove the others off. It was xxx a dreamland, Lord Luton, and it seems so long ago.'

Then, putting her own affairs aside xxxxxxxxxxx and grateful for the domestic felicity she had attained, she asked: 'Where are your other three? That delightful young fellow who cared for me so thoughtful? WASN'T HIS NAME PHILIP?'

When Luton could not bear to answer, Foagrty said gently: 'Dead. DROWNED. Those boots you warned him about. They xxx dragged him down.'

Uttering a small cry of grief, she covered her face and soon she was sobbing: 'I told him he was too young to go.' Then she asked: 'Carpenter, the nice one?' NICE

'Dead. Scurvy in the second winter.'

'You spent two winters? How about the other one, who quoted poetry at night?'

'Dead.'

'Oh my God, what happened to you men? Did you miss the easy route or something?'

Neither Luton nor Fogarty was prepared to DARED answer that terrible question, but after a moment the former EVELYN asked: 'And you? How did you negotiate the Mackenzie? Then One your second try, that is?'

'Come early spring we're back at Athabasca Landing, same four Germans sell xxxx our group, three couples, a new boat, bigger and stronger this time, and the rest was easy.'

Lord Luton could not refrainx. 'Easy?' he LUTON asked in his distant, displeased manner.

'Yes. In the THAT fall WHEN YOU PUT ME ON THE BIG BOAT the ice chased us up the river. In the spring IN OUR OWN BOAT we chased it down. BACK Like everyone with good sense advised us, we found the Peel, then the Rat where we cut our boat in half along the line the Germans had painted on it, and we hauled it inch by inch.... what hellish work, ... over the Divide, but when we reached that other little river, what do you call it?'

16

it rotten luck.' Then, to his own surprise he asked: 'Have you ever known anyone who stood this close to death from scurvy...the slow toring away of the human body?' And he held his thimb and foregfinger only a milimeter part.

'So now it's back to England and a castle somewhwre I suppose?'

'Yes, I do have a castle, and many responsibilities.'

A gush of tears overwhelmed her, and at the end she said: 'I can see the faces of each of your three men, of my three farmers. They will be with us forever.'

When Luton said nothing, she concluded: 'On the first time we parted, you refused to accept my kiss of thanks. Don't refuse me again,' and he rose, stood very erect, and, striving to mask his distaste, he allowed her to kiss him, but she had to stand on tip-toe to do it. Then he asked: 'What will you do when the goldfield ends?' and she shrugged her shoulder as she replace her kepi: 'Who knows? Who can guess what you will do? We are voyagers headed for destinations we cannot see. But like traveling the Mackenzie. If it throws you back the first time, you still keep trying.'

Signaling to Foagrty and her husband, she joined them and watched Lord Luton briskly climb the gangplank and turn at the railing of the Jos. Parker to salute them in farewell. 'Where you heading?' the big Australian shouted and he called down: 'Back to civlization,' and with a kind of sardonic amusement he lingered there, watching the three as they disappeared: 'There they go, an upstart Irish peasent trying to be better than he is, a hulking Australian with no neck or command of English, and a Yankee farm girl of no background whatever.' He shook his head in a gesture of surrender and mumbled: 'Barbarians take over the world while wise men huddle like bears in icy caves.'

But that cynical comment was not to be Lord Luton's final judgment on his well-lanned expedition to Dawson. It could not be; he was far too good a man for that, for as he watched Irina Kozlok disappear from view, swinging along with her mates in that free and easy stride, her fine uniform glistening in the sun, her kepi properly cocked, he suddenly uttered an impulsive cry that startled others lining the rail and he felt no embarrassment in disturbing them in this highly improper way.

'Oh God!' he cried, his heart torn with anguish and his brain at last prepared to face the truth. 'She spent ten weeks going the right way. I spent one hundred in going the wrong.' He trembled, still looking at the empty space she had vacated, and then like a pentitent anchorite in his medieval cave he mumbled his proud head bowed: 'Oh merciful God, Let the souls of those three precious men forgive me.'

17

BEFORE (3)

onto the waiting ship.

Thoughtful biographers of the ninth Marquess of Deal, ~~which he became~~ to which title he was elevated in 1909, judged that his disastrous expedition to the Klondike had not been all loss:

> He spent twenty-three months covering the two-thousand and forty-three miles getting to Dawson and remained three hours, but more than it was this prolonged and dreadful experience, in which he lost three of his party, including his sister's only son, that put steel into the heart of the Marquess. When Lloyd George tapped him in 1916 to whip the British industrial effort into line so that Britain could muster its full strength against the Kaiser, he was as well prepared as a man could be to discipline the private sector.

> A blue-blooded nobleman and a man who in the privacy of his club had dismissed Lloyd George as 'that insufferable little Welshman, no gentleman at all,' he rallied to his assignment, became one of Lloyd George's most trusted adherents, and performed wonders in helping to throw back the German might. In dealing with refractory industrialists who came to him complaining that they simply could not accept the difficulties involved in this wartime measure or that, he never referred to his two years in the arctic, but he did look the man in the eyes, stare him down and ask: 'Difficulties? Do you know what difficulty really is?'and because everyone knew of his experiences in the arctic, he got his way.

> with what was known as 'evelyn's sident sneer.'

> But that was not the characteristic which enabled him to ~~succeed~~ become one of the most effective ministers of war, for as Lloyd George remarked in one of his cabinet summaries: '

> ~~What profound alteration in his attitudes occurred there we may never know, but Lloyd George in one of his cabinet notes said of him:~~ 'The Marquess of Deal ~~could~~ reach a decision quicker than any man I ever knew, ~~and boldly defend it, but he was also prepared to reverse himself if proved wrong, a trait which disturbed me. I asked him once: "Deal, why in God's name do you allow them to argue you down, when you're strong at the start?"~~ and he gave a cryptic answer: "Because I learned in the arctic that there is no sense in bulling your way ahead if you suspect in your heart you're wrong." ~~And~~ I do believe his willingness to listen to others ~~and keep production steaming~~ helped us ~~to~~ win our war against the ~~Hun~~ Boche.'

STET COULD

to bend his will to theirs, anyhting to keep production huming.

defend it with brilliant logic and ram it down the throats of any who opposed. But if his opponent~~s~~ marshaled relevant facts to support his case, Deal was pfepared to listen and even to reverse himself, acknowledging with disarming grace: "I could have been wrong." I asked him once: "Deal, how in God's name can you be so overpowering when you first thinder out your decision, then so attwngive when the other fellow argues his case? And how did you school yourself to surrender so graciously if his arguments prove ~~to be~~ superior to yours?" and he gave a crypticе answer: "

18

Editing the 'Despair' Galleys

Looking at the next two sets of pages, those showing the text as it appears in actual type, evokes nostalgia. How different bookmaking is today from when I started! A revolution of such staggering dimensions has occurred because of mechanical marvels that I can scarcely believe are possible. Merlin and his magic wand must have been at work.

When I was an editor at the Macmillan Company, we received galleys from the printer in the form of long white sheets of paper, each containing two or three normal book pages of copy, and editorial work consisted of manipulating those galleys skillfully and intelligently. The problem was this: the author's words had now been set by Linotype into hard lead, and to change even one word involved an intricate process. The line of lead containing the error had to be located, lifted out, and corrected, but if that one line was in any way altered as to length—either lengthened or shortened—all subsequent lines in that paragraph also had to be reset, and the cost could be substantial. So the governing rule was this: 'If the error is in the last line of the paragraph, correct it. At the beginning of a long paragraph, either limit the correction to that one line or forget it.'

Suppose the error did occur in the first line of a fifteen-line paragraph. To make a correction involving a change in the length of the line and the recasting of the fourteen following lines could cost not pennies but dollars, and such expense reflected poorly on the editor, so we became unbelievably skilled in restricting changes to one line, and an editor's desk customarily contained paper on which lines were matched letter for letter, so that the change could be confined to that line. For example, here is how one might make a correction in a murder mystery where the killing had to take place on the eighth floor, but the text read otherwise:

in their apartment on the ninth floor
in their rooms on the eighth floor
in their quarters on the eighth floor

The first correction, *rooms*, doesn't work, but the second is a perfect fit.

I became a wizard at making the most intricate corrections within one or two lines; I would type out six or seven clever alternatives, rarely failing to find a fit, and this skill served me well when I became a writer, because now the expense of resetting a fifteen-line paragraph fell on me. The cost was deducted from my royalty check, and I believe that in a long book I failed to engineer a perfect fit only once or twice, but even those few failures irritated me.

There is a manuscript extant in which Mark Twain, a canny man with a farthing, faced a disaster at the start of a very long paragraph in *Huckleberry Finn*. He had written: 'So Tom and I got our canoe . . .' but his editor pointed out that in the preceding chapter the rascals had clearly lost their canoe. Something had to be done, and Twain was equal to the challenge; he changed the clause to read: 'So Tom and I found a canoe . . .'

Today computer typesetting permits alterations, often of a substantial nature, at any point in a paragraph; even so, I sometimes find myself hesitating about changing a word at the beginning of a paragraph. However, my editors tell me: 'Make the change. Nowadays it costs pennies and we absorb the cost.' The galleys that follow show how energetically editors and authors now make changes.

In the old days, after the long galleys were corrected, a crucial step was taken; the copy was rearranged into numbered pages, and they became sacrosanct. Corrections had to be limited not only to single lines but also to one page, and again people like me with a publishing background became skilled in adhering to the rules. Today the computerized press can repage an entire chapter or even a whole book with a touch of a button, and these galleys illustrate that freedom.

with a bit of jog,' and with that he stepped out into the bitter February cold. As he walked unsteadily toward the running track he paused one fleeting moment to whisper to Fogarty, but what he said, Lord Luton could not hear.

The two men in the hut agreed that spurring him to action had been salutary, but since they did not continue to monitor him as he ran right past the track, they did not see him slow down because of gasping pain near his heart or, when he was out of sight, begin to take off his outer garments one by one. Heavy parka, gone! Woolen jacket with double pockets, thrown aside! Inner jacket, also of wool, away! Now his good linen shirt came off and next his silk-and-wool undershirt, until he stumbled ahead, naked to the waist in cold that had returned to below minus forty.

There was no wind, so for a few minutes he could move forward, but then his scurvied legs refused to function and his lungs began to freeze. Grasping for the branches of a stunted tree, he held himself erect and in that naked position froze to death.

When Harry's return was delayed, Lord Luton said to Murphy: 'Good, Harry's whipping himself back into shape,' but when the absence became prolonged, Luton said with obvious apprehension: 'Fogarty, I think we'd better look into Harry's running.' From the cabin door they stared at the track, but they saw nothing.

'Whatever could have happened?' Luton asked, and Fogarty had no reasonable surmise. They walked tentatively toward the running oval, and Fogarty spotted the red-and-gray parka lying on the ground and rushed forward to retrieve it. As he did so, Luton, coming behind, spotted the woolen jacket, and then the inner jacket and not far beyond the erect corpse of Harry Carpenter, already frozen almost solid. When they returned to the shack, a distraught Evelyn could not accept the death of his friend as merely the kind of accident one could anticipate during a protracted adventure. In a voice trembling with anguish and

seen at the mouth of the Peel. Toward them walked a robust man, dark-faced and with black hair neatly cropped above his eyes, and a lively little woman adorned with strands of seashells around her neck with intricately beaded shoes upon her feet. They halted a few yards before the two men and dropped to their knees. From their manner of probing into everything and even inspecting the knapsacks, Fogarty concluded that they had come, with friendly intentions, across the tundra to see whether the white men were lost and needed help.

Luton, with a bounding joy which cleared his tormented brain, rushed toward the startled Indians, shouting to Fogarty: 'You see! There is a track through this wilderness! They've come to show us!'

He was correct, for the Han had seen the wanderers from a distance and had deduced that they were lost and in grave trouble. Their tribe made their summer camp along the edge of this inhospitable land and various members had made the long excursions to the Hudson's Bay establishment at Fort Norman where they had traded furs for the rifles, axes, and iron cooking pots they treasured. They were not engaged in such travel now, for it would have been unlikely that any Han man would take his wife on such a trip trading among strangers, especially when the latter were white. They were in this harsh land only to hunt the Arctic hare, but this intent was discarded now, for to succor men who were obviously lost was another matter.

However, Lord Luton could conceive of no way to converse with these people who had no command of English and no proficiency in any language other than their own, and he was angry with himself at being unable to explain to them the extremity in which he and Fogarty found themselves. But the Irishman was encountering no difficulty in discussing his predicament with the Indians, for with vigorous and imaginative gestures he described Fort Norman, and the Mackenzie River and the Peel with its ugly rapids, and the journey through the western range, and the mosquito attacks.

163

But when in his enthusiasm he reached the Indians he stopped as short as if a mighty hand had been thrust in his face, for the Indians were engulfed in a most putrid stench. However, when Fogarty came close he burst into laughter and wiped the face of the man: 'Bear grease, probably rotting, mixed with some special herbs. Keeps away mosquitoes, but but it does stink.'

Luton was correct in vuessing that the Han come to help; they had seen

shared their last frugal meal, Lord Luton addressed his saviors in flowing and gracious words they could not possibly have understood: 'Beloved friends, guides and helpers, when I first saw your people engulfed in the strangeness of Edmonton, I saw you as savages. When you helped us find the mouth of the Peel I chuckled at your confusion about the telescope. I was vain and arrogant, and I pray you will forgive me. And even when I saw you coming as our saviors as I knelt by that fetid lake I tried to shoot you as if you were animals. I was vain and blind and arrogant, and I pray you will forgive me, for I owe you my life.'

They could make nothing of his words, of course, but Fogarty ingnored that deficiency by indicating that he, Luton and the Indians had shared the same camps and the same food. They had marched together, had fought the mosquitoes, had prayed together at the graves and had crossed the land of death. This sharing had made them brothers, and both he and Luton wished to give them presents. Having made this clear, he asked Luton for some Canadian money. With elaborate gestures he started to explain that these pieces of paper could be exchanged . . .

The man stopped him. He knew what money was. He had worked along the Yukon. He would take the money and buy his wife a blanket and himself a supply of bullets for his gun. Luton, visualizing the spirited little woman in her blanket, nodded gravely and held out his hands toward her. For a moment Fogarty suspected that Luton might be about to embrace her, but Luton held back, for a gesture like that would speak of too easy a familiarity.

On the final morning there was an impasse, for although the travelers were safely through the desolate land, where assistance from the Han was vital, they still faced a taxing journey to Dawson, and they must now choose which of two radically different routes to follow. Each path, as the Han indicated, had been well marked by the passage of many Indian feet in decades past and even some white men's traces in recent years.

The first was the easiest and most inviting: a northwest trail

166

as members of mankind's common family they would place their final beds side by side. Before they fell asleep Luton whispered: ''I've almost grown to like theyr ~~smell~~ stench. Reminds me of slvation from the mosquitos and that wilderness of lakes.

Editing the 'Desolation' Galleys

I had titled the third portion of the manuscript 'Despair' because I focused on the experience of the two men trapped in that bleak Arctic wasteland between the two mountain ranges when they could find no path through the mosquito-infested tundra. My work in wartime naval aviation had required me to circulate to airmen instructions regarding their behavior if forced down in the areas north of the Arctic Circle, and I was awed by the basic instruction: 'If you land on the Arctic tundra during the mosquito season without a net to cover your entire body, you will be driven crazy by the end of the first day, and by the end of the second you will be dead.' I therefore saw the predicament of the travelers in these spring months, the worst of the season, as doomed, and 'despair' was the word to depict their plight.

But anyone who chanced to work on the manuscript in either Toronto or New York felt that this word prejudiced the flow of the story: 'After all, they do survive, and the reader is entitled to that ray of hope. Focus on the land, not on their defeat.' So the title of the chapter became 'Desolation,' which I must admit was an improvement. The men did survive because Lord Luton would not permit the terrors of the land to defeat him.

The preceding paragraph may give the impression that the manuscript was a basket case on which eager medics performed miracles, but that was not the case. Moreover, I had published many of my books with minimal or no help from editors. *The Bridges at Toko-Ri,* for example, which I wrote to prove that I could turn out the orderly short novel that was true to the Aristotelian proprieties, was printed much in the form that it left my typewriter, as were my works on Japanese art, but because of my peculiar background in publishing I saw a book as the end product of the cooperation of many talents and not as the solo flight of one intellect. I was, of my generation of writers, one of the few who had worked as an editor, and I knew at intimate first hand what the fruitful relationship between writer and editor and copy editor could be. I also knew that many of our greatest writers in past centuries had tailored the conclusions of their novels to meet the dictates of their publishers, often with excellent results. So I saw publishing in a way that was rather different from how others might view it. I sought professional suggestions and profited from them. I certainly did not accept editorial dictation, nor did I ever receive any that I can remember, but I did maintain a voluminous correspondence with the skilled editors who saw my books through the press.

In these galleys I recognize the handwriting of my longtime copy editor at Random House in New York, the estimable Bert Krantz, dictator of the appropriate phrase. Her task was to run the completed Canadian manuscript through the American system, and she was incapable of letting go any galley without tidying up some phrase. I often wondered what she would do if Random House were to publish Lincoln's 'Gettysburg Address.' But many times she saved me from grotesqueries or downright error.

I was not aware when I wrote the notes to the preceding segment that at the bottom of page 189 I had explained to my Canadian editors why I justified—that is, equalized—wordage when a line already set in type had to be corrected. But there it is, as in the old days.

Between my own Palgrave and a beautiful old 1861 edition that someone lent me, was able to check the poetry. (Note that the While is correctly in the poem in your last chapter.) The word keel niggled my memory, and I went back to Albert's notes, where he had made mention that the word should be checked. So - here is clip from Webster's, where, serendipitously, there was the line itself! Bert

Ever since we left the Athabasca Landing I've been such a mariner,' and after laughing at himself he cited a few more effective opening lines: "It was a beauteous evening, calm and free" and "Oft in the stilly night."

But then he shifted sharply: 'I've come to think that how a work of art ends is just as important as how it begins. A good opening entices us, but a strong finish nails down the experience.' Now he had to consult Palgrave, for not even he was as familiar with the good closings as with the lyrical openings. He deemed one of blind Milton's to be impeccable: They also serve who only stand and wait.' But as a young man in love, a condition he had so far revealed to no one, not even the young lady, he also favored: I could not love thee, Dear, so much, Lov'd I not Honour more.

But he surprised his listeners by praising extensively the rough, harsh ending of one of Shakespeare's loveliest songs: 'It has one of the perfect openings, of course: "When icicles hang by the wall" and it continues with splendid lines which evoke winter, such as: "And milk comes frozen home in pail" and "When roasted crabs hiss in the bowl." But when all the niceties of the banquet hall have been exhibited he takes us into the kitchen with that remarkable line which only he could have written: "And greasy Joan doth keel the pot" to remind us that somebody has to do the cleaning up.'

In the silence, men thought of winter, for they had known it as few do, and finally Philip asked: 'What does keel mean?' and Trevor said: 'I dunno. Must mean scrub or wash away the grease. Joan was greasy, you know.'

He then came to his conclusion: 'Point I've been wanting to make, the real poet has the last line in mind when he writes his first, and there's no better example of this than the ending to that special poem of Waller's whose opening stanza I praised many months ago, the one beginning: "Go, lovely Rose!" Do any of you remember how it ends? Neither did I, and I'm not

keel---more at cool. vt 1 now dial: cool; specif: to keep esp. by stirring or skimming from bliling over ‹while greasy Joan doth ~ the pot---Shak.›

keekwilee-house \'kēkwə(,)lē-\ *n* [Chinook jargon *keekwilee* below, fr. Chinook *gigwalix*] : an earth lodge partially below the surface of the ground used by the Indians of the northwest coast of No. America — compare BARRABORA

[1]**keel** \'kēl, *esp before pause or consonant* -ēəl\ *vb* -ED/-ING/-S [ME *kelen*, fr. OE *cēlan*, fr. *cōl* cool — more at COOL] *vt* **1** *now dial* : COOL; *specif* : to keep esp. by stirring or skimming from boiling over ‹while greasy Joan doth ~ the pot —Shak.› **2** *obs* : to make less ardent or violent in feeling ~ *vi* **1** *now dial* : [4]COOL **2** *now dial* : to become less ardent or violent in feeling

[2]**keel** \"\ *n* -S [ME *kele*, fr. MD *kiel*; akin to OE *cēol* ship, OS & OHG *kiol*, ON *kjōll* ship, Gk *gaulos* milk pail, kind of ship, OE *cot* small house — more at COT] **1 a** (1) : a flat-bottomed ship; *esp* : a barge used on the Tyne to carry coal from Newcastle (2) : a barge load of coal **b** : a British unit of weight for coal based on the amount one keel can hold now equal to 21.2 long tons **2** : a long ship of the early Norsemen

[3]**keel** \"\ *n* -S [ME *kele*, *keole*, fr. ON *kil-*, *kjölr*; akin to MD & MLG *kiel*, *keel* keel, OE *ceole* throat, beak of a ship — more at GLUTTON] **1 a** (1) : a longitudinal timber or series of timbers scarfed together extending from stem to stern along the center of the bottom of a boat, often projecting below the bottom, and constituting the boat's principal timber to which the ribs are attached on each side — compare CENTERBOARD, FALSE KEEL; see SHIP illustration (2) : a bar keel or plate keel on a metal ship (3) : KEELSON (4) : BILGE KEEL **b** (1) : BOAT, SHIP (2) : a boat or ship having a keel as opposed to one having a centerboard or a flat bottom ‹the shipyard laid down ten

When Luton finished reading, Trevor reached for Carpenter's hand and whispered in a voice so weak it could scarcely be heard: 'When we reached home I intended speaking with your cousin, Lady Julia. Please tell her.' Then he turned his ravaged body toward Luton: 'Oh, Evelyn, I'm so sorry.'

'For what?'

'For having let you down,' this in a gray, deathly voice.

'Forget that!' Luton said heartily. 'Sleep now and mend yourself.'

He was long past mending. That remorseless killer, scurvy, had so depleted him, stealing his sources of strength and destroying his capacity to rebuild, that all he could do was look pitifully at his three companions and gasp for breath, even though he knew the cool, clean air would do him little good.

Fighting valiantly to maintain control, he reached out to clasp Evelyn's hand, failed, and watched with dismay as his fingers fell trembling on his blanket. Knowing that he was near death, he tried with harsh rasping sounds that formed no syllables to bid farewell to his companions, fell back, and with one last surge of energy turned his face to the wall to spare them his distress. Thus isolated, this compassionate young man, so full of promise but with his love undeclared, his poems unwritten, died.

As before, the end of February was the time of hell and ice, except that this year there was no spring like break in the middle, and much of the misery it brought stemmed from the fact that the days were lengthening, visibly so, but the rate was slow and the persistence of the cold so deadening that it seemed a perversion, a teasing of the spirit. Spring was due but it did not come.

Camp routine continued as before. Lord Luton shaved, and tended his clothes, and protected his five cans of meat and marched erect rather than bent over as the others did in order

and the interminable lakes, little more than collected swamps with marshy edges, obliterated whatever tracks there might have been between the two mountain ranges. They did not go to sleep that night assuring each other: 'Tomorrow we'll find the way' because neither man believed they would.

The next day, their first full one in the barren tundra, was a horror of wrong choices and blind guesses as the light mists of the previous night had turned to heavy cloud and pelting rain. At times they seemed to go in circles, or to lose themselves in swamps much deeper and tenacious than before, so that any hope of completing an orderly transit of the valley vanished, and Fogarty, always the realist, said at dusk when the rains ceased and the clouds in the east lifted: 'Milord, we are close still to the hills we left yesterday. I still see where we came out of them. I know where the trail back is, and if we start right now we can retrace, go down the Peel, regain the Mackenzie and reach Fort Norman before our third winter strikes.'

Luton, poking about among the bogs to find a place to catch some sleep, stopped his search, turned to glare at Fogarty and said very quietly: 'I did not hear what you just said. Tomorrow, bright, I shall explore some distance in that direction. You'll do the same in the opposite, each of us keeping the other in sight, and we shall try to intercept the missing path. It has got to be here. It stands to reason.'

So on the second full day, when the thick clouds in once again and the escape route back to the Peel was no longer visible, the two men scouted exactly as Luton had devised, he to the north flank, Fogarty to the south until each was almost lost to the other. Finding nothing, they would shout, wave arms, and reconvene in the swampy middle, march forward, then launch a new probe outward. They accomplished nothing and at dusk had to acknowledge that they were truly lost.

But not hopelessly so, for Luton said grimly as they ate their meager rations: 'There has to be a path through this morass. Tomorrow we find it and gallop off to Dawson.'

themselves, in their forties, with playing the cello, reading good books and needlework.

When such thoughts assailed him he recalled Trevor's commission: 'When we reached home I intended speaking with Lady Julia. Please tell her.' He was certain now that he would not be reaching home, which meant that Julia would never know that a young poet of marked talent had loved her. He became so obsessed with his failure to deliver the message that for two days he chastised himself, then asked for one of the last precious pieces of paper on which he tried in vain to tell Julia of Trevor Blythe's death and of the young man's last request: that she be told he would have been coming home to marry her. But he had neither the strength nor the concentration to finish the letter, and as the pencil fell from his almost lifeless hand he realized the true significance of death and murmured in a voice too low for his companions to hear: 'It means that messages of love will not be delivered.'

That night Lord Luton, seeing the desolation of spirit which had overcome his chief lieutenant, cried brightly: 'I say, men! Isn't it time we attacked another can of our Fort Norman supply,' and as before, Fogarty chopped the can open and brought out the saucepan. This time he was able to throw in a small collection of roots he had grubbed from the thawing soil, and when stew was rationed out, it was twice as tasty as before and the three diners leaned back and smacked their lips, remarking upon what a civilizing effect a substantial hot meal could have upon a hungry man.

But Carpenter was so debilitated that his high spirits did not last the night, and in the morning he had neither the strength nor the resolve to leave his bed. Luton, lost his composure, and, sick at heart over the weakening condition of his friend, sat beside Carpenter and took him by the shoulders: 'Look here, Harry, this won't do. It won't do at all.' Harry, thinking he had been rebuked for purposely malingering and unable because of his illness to see that Luton was merely using the hale-and-hearty one he would cry out as if it were he who was at the end of his tether: 'Milord! This one looks inviting. I'm near spent,' and he would throw down his pack as if he could proceed no farther.

This enabled Luton to play the game of wanting to forge ahead but agreeing grudgingly to a pause for his companion's sake. After a rest which each man needed, Luton would be the first on his feet, as if he were impatient to get on with the climb, but almost without betraying that he was doing so, Fogarty would hoist Luton's ~~second~~ knapsack onto his own back, and the two would resume their climb.

SMALL

Now the miracle of the Arctic abetted them, for the days of late spring were practically endless, more than twenty hours long during which they could climb as they wished. They kept pushing painfully upward through the silvery dusk, stopping for rest and even unplanned sleep, then rising again as if it were dawn to strike for higher ground. However, real night, shadowy though it was, did eventually come upon them, forcing them to face the problem of what to eat and this caused tension.

??? EDITOR

'We can't go on climbing like this without something to eat,' Fogarty said on the second night, staring at the ~~knapsack~~ in which Luton kept the remaining cans of meat. Luton replied: ~~'You boasted you were a poacher. Poach!' and an evident distaste~~ glared in his eyes. Luton absolutely refused to discuss the possibility of slashing open one of the cans: 'No! No! We must still have scraps of that meat the Indians gave us,' and they scraped their bags for fragments of food, chewing on them in triumph when they found a few edible morsels.

rucksack

rucksack on previous page contains the cans.

'IT'S UP TO YOU. YOU'RE THE POACHER. FOR GOD'S SAKE, GET GOING!' AND DESPERATION

When they neared the top of their exhausting climb, Fogarty succeeded in bagging an adventurous goat, a remarkable feat considering the wariness of that beautiful animal, and this kept them going for the last painful days. On each occasion when they built a fire with such twigs as they had gathered during that day's struggle and they could smell the meat beginning to roast, Luton said generously: 'Excellent shot, that one, Fogarty. Never

THIS FITS THE SPACE, USING BLANKS AT END OF PARAGRAPH.

AS AN OLD TIME EDITOR I ALWAYS JUSTIFY LINES WHEN TYPESET

189

('you boasted you were a poacher. Poach!' and an evident distaste)

'It's up to you. You're the poacher. For God's sake, get going

and esperation

26

The Published Version

young women like Julia, radiant and of great power but not particularly marketable in the marriage bazaars, and if they failed in their twenties to find the one good man who could appreciate their inner beauty, they might find no one, and have to content themselves, in their forties, with playing the cello, reading good books and doing needlework.

When such thoughts assailed him he recalled Trevor's commission: 'When we reached home I intended speaking with your cousin, Lady Julia. Please tell her.' He was certain now that he would not be reaching home, that Julia would never know that a young poet of marked talent had loved her, nor would she receive the gift that would express this love. He became so obsessed with the thought that he would fail to fulfill this mission that for two days he chastised himself, then asked for one of the last precious pieces of paper, on which he tried to tell Julia of Trevor Blythe's death and of the young man's last request: that she be told he would have been coming home to marry her. But he had neither the strength nor the concentration to finish the letter, and as the pencil fell from his almost lifeless hand he realized the true significance of death and murmured in a voice too low for his companions to hear: 'It means that messages of love will not be delivered.'

That night Lord Luton, seeing the desolation of spirit which had overcome his chief lieutenant, cried brightly: 'I say, men! Isn't it time we attacked another can of our Fort Norman supply,' and as before, Fogarty chopped the can open and brought out the saucepan. This time he was able to throw in a small collection of roots he had grubbed from the thawing soil, and when stew was rationed out, it was twice as tasty as before and the three diners leaned back and smacked their lips, remarking upon what a civilizing effect a substantial hot meal could have upon a hungry man.

But Carpenter was so debilitated that his high spirits did not last the night, and in the morning he had neither the strength nor the resolve to leave his bed. Luton, sick at heart over the weakening condition of his friend, sat beside Carpenter and took him by the shoulders: 'Look here, Harry, this won't do. It won't do at all.' Harry, thinking he was being rebuked for purposely malingering and unable because of his illness to see that Luton was merely using the hale-and-hearty approach of the regimental marshal, took offense at his friend's chiding.

Hiding his distress, he rose on pitifully weakened legs whose sores had never healed but only worsened, put on his heaviest clothing, and said cheerfully: 'You're right, Evelyn. I could do with a bit of jog,' and walking unsteadily, he started to step out into the bitter cold, pausing for one fleeting moment to whisper to Fogarty. But what he said, Lord Luton could not hear.

The two men remaining in the hut agreed that spurring him to action had been salutary, but since they did not continue to monitor him as he ran right past the track, they did not see him slow down because of gasping pain near his heart, nor when he was out of sight, begin to take off his outer garments one by one. Heavy parka, gone! Woolen jacket with double pockets, thrown aside! Inner jacket, also of wool, away! Now his good linen shirt came off and next his silk-and-wool undershirt, until he stumbled ahead, naked to the waist in cold that had returned to many degrees below zero.

There was no wind, so for a few minutes he could move forward, but then his scurvied legs refused to function and his lungs began to freeze. Grasping for the branches of a stunted tree, he held himself upright, and in that position froze to death.

When Harry's return was delayed, Lord Luton said to Fogarty: 'Good, Harry's whipping himself back into shape,' but when the absence became prolonged, Luton said with obvious apprehension: 'Fogarty, I think we'd better look into Harry's running.' From the cabin door they stared at the track, but they saw nothing.

'Whatever could have happened?' Luton asked, and Fogarty had no reasonable surmise. They walked tentatively toward the running oval, and Fogarty spotted the red-and-gray parka lying on the ground and rushed forward to retrieve it. As he did so, Luton, coming behind, spotted the woolen jacket, and then the inner jacket and not far beyond the erect corpse of Harry Carpenter, already frozen almost solid.

When they returned to the shack, a distraught Evelyn could not accept the death of his friend as merely the kind of accident one could anticipate during a protracted adventure. In a voice trembling with anguish and self-doubt he asked: 'What did he whisper to you, Fogarty?' and the Irishman replied: 'He praised you, sir.'

'What did he say?' Luton cried, his voice an agitated demand, and Fogarty whispered: 'He told me "Keep Evelyn strong for crossing the mountains." '

'Why would he have said that?' in higher voice.

'Because he knew we were trapped . . . by those mountains Mr. Trevor wrote about.'

Luton and Fogarty were to experience an additional horror in Harry's manly suicide. Unable at that moment to dig a grave, and not wishing to bring the corpse into the cabin, they collected his strewn garments and placed them like robes over the stiff body, which they laid in the snow. When they returned the next day they discovered what food the ravens of the arctic fed upon.

March was especially difficult, for with the coming of the vernal equinox, when night and day were twelve hours long at all spots

on the earth, the two survivors had visible reason for thinking that spring was already here, and desperately they wanted the snow and ice to melt so they could be on their way. But this did not happen, for although the days grew noticeably warmer and those fearful silent nights when the temperature dropped to minus-sixty were gone, it still remained below freezing and no relaxation of winter came.

It was a time of irritation, and one day when Luton was beginning to fear the onset of scurvy himself, he railed at Fogarty: 'You boasted last year that you were a poacher extraordinaire. For God's sake, let's see you bag something,' and Fogarty merely said: 'Yes, Milord,' but was unable to find anything to shoot.

Even in the closeness of the cabin, Lord Luton maintained separation by caste. Fogarty was a servant, an unlettered man who had been brought along to assist his betters, and never did either man forget that. During two winters, each more than seven months long, Luton never touched Fogarty, although Fogarty sometimes touched him when performing a service, and it would have been unthinkable for Luton to have addressed him by a first name. And had Fogarty referred to His Lordship as Evelyn, the cabin would have trembled as if struck by an earthquake. From these strict rules, hammered out over the centuries, there could be no deviation. If Fogarty had to address Luton directly, it was 'Milord' and nothing else; Luton would have considered even 'sir' too familiar.

And yet there was mutual respect between these men. The Luton party had started with five, and now only two were left, and at times Luton had entertained but never voiced the judgment that if in the end there was to be only one to reach Dawson, it would probably be this happy moon-faced Irishman. 'Damn me,' he muttered to himself one day as he watched Fogarty running his laps on the oval track where mud was

king farther toward the western mountains, wherever they might be, was preposterous. When night finally came, and a smudge fire was coaxed from damp twigs to keep the insects at bay, Luton and Fogarty had to sleep side by side to share and tend the fire, and before they fell asleep, Luton said: 'This was not a good day, Fogarty. A few more of these . . .'

'I'm sure I can still find the Peel . . .'

At the mention of that repugnant river Luton shuddered and said: 'We're engaged in a challenge, Fogarty, and the more hideous it becomes . . .' The Irishman, formulating his own finish to the sentence, thought: He intends to move forward until we perish. Making the sign of the cross, he vowed: And I shall stay with him till he does. But then he added: The minute his eyes close for the last time, back to the Peel and Fort Norman.

The next day was the worst the two men would know, for with the coming of dawn and the dying of the smudge fire, the hordes struck with renewed fury, attacking any centimeter of exposed skin. They simply engulfed an area, sinking their proboscides deep into the skin, and their bite carried such a potent irritant, that once they struck, Luton and Fogarty had almost uncontrollable desires to scratch, but if they succumbed, they exposed more skin, which was immediately blackened by new hordes. 'My word, this is rather frightening,' Luton cried as he adjusted his netting to keep the little beasts from his face and eyes, but Fogarty expressed it better when with ghoulish humor he muttered as they attacked him in a score of different places: 'Stand fast, Milord, or they'll fly off with you.'

The two men found macabre delight in chronicling the ingenuity of their foe. Luton said: 'Look at this rivet on my glove. You'd think not even a gust of air could force its way in there, but they do.' Belatedly, Fogarty found that the insects were assaulting his face by forcing their way through a minute hole

in his net; they had detected it in the first moments of their attack. No opening, no gap in clothing could be so insignificant but what these murderous creatures exploited it. And they were murderous, for tradition in the arctic was replete with stories of unprotected men who had been caught in summer and driven to suicide by millions of mosquitoes which assaulted them without respite. There were many cases in which caribou or horses had been killed by overwhelming and relentless attacks.

In all of nature there was no comparison with the arctic mosquito; mercifully, it appeared only for a few weeks in late spring and summer, but when it did men shuddered and animals sought high ground where breezes would keep the pests away.

On this hideous day the two men were not to find their escape on high ground, for there was none that they could see, only the remorseless tundra swamp populated by myriad mosquitoes which maintained their attack in unbroken phalanxes. At one point in the early morning Lord Luton was so beleaguered by a black swarm—perhaps five hundred thousand coming at him in waves that darkened the sky—that he clawed at his face in despair as the hordes broke through a tear in his netting. In that moment he realized that if the assault were to continue with such fury throughout the day, he might indeed go berserk as caribou were said to do when the mosquitoes pursued their relentless assault.

Fortunately, Fogarty spotted the break in Luton's protection and repaired it with grasses that he wove through the surrounding interstices, and in this way Luton was saved, but neither man had much hope that if such conditions persisted for several days, they could survive, especially since they had only limited food and no clear understanding of where the western mountains lay.

They did have drinking water, of course, and Fogarty sug-

good humor that Luton did not resent the familiarity which would have appalled him a month ago.

On the next evening Fogarty ended the day's climb so famished that he feared he might topple over, and he pleaded: 'Milord, let us open another can,' but Luton was adamant: 'We shall hoard them against the day we face a desperate crisis,' and Fogarty asked weakly: 'Will my death be considered such a crisis?' Luton replied: 'I am determined that we shall reach Dawson, you and I. And these cans may be the agency that enables us to do so.' Ostentatiously he used the rucksack containing the cans as his pillow, and fell asleep with the rifle across his chest.

They struggled up the last rocky tor, sustained only by their primordial courage, which all men can call on in extremity but which only a few are ever required to exercise. Fogarty, gasping up the final slope, was in the van, with Luton's extra pack draped about his shoulders, when he saw with mute joy that the apex had been reached. Staring down the forested valley that awaited to the west, he turned and said quietly: 'From here on, Milord, it's all downhill.'

Luton affected not to hear, nor did he look ahead to the route that lay revealed before them; he stood with his back turned to his destination, his gaze reserved for the dreadful steeps they had climbed with such pain. As he stood there exhausted, his back bent, even though Fogarty was bearing half his burden, his thoughts wandered down the slopes, beyond the horizon and the hidden Peel River, to the lonely shack in which Trevor had died and from which Harry had walked to his death. It was impossible for him to experience any sense of triumph in having conquered the mountains.

But then Fogarty tugged him away from the doom-ridden past, turning him to face the more promising future, and when

he had Luton's attention he repeated his encouraging words: 'From here on, all downhill.' Luton, ignoring Fogarty's efforts to inspirit him, continued looking back at the brutal path they had taken, and his shoulders sagged so perceptibly that the Irishman wondered if Luton was weeping. Then, with a sigh that caused Fogarty to shudder, the noble lord said: 'There must have been a simpler way through the tangled rivers and the mountains but we were not allowed to find it.' Even at this near-conclusion to their terrible ordeal he resisted accepting responsibility for the fatal choices taken: it was still implacable nature that was to blame.

But as he spoke these words by which he absolved himself, he felt intuitively that he really must present a more resolute impression to his servant, so he straightened suddenly, hoisted his heavy main pack, recovered his secondary one from Fogarty, and stepped boldly into the lead, uttering a command that fairly rang with enthusiasm and authority: 'Let's get on with it, Fogarty! Dawson's got to be hiding behind that bend.' Off they strode on the last leg of their journey, elated to know that they had at last penetrated the mountains that had opposed them from the beginning.

Then on a memorable day in June, Fogarty in the lead position went around a bend and shouted: 'Milord, there it is!' When Luton hurried up he felt dizzy and had to shake his head to clear his eyes, for below him, on a narrow ledge of land fronting a great river, stood the tents and false fronts of what had to be Dawson City. Seeing it nailed down in reality, and not a chimera, the two men stood silent. They had defeated scurvy and temperatures of minus-sixty, and rapids up which their boat had to be hauled by bare hands, and murderous mosquitoes, and they had reached their destination after twenty-three months and nearly twenty-one hundred miles of hellish travel.

Neither of the men exulted or gave cries of victory, and neither revealed what prayers or thanks he did give, but Lord Luton, in this moment of extraordinary triumph, knew what any gentlemen must do. Instructing Fogarty to conceal their camp in the treed area that sloped away from the river, lest anyone down in Dawson see them before they were prepared, he said: 'Fogarty, we'll enter in style.' For two days he kept himself and the Irishman less than a mile from their destination while they cleaned their gear, dusted their clothes, and made themselves generally presentable. From a tiny military kit which he carried, Luton produced a needle and thread, and for much of the second day he perched on a rock mending the tears in his jacket. Fogarty's beard presented a problem. 'It must come off,' Luton insisted. 'It would look improper for me to present myself clean-shaven while I allowed you that wandering growth. Would look as if I didn't care.'

'I'd like to keep it, Milord. It was most helpful with the mosquitoes.' But there was no reprieve, and during most of the second afternoon, Fogarty heated water, soaped his heavy beard, and hacked away at its edges, wincing when the pain became unbearable. Finally he threw down the razor: 'I cannot,' whereupon Luton retrieved the razor and cried: 'Well, I jolly well can.' And for the first time during this long journey Lord Luton touched his manservant voluntarily.

Perching him on a log and covering his heavy beard with as much lather as their last shreds of soap would produce, he grabbed Fogarty by the head, pulled his face upward toward the warm June sun, and began almost pulling the hairs out by the roots. It was a process so painful that finally Fogarty broke loose, leaped to his feet, and cried: 'I'll do it meself!' and the rest

of that day and into the evening, using the tired old razor which he stropped at least fifty times, he fought the battle of the beard, exposing always a bit more clean Irish skin. At bedtime he looked quite presentable, a lean, capable, rosy-faced man who, as much as Lord Luton, had held the party together.

That night when Fogarty was not looking, Lord Luton took from his pack one of the two remaining cans of meat, placed it on a flat rock, and laid the hatchet quietly beside it. When Fogarty finally spotted it, he was overcome, and after a painful joyous pause in which neither man spoke, the Irishman lifted the hatchet by its cutting end and pushed the wooden handle toward Luton: 'It's your can, Milord. You got it here and you shall do the honors.'

When the can was neatly severed, Fogarty ransacked the gear for whatever scraps were still hiding and made one final stew, which he served elegantly to his master: 'One spoonful for you, one for me, and, Milord, never on this entire trip did any of us break that rule about eating. We never ate secretly nor at expense to the others.' When Luton made no response, the Irishman added: 'And you arrive as you said you would, with your meat to spare. You got us here.' Only then did Luton speak: 'It's like dear Mr. Trevor said that night in the tent. A good poet always has in mind the closing lines of his poem. So does the leader of an expedition. He intends to reach his target.' He fell silent for just a moment, but then his voice hardened: 'Scurvy or arctic freeze, pushing or pulling, he does reach his target.'

Real trouble arose at dawn when Fogarty wanted to throw into a nearby ravine the unnecessary gear that he had lugged so laboriously and which was now useless. 'Let's toss all this in the ditch, with the last bloody can of meat!' he cried, but before he could do so, Luton restrained him with a warning cry, and when Fogarty turned he could see His Lordship's face was gray with anger.

'Fogarty, we have come so far, so very far. Let us today march into Dawson as men of honor who remain undefeated,' and to Fogarty's bewilderment he spread on blankets what gear their rucksacks could not contain and gave a demonstration of how it should be properly packed, with the corners neatly squared.

When all was in readiness, Luton supervised the placement of Fogarty's pack on his back and then inspected the Irishman's clothes, brushing them here and there: 'Let us enter that sprawling mess down there as if we were prepared to march another hundred miles,' and when Fogarty said truthfully: 'Milord, I could not go another hundred,' Luton said: 'I could.'

At eight in the morning of 21 June 1899, Lord Luton, tall, erect and neatly shaven, led his servant Tim Fogarty, who marched a proper three paces behind, into Dawson City as if they were conquerors. When Superintendent Samuel Steele of the Mounties heard that Luton had arrived, he hurried down the false-fronted street to meet him, bringing several packets of mail and a list of inquiries from London. But Luton could express no interest in such things; his only concern was to dispatch immediate telegrams to the families of his three dead companions. Each message concluded: 'His death was due to an act of God and to human miscalculations. He died heroically, surrounded by his friends.'

Satisfied that he had discharged his obligations, he was about to leave the rude shack that served as telegraph office when Fogarty said quite forcefully: 'I'd like to inform my people, too.' Luton, striving to mask his astonishment at a servant's presumption, said: 'Go ahead,' but Fogarty said: 'I have no money, Milord.' Luton asked: 'All that money you earned cutting hair?

Four customers, almost two years.' Fogarty looked squarely at the man who'd brought him so far from Ireland and said: 'I'm keeping that money, as I may need it to buy me a gold mine.' Luton smiled icily at the cheekiness of his ghillie and told the clerk: 'I'll pay for one more. To Ireland.' Fogarty, after careful calculation, sent his wife seven words: ARRIVED GOLD FIELDS ALL WELL WRITING SOONEST.

While Fogarty was drafting his message, Steele informed Luton that a generous supply of funds had been received from London 'to be delivered to Lord Luton's party, should it ever arrive.' The sender, the Marquess of Deal, had expected his son to reach Dawson in the summer of 1898; he was a year late.

Steele's message reminded Luton of the package of mail he still held, and he tore open a thick envelope addressed in his father's strong hand and quickly read the first page. His back stiffened, and Steele inquired if the letter had brought bad news. Luton stared at the man as if he were not there, folded the page, and slid it back into its cream envelope. His older brother, Nigel, dead in a hunting accident on their Irish estate. Luton's stern, imperial face betrayed no hint of the conflicting emotions sweeping over him: shock at his new responsibilities as heir to the marquisate; grief at news of his brother's death, for he had loved and respected him; and confusion regarding his cheerless victory in having at last reached Dawson despite intolerable defeats along the way. Head bowed, he mumbled: 'Mostly it was bitter gall. But there were moments. And every man on our team did behave well. They really did, including Fogarty.'

When Steele asked: 'Will you be heading for the gold fields?' Luton stared at him in amazement and said nothing. Gold was not on his mind or even in his consciousness; he could not recall how he had ever become interested in it, and certainly it was no concern of his now. Later, when Steele related the story, he said: 'He looked as if he had never heard the word. But then most of the people who reached Dawson from Edmonton never went to the gold fields. They seemed content merely to have got here alive.' Steele's people later compiled this summary of the Edmonton traffic:

> There left that town in the years 1897–1899 some fifteen hundred persons, men and women alike, Canadians and foreigners with no distinction. More than half turned back without ever reaching the Klondike. At least seventy perished en route, and they among the strongest and best prepared of their societies. Of the less than a thousand who reached the gold fields there is no record of anyone who found gold and only a few cases in which claims were actually staked, invariably on nonproductive streams. Most who did succeed in arriving here turned right around and went home without trying to visit the fields, which they knew had been preempted, the most famous case being that of Lord Luton, the future Marquess of Deal, his older brother Nigel having died.

Luton achieved local immortality by the boldness of his actions that day in Dawson. He arrived with Fogarty at eight, received his accumulated mail at nine with indifference, not even bothering to open most of the letters, sent his cables, and at ten, after having given depositions concerning the deaths of three members of his party, spotted the old sternwheeler *Jos. Parker* anchored at the waterfront. Inquiring as to its destination, he was told: 'The young feller at Ross and Raglan can explain.'

Hesitating not a moment, he marched down the muddy street to the store and demanded two passages to Seattle. A bright

young clerk said: 'Boats from here have too shallow a draft. Ours goes only to St. Michael.'

'What do I do then?' Luton asked severely, and the clerk replied: 'Oh, sir, one of our fine, new steamers bound for Seattle will be waiting to pick you up the moment you arrive.' As Luton signed his name to the manifest, the young man said: 'Evelyn, that's a funny name for a man,' and the noble lord stared down at him as if from a great height.

As he started to leave he grumbled to himself: 'I came through Edmonton to avoid America. Now I'm heading into the heart of the damned place.' He shook his head: 'The only other course is to return the way I came, but that would be insanity.'

Turning to Fogarty, he held out a ticket for the steamer, but he did this with a gesture so impersonal and demeaning as if to say: 'Here it is, come aboard if you wish,' that the ghillie ignored it, and to Luton's surprise, said rather blithely, 'No, Milord, I came to find me a gold mine and I shall.'

'You mean . . .' Luton fumbled, 'you're not coming?'

'No, Milord,' Fogarty said brightly. 'We've come to a free land and I aim to run me own gold mine . . . me own way.'

There was no rancor in what he said or how he said it, and that afternoon when the flustered nobleman started for the gangway that would separate him forever from Fogarty, the Irishman demonstrated his good will by offering to carry Luton's two small pieces of luggage, one containing new clothes he had purchased in Dawson, the other the rucksack he had carried so far and with such uncomplaining determination. 'No,' Luton said, returning the rucksack, 'this is for you. To help you on the gold fields,' and he strode on ahead as was his custom.

But as he approached the steamer he knew that he could not

THOUGHTFUL BIOGRAPHERS of the ninth Marquess of Deal, which title he inherited in 1909, judged that his disastrous expedition to the Klondike had not been all loss.

He spent twenty-three months covering the two thousand and forty-three miles getting to Dawson and remained only a few hours, but it was this prolonged and dreadful experience, in which he lost three of his party, including his sister's only son, that put steel into the heart of the Marquess. When Lloyd George tapped him in 1916 to whip the British industrial effort into line so that Britain could muster its full strength against the Kaiser, he was as well prepared as a man could be to discipline the private sector.

A blue-blooded nobleman and a man who in the privacy of his club had dismissed Lloyd George as 'that insufferable little Welshman, no gentleman at all,' he rallied to his assignment, became one of Lloyd George's most trusted adherents, and performed wonders in helping to throw back the German might. In dealing with refractory industrialists who came to him complaining that they simply could not accept the difficulties involved in this wartime measure or that, he never referred to his two years in the

Arctic, but he did look the man in the eye, stare him down with what was known as 'Evelyn's silent-sneer' and ask: 'Difficulties? Do you know what difficulty is?' and because everyone knew of his experiences in the Arctic, he got his way.

But that was not the characteristic which enabled him to become one of the most effective ministers of war, for as Lloyd George remarked in one of his cabinet summaries: 'The Marquess of Deal could reach a decision quicker than any man I ever knew, defend it with brilliant logic and ram it down the throats of all who opposed. But if his opponent marshalled relevant facts to support his case, Deal was prepared to listen and even reverse himself, acknowledging with disarming grace: "I could have been wrong." I asked him once: "Deal, how in God's name can you be so overpowering when you first thunder out your decision, then be so attentive when the other fellow argues his case? And how did you school yourself to surrender so graciously if his arguments prove superior to yours?" and he gave a cryptic answer: "Because I learned in the Arctic it's folly to persist in a predetermined course if in your heart you suspect you might be wrong." I do believe his willingness to listen to others, to bend his will to theirs, anything to keep production humming, helped us win our war against the Boche.'

Among the few personal items Lord Luton carried back to England was Trevor Blythe's battered copy of Palgrave's *Golden Treasury.* He would complete Harry Carpenter's mission and bring Trevor's message of love and his precious book to Lady Julia. But before making the presentation he had put

together in an elegant limited edition for family and friends a slim volume consisting of three parts: a selection from those Palgrave lyrics Trevor Blythe had read during the night sessions near the Arctic Circle, extracts from his own journal of the expedition, and, most precious of all, disjointed fragments of a poem cycle Blythe had intended to call *Borealis.*

In selecting the Palgrave poems, Luton chose those which he and the others had especially prized, and that collection is here reprinted in part. The editors express gratitude to the tenth Marquess of Deal for allowing access to this treasured family heirloom, which is now part of the library collection at Wellfleet Castle.

In justifying his choices Luton explained: 'Three of us were not yet married, so it was understandable that we would find great pleasure in the love poems, and Trevor read to us some of the most beautiful, none better than this first one which we all cherished.'

LXXXIX

Go, lovely Rose!
Tell her, that wastes her time and me,
That now she knows,
When I resemble her to thee,
How sweet and fair she seems to be.

Tell her that's young
And shuns to have her graces spied,
That hadst thou sprung
In deserts, where no men abide,
Thou must have uncommended died.

Small is the worth
Of beauty from the light retired:
Bid her come forth,

It Never Gets Easier

When, after this painstaking work in Toledo, New York and Miami, the book Journey was finally published, it was well received in Canada, became a major book club selection in the United States, and was published abroad in England.

So the determined effort and the scores of pages rewritten were worth the hours spent. It became a book which many readers assure me they will cherish. Could there be a more gratifying success?

After this protracted work in Toronto, New York and Miami Journey was published

After this protracted work in Toronto, New York and Miami, Journey finally appeared as a book. In Canada it was well received. In the United States a major book club elected it. And in Europe it was published in England, Germany and France. So the determined effort and the endless corrections and refinements proved worth the effort. It's a book they will Many readers have assured me they will cherish it. Could there be a more gratifying outcome?

And so, after intensive work in Toronto, New York and Miami, this rejected segment of a chapter blossomed into a book which was well received in Canada. In the United States a foremost book clubs made it a major selction, and in Europe publishers in ten different countries translated it, including Germany, France, Italy and Spain, with Great Britain circulating it through the empire. Our hard work was rewarded, and readers from various nations have told me it's a book they will cherish, for it depicts the tragedies and triumphs of the human spirit.

So, after intensive editorial work in Toronto, Mew York and Miami, this rejected segment of a chapter matured into a book which would be well received in Canada, designated a book club main selection in the United States, and find translation into nine foreign languages including German, French, Swedish and Hebrew. Great Britain would circulate its edition throughout the Commonwealth, and readers from various nations would tell me: 'It's a book I'll cherish, for it depicts tragedy and triumph.' The hard work was worth the ffort.

And so, after intensive work in Toronto, Miami and New York, this rejected segment of a novel manuscript matured into a novella which was acclaimed in Canada, became a main selection of a mjor book club in the United States, and achieved translation into nine foreign languages including German, French, Swedish and Hebrew. The British edition was circulated throughout the Commonwealth, so that the work we had done to salvage this tale proved worth the effort.

THE WORLD IS MY HOME

Three Segments from a Nonfiction Book

Getting Started

When I finish writing and correcting a manuscript to my own satisfaction, I ship it off to my publisher in New York, and it is about fourteen months before I see the finished book because editors, lawyers and copy editors have much work to do on the project. During those months there is a good deal of correspondence between the editor and me, but the queries from New York come at spaced intervals, and that still leaves me time to think about my next book.

Because I have a fertile mind, I seem always to have seven or eight viable choices for the next project, and with great care I ponder which to choose. Upon closer inspection I find that of the seven or eight for which I had secure hopes, four or five are not as promising I had thought or my expertise in those fields is inadequate. I junk those and never look back.

That still leaves me with three or four eminently eligible subjects, and I do a vast amount of reading and even outline plots, but on some morning in the ninth or tenth week, a bell seems to ring and a clear voice tells me: 'All right, Buster. For better or for worse, this is it!' And a choice is made: 'I'll do this one and forget the other three.'

On that day of decision I roll a clean sheet of paper into my manual typewriter and type out in the upper-right-hand corner a brief statement about the frame of mind I was in when I made my decision. I spend the rest of that day contemplating the magnitude of the task I've set for myself: the year of research, the two years of sitting at my typewriter seven days a week for more than a hundred weeks.

As explained earlier, on the next day I type out in the upper-left-hand corner of the same page a kind of summary of the content of the proposed book, and then I immediately outline in the space left the ten or twelve or fourteen chapters that I suppose will constitute the book. Remember, I've been thinking about this for more than a year, so it is not surprising that I am able to list most of the chapters and in the order I hope to tackle them. Never do I get them all right; rarely do I get more than one wrong. Notice that in this case of a book of reminiscences I erred in the placement of 'Reading' and corrected it immediately, but what is not apparent is that I missed entirely what was going to prove one of the best topics of the entire book, 'Travel,' segments of which are dealt with in this present essay. To make way for it, belatedly, I dropped 'Reading.'

The subjects entered that second day appear in black ink. Everything subsequent is marked by the appearance of ink in another color. Note that I did not know, at the beginning, what subtopics I'd be dealing with in IX 'Trios' and XI 'Bestseller.' Even late in the day I had not yet made up my mind.

If I work two years on one of my large books, having done a wealth of work prior to starting, that's 730 workdays, and if the book contains 730 pages, it's obvious that I produce one page of work a day. Of course I do better than that, counting the heavy rewriting I do and the time I must take off for nonwriting obligations. On a good working day when all goes well I can complete six or seven pages, between 7:30 A.M. and 12:30 P.M., never in the afternoon and not more than three or four nights a month. I get it done in the morning or I don't get it done.

Have I ever got fairly well into a manuscript and abandoned it? Three times. I had a novel on Mexico more than half written but then I lost forward motion, abandoned the manuscript, filed it away and lost it. Happily, some thirty years later I recovered it and was able to complete the novel. I was well into a vast novel on the siege of Leningrad when health problems knocked it cold, and an attempt on another subject proved abortive. But if I suffered pain at their demise, I did not experience regret, for an inner monitor warned me: 'The project died for a logical cause,' and I was content to turn to a better.

I have rarely attempted any book without having considered it for at least ten years, and in two cases I have notebooks and photographs that prove that a subject on which I had done much preliminary work did not come to fruition until forty years later.

8 March 1988

I spent a good deal of thought last night as to how this task could be tackled, and when I rose this morning I had before me this sheet of paper with the fourteen spaces identified for the contents of the book, but with nothin to fill the blank spaces. Filling in the titles of the chpaters was relatively easy, furs half no writing, second half all writing. I jotted down the proposed titles and was quite pleased with the coverage and the balance. I then added the topic sentences in black ink and shall add efterhoughts in some other colc I'm eager to get at the cirst seven chapters to rediscover what ade me the way I am, but the meat of the book comes in the last seven, for there I have to justify myself, and that is never easy, esoscially since I refuse to do so when people talk with me. Big question: Can I wr te a book which will interest others The material's there if I can dredge it up.

I. MUTINY. STARTED LONG AGO.
RICHMOND- TRAVEL ORDERS

II. VICE. UNCLE ARTHUR. VICTROLA.
BOOK OF THE OPERA. WILLARD
METCALF. MORLAND

III. TRAVEL.
ROAD BY HOUSE. RTE. 34
EUROPE. BRUCE LINE

IV. PEOPLE.
BARRA. the Poet

V. POLITICAL
RUN FOR OFFICE. 5 TIMES 3/2.
WORK IN WASHINGTON

VI. READING
Mom. Dickens, thack SINRIEN
READE. BALZAC, DOSTO, FLAUB

VII. IDEAS. 1. BROTHERS. 2. WAGES
3. LONG BOOKS VS. T.V.
EUROPEAN

7 March 1988

People have asked constantly: 'When are you going to write your autobiograhpy?' and I always reply: 'I've though aBout it, but zomething more important always intrudes. Probably never get around to it.' But during ship travels, when I sit around qith nothing to do, many people come up to tell me: 'You really owe it to us to put down in writing the things you've been telling us, so others can profit.' So repeatedly has this been said thst I judge I'm about ready to take a stab at a most demanding project, but I'll want it to rock-bottom honest and different from the usual accoibt. I visualize a book in XIV parts I-VII as if I'd never written anyth ng, VIII-XIV as if that's all I did. If I could do this with style I do think I might come up with something worth sharing, but the two parts would have to be sharply differnt, concise and illustrative of vital values. I think I see tonight how it might be done and, if after two or three chapters are cokpleted it still looks promising, I believe I'll move ahead. Should be an interesting recapitulation, at least for me.

VIII. WRITING. WHY SO LATE? GOALS.
NARRATIVE. EXTENSIVE READING
EUROPEAN

IX. TRIOS. HEGGEN-LOCKRIDGE-BURNS.
MAILER-VIDAL-CAPOTE WOMEN
ONE MORE 3

X. EQUIPMENT.
PSYCHOL-INTELLECTUAL-TESTS
1. IQ 2. GRE
3 NAVY GENIUS
VAST READING. LANESS.
PELLE/THE PEASANTS. NEXO.

XI. BESTSELLER.
???

XII. HEALTH. YEARS OF GREAT PAIN.
(INTERMITTENT) OPERATIONS
MAYBE THE PRINCESS

XIII. WEALTH. DERIVATION OF MY
CURIOUS ATTITUDES. DEPRIVATIONS.
CHILDHOOD-DEPRESSION- NO MONEY
TRAVEL- NONE IN EUROPE

XIV. MEANING. AMBITIONS O. PLANS O.
PROMOTIONS O- SALARY RAISES O.
ROYALTY O. ST. PAUL. ST. JAMES.

Research Methods

For reasons I am not sure I understand, my writing has been strongly driven by geographical factors. I've been an invetrate wanderer, not because I was dissatisfied with my homeland but because I had an insatiable desire to see and know the rest of the world. This impulse has carried me to more than a hundred nations and innumerable corners of all the continents except Antarctica, an omission that galls me.

In tackling a new subject, even one on which I am well informed, I am never easy until I have drawn with reasonable care and accuracy a set of maps depicting the areas to be covered, and the casual observer might be astonished at the pains I take in addressing this task. For *Alaska,* to cover the intricacies of Canadian scenes—Alaskan, Siberian, and Russian—and the seas and seaports like Seattle, I drew some thirty major maps, many of them repeatedly until I knew exactly where the great Mackenzie River flowed and how the Chinese-Russian entrepôt Kyakhta in Mongolia related to Lake Baikal and Irkutsk. I drew as many for *Hawaii* and *Texas* and almost as many for the South African novel.

For *The World Is My Home,* the subject for the second half of this workbook, I required only two major maps, which showed where I had traveled and written about: Asia and the Pacific Ocean in the front inside cover; the United States and the Atlantic at the back. By using red lettering to indicate areas about which I'd written complete books and black to show those towns and locations about which I'd written substantial chapters, I hoped to show the wide scatter of subject matter I'd dealt with.

The map shown opposite is constructed of half of each of the rough endpapers I had provided. The work I've done in Europe and America is thus ignored, but since I'd done so much work in Asia and the Pacific I preferred to stress those areas. And the map does fit nicely into my work program. There was no sensible place to use as a marker for *The World Is My Home,* since it dealt with all areas, but because one of the episodes dealt with in this workbook is Tonga, I have indicated that island on this map and on the two smaller maps that cover the areas adjacent to that island. These were study maps only and were not intended for publication.

I also had the practice of drawing architectural schematics for any major buildings or settings with which I would be dealing, and although I am neither a skilled draftsman or a capable sketcher, I could create usable pictures of the items that interested me. I did this for almost all the books on which I worked, so that in total I must have made well over a hundred maps and sketches.

This is interesting in that I have never taken notes, in the college sense of the phrase, and certainly never worked with three-by-five index cards. My mind does not work that way, for I learned early on in my college education that I wasted time filing information away because I never returned to it later. But what I do is turn to the very last blank page at the back of any book I'm using and list there the page numbers and a one-word index of data to which I might want to return later. An important research book might contain as many as fifteen citations, each of them referencing a significant bit of data. In that way I can keep three or four hundred books at my fingertips when needed. Upon completing a manuscript after two years of such intensive study, I have acquired such a breadth of knowledge that I could probably teach an advanced course on the subject. But when the job is done, I quickly cleanse my mind of that vast accumulation, and some years later am unable to cite even three good research studies on a subject like Hawaii, Poland, or the astrophysics of space.

One aspect of my research in arcane documents, maps, diagrams, and general information deserves comment. Through the years my friends and I have heard repeated and quite circumstantial rumors that I employ a large staff of researchers to do my legwork and even to write major portions of my books. The truth is that I do all the research myself, but I have an assistant, John Kings, who looks after the business details of my office and schedules the appointments and speaking engagements. He is a manager whose help is invaluable. I can tell him at the start of a day that I need, say, a good biography of Tennyson, and since the University of Texas at Austin, where he works, has twenty-three different highly specialized libraries on the campus, I expect to have almost any book I require on my desk by five o'clock on the day I ask for it. Never have I been disappointed. Moreover, Mr. Kings knows that in that instance I need not only one biography of the poet but three or four, and there they are.

However, I do all the reading myself, all the research, and all the writing. When I wrote *Texas* I had the assistance of two doctoral candidates to locate materials for me, but it was I who did the reading and the writing. For *Sports in America* I had the assistance of a longtime sportswriter who found the batting averages and other records of the athletes I wanted to write about. He was proficient, but I did the writing. But when a manuscript is finished I usually employ, at my expense, some local expert to tear it apart and identify where I might have gone wrong. Such help has enabled me to avoid gross error, but despite such research and such attention to detail, I have published no book that has been free of error, and some of them have been infuriating.

A major aspect of the art of writing is the art of paying attention.

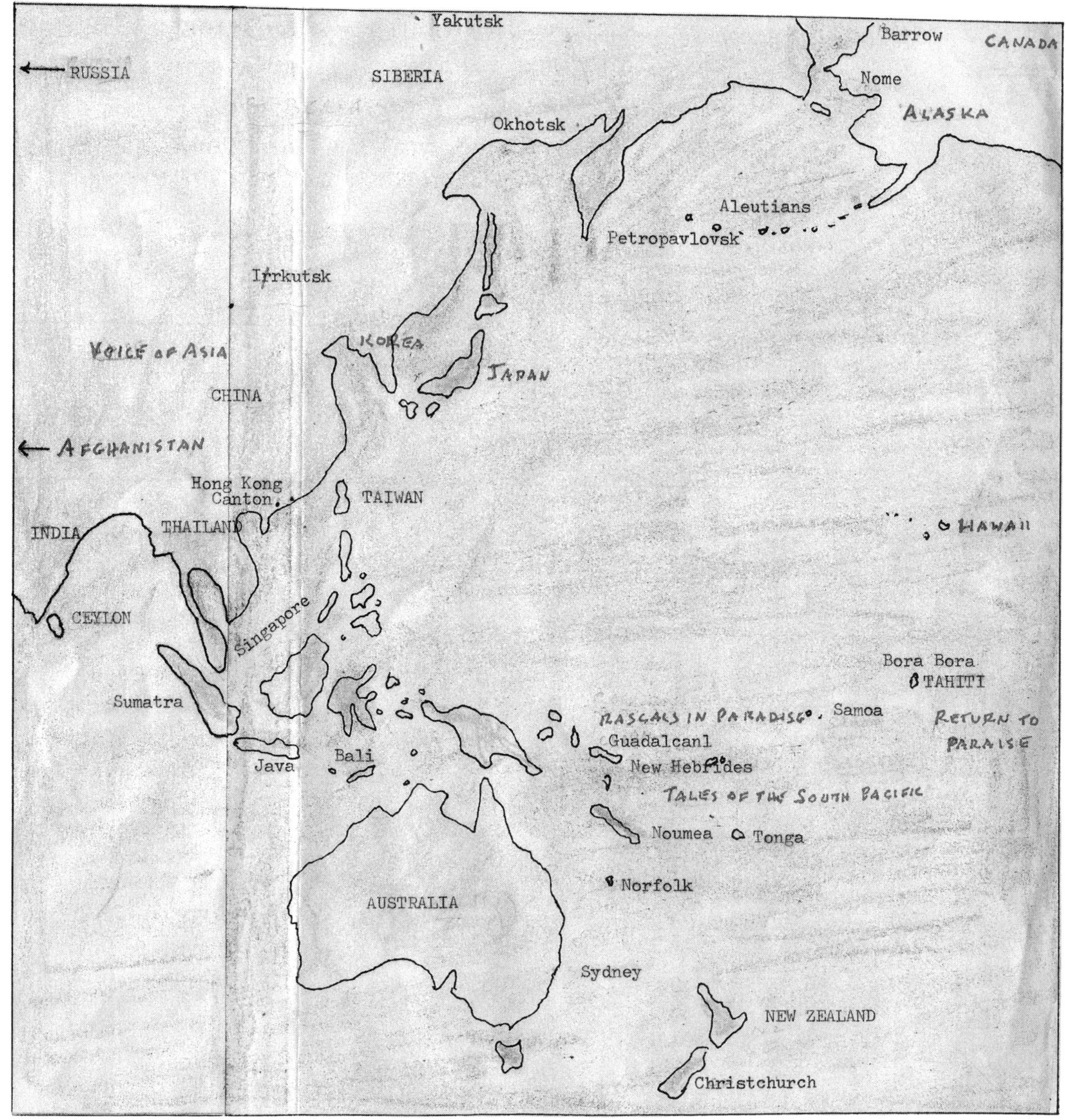

Travel Orders

I fought a long and curious war in the South Pacific. Although exempt from the draft on two counts—I was overage and a Quaker—I fell into the hands of a draft board chairman who despised my guts and was determined to make me serve. When he hounded me into the Army despite my age, I could still have claimed exemption because of my religion, but as a professor of history I had known for some time and had taught that Hitler and Tojo were world-class menaces, so I felt that the honorable course was to fight them.

Ordered to report to the Army at Fort Dix on Friday morning, on Thursday afternoon I cut a deal with the Navy that allowed me to enlist as an ordinary seaman. I said I would rather ride to war on a battleship than march over uncertain terrain, but what convinced the Navy that they could use me was the fact that in my early twenties I'd had papers in the British merchant navy—honorary, to be sure—but I did know the Mediterranean, the North Sea, and the Baltic, the first intimately. When the officers heard about this they grabbed me, saying: 'We need men for the battles that will come in the Mediterranean,' but the word did not trickle through to the proper authorities, for I was sent immediately to the South Pacific as an aviation expert.

There I provided our forward aviation units with maintenance instructions as we took one island after another from the Japanese. I flew in almost everything that had wings and participated in bombing runs on Rabaul and Kavieng, but, to be truthful, except for a stint in Samoa, I never did anything a capable woman secretary couldn't have done better.

When my assigned tour of duty was ended and I was scheduled to return home as a certified hero—I had worked a lot of the battle areas and survived two plane crashes—the officers in Washington responsible for staffing the Navy saw in my records that I had attended some nine universities or the equivalent, where upon they sent an urgent message to Admiral Halsey's staff: 'Admiral Samuel Eliot Morison, Chief Naval Historian, needs a good legman in the South Pacific. Lieut. James A. Michener in your command looks the type. Although he is scheduled to come home, see if he will extend his stay for another full tour.'

When faced with this proposal I did one of the smartest things I ever did: I played dumb and said I was eager to go home, whereas in truth I was not eager at all. My wife had also enlisted, in the WAAC, and was serving with distinction on General Eisenhower's London staff, so there was no home to go to. As I had suspected, the Navy was so eager for me to re-up, as they called it, that they enticed me with a set of the finest orders an officer ever had: 'FAGTRANS to all bases in the South Pacific,' the acronym meaning First Available Government Transportation. The 'available' was all-important; it carried no priority, but it did mean that if I could glom on to anything that was moving, I could travel about by air, ship, or, in Australia and New Zealand, train.

On those orders I traveled to forty-nine different South Pacific stations and in time came to know the area as few Americans ever would, from the minute frontline posts like Sterling, Tulagi, and Emirau, to cities like Sydney and Christchurch, to the heavenly spots like Samoa, Tahiti, and Bora Bora, and the remote islands like Pitcairn, Easter, and the Marquesas that the war never touched.

In *The World Is My Home,* my recollection of those days written in 1988 and published in 1991, the long Chapter II 'Tour,' recounts the crazy happenings during one of my extended visits to various islands as I collected materials for Admiral Morison, whom I was fated never to meet. I doubt that my reports ever reached him or that he would have made much use of them if they had.

In the pages that follow, I borrow two typical incidents from that tour to illustrate problems that writers encounter when publishing nonfiction. The first describes how an early memory of 1944 was ineffectively recalled in 1988, but is later saved by the almost magical reappearance of the principal details I had reported forty-four years earlier. The second deals with an appalling mistake I made when writing about Tahiti.

Mapping the South Pacific

The segment 'Tour' from my memoir concentrated on that watery empire known popularly as the South Pacific. This name has no meaning for serious geographers, but in common parlance it does exist and is defined by the lower half of the map shown here. It extends farther west to include important sites like Bougainville, Rabaul, Kavieng, and sprawling New Guinea. The islands of the South Pacific have always had an aura of romance.

Consider the gifted writers who fell under their spell: Melville and Maugham in the Marquesas; Loti, Nordhoff and Hall in Tahiti and Pitcairn; Frisbie at Pukapuka; Margaret Mead in Samoa; the noteworthy Louis Becke, the violent Jack London, the poetic dreamer Rupert Brooke in the islands generally; Richard Tregaskis at Guadalcanal. And Gauguin's *Noa, Noa,* a lovely piece of illustrated writing (or writing with some sketches) is widely read and admired in the South Pacific. Two American popularizers helped create the illusion of paradise: Frederick O'Brien, whose 1919 book, *White Shadow in the South Seas,* inflamed imaginations that were subsequently titillated by the motion picture travelogues of James Fitzpatrick that were shown throughout the world. Each of the films ended with a syrupy good-bye: 'And so as the sun sinks beyond the horizon we bid a reluctant farewell to this beautiful island. . . .' It was to such idyllic places in the South Pacific that my precious FAGTRANS carried me.

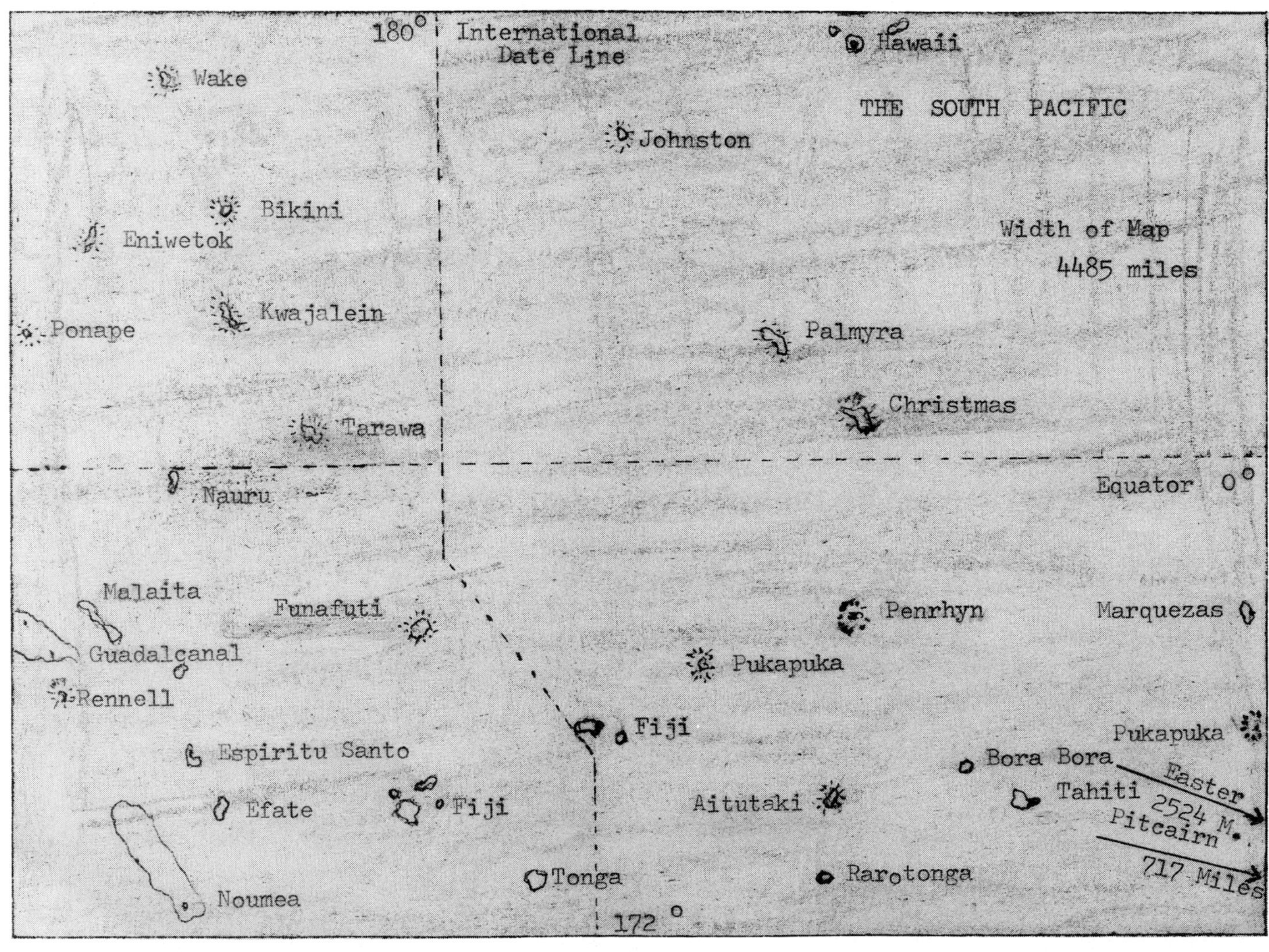

Planning a Hectic Chapter

If you look back at the original outline of the book *The World Is My Home*, you will see that it contained no chapter entitled 'Tour,' nor did it surface when the first seven chapters were rearranged. In fact, when I started writing, it was still not part of the plan, but I was only a short way into the manuscript when I realized that the authenticity of the dramatic change in my life that came one night on a deserted airstrip in Noumea would lack emotional and intellectual preparation if I failed to explain the impact of the war on my thinking. In my first tour of duty I had seen my nation methodically develop awesome power, I'd seen the Japanese bastions at Rabaul and Kavieng rotting in the sunlight along with their men, and I'd watched the loss of good men at Guadalcanal and the heroism of others who flew rescue missions on the Black Cats out of Tulagi; I barely survived a couple of bad crashes myself. Then, suddenly, I was catapulted into a languorous paradise, and that was a story of a much different character.

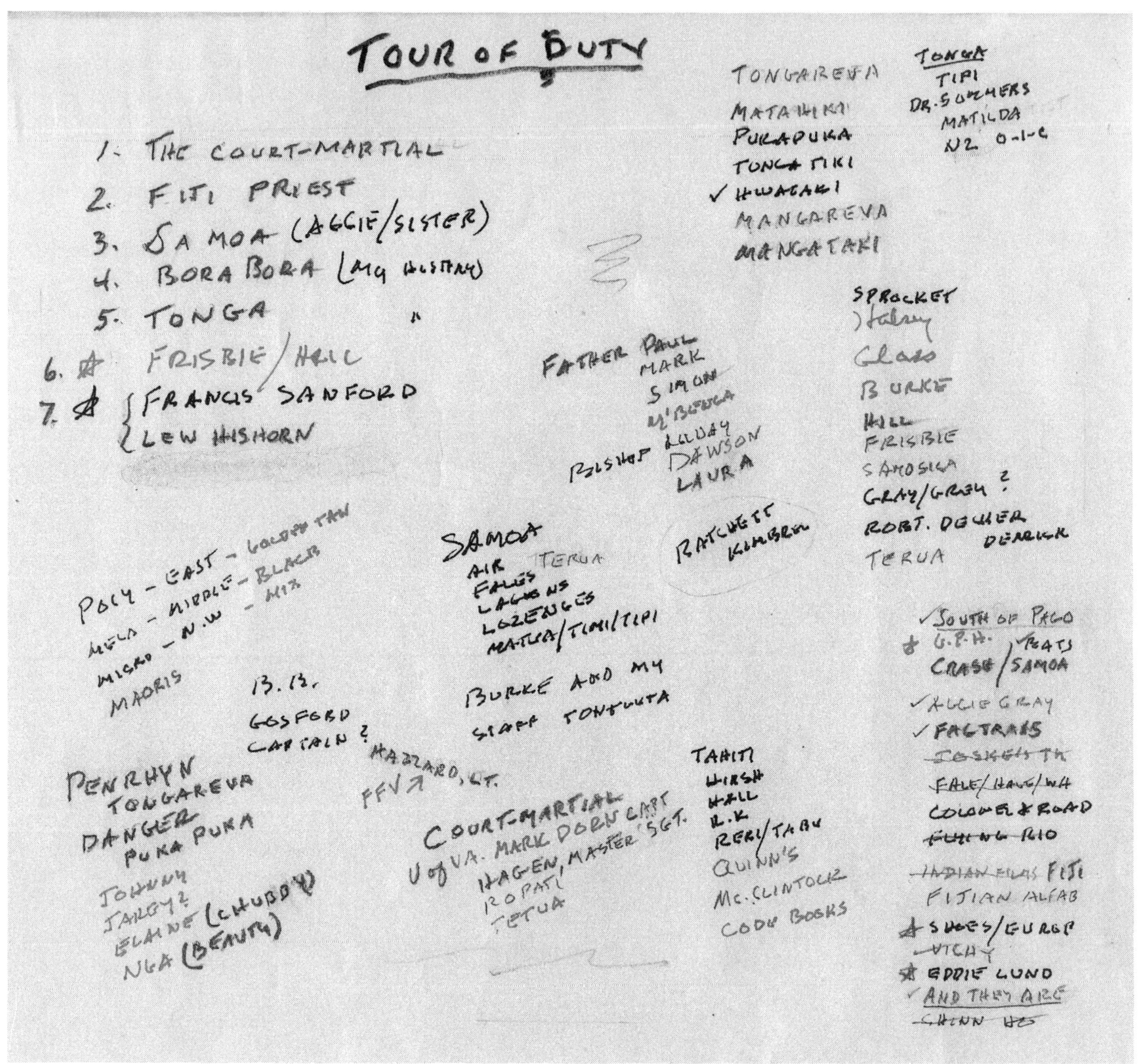

A Source of a Firsthand Account

The name Tonga* rings in my memory like a golden bell that alternately peals joyous and mournful music. My association with the island started when the admiral in Noumea delivered a directive that was both succinct and mysterious: 'Grab the first flight to Tonga and find out what in hell's going on . . . and about that little red truck. Isn't anyone in charge?'

The good part of my assignment started the moment I landed, for I found myself among some of the gentlest people of the South Pacific, who lived on more than a hundred and fifty separate islands, with the tidy little town of Nukualofa as capital. The islands boasted an odd assortment of treasures: a majestic queen who stood six feet eight inches tall and weighed three hundred pounds; a great sea turtle that was known to be two hundred years old and maybe three; a gigantic stone assembly shaped like the Greek letter *pi* whose origins no one could decipher; and the largest collection of fruit bats in the world, which darkened the sky as they flew out at nightfall.

The morning after I arrived I got to work, reviewing records and interviewing scores of Americans and Tongans alike. When I felt that I had a fairly good grasp of what had happened when the admiral wasn't looking, I wrote a rather full report of what had obviously been a hilarious and most unmilitary affair. But all that happened in 1944—decades ago—and unfortunately I did not have at hand a copy of my on-the-scene report to refresh my memory of the outrageous affair. I could not recall details or believe that they could have happened when I did remember them. My first draft, which appears on pages 85–90, was a drab affair, but I did not lose hope that the situation would improve: 'When more details start coming back to me I'll be able to build something usable on this shaky underpinning.'

Then a remarkable coincidence saved me. Some years back I had told my literary agent, Owen Laster, about my wartime adventures on Bora Bora and Tonga: 'Years from now some researcher in Navy files will come upon my extensive reports on those two islands, and he'll be able to combine them into a hilarious portrait of how the United States Armed Forces operated in the South Pacific when the fighting war passed north to Iwo Jima and Okinawa. He'll have a gold mine.' This possibility so excited Laster that he initiated a search for the missing documents, and although his aides failed to locate them, they did encourage the Navy archivists to search for and discover a later report that quoted so copiously from my earlier work that I was able to reconstruct details I had forgotten, such as my mission to help keep the islands near Tahiti on the side of de Gaulle's Free French rather than with the traitorous Vichy French, who were so strong in the area. How these long-lost summaries came into my hands was a miracle that I shall describe later.

When I read my report about Tonga, wonderful images began to flood back: an island girl of enchanting beauty, American soldiers firing at the millions of fruit bats as the creatures came out of their caves at night, a huge warehouse, an ineffectual island commander, a gung-ho medical doctor who had always dreamed of military glory, a thieving rascal named Tipi (one of the most capable foreign agents ever to confront the Navy), and the Little Red Truck.

This oblique glance at my report gave me the help I needed, for I had written about the everyday life of Tonga: the riots, the night raids, the placing of docile natives under house arrest, and the social life of Nukualofa. What a cascade of emotions my long-dead report awakened! How eagerly I went about the task of re-creating those exciting days.

At the close of this Tongan segment I reprint the final edited version as it appears in *The World Is My Home*, and there I have marked those passages that survived from the rough draft. How few they are! How little they contribute to the vitality of the story. I think this illustrates the value of firsthand data. Also, remember that I was relying not on my manuscript but on reactions by an outsider who was not interested in the things that particularly interested me. But those passages about events nearly half a century ago exploded in my mind, evoking passionate images and sounds and the craftiness of that truck.

*Discovered in 1616, became a monarchy in 1845 and a British protectorate in 1900; a fully independent monarchy since 1968 and a member of the Commonwealth of Nations.

Why, if my memories of Tonga are now so joyous, did I say that my experience ended dismally and with lasting frustration? Alas, my two reports—one on Bora Bora, the other on Tonga—have never been found. They were written with what I can only call love. I was describing how American GIs made contact with Polynesia, one of the world's most alluring and hypnotic areas. I shall always be grateful that I was allowed to witness this bewildering, lovely, and instructive confrontation, and recalling it now makes me think that had I been an Air Force historian serving in Saudi Arabia from August 1990 to April 1991 I could probably have written just as compelling unit histories about our troops there as I did about our men in the South Pacific. And I suppose that when I had done so, some older academic historian working for the Air Force in 1996 would say: 'The kind of rot Michener wrote about ought not to be part of the official record. Makes the Air Force look bad.' And he would burn my reports, but not before borrowing the best passages for inclusion in his own. The passages he borrowed would save my account.

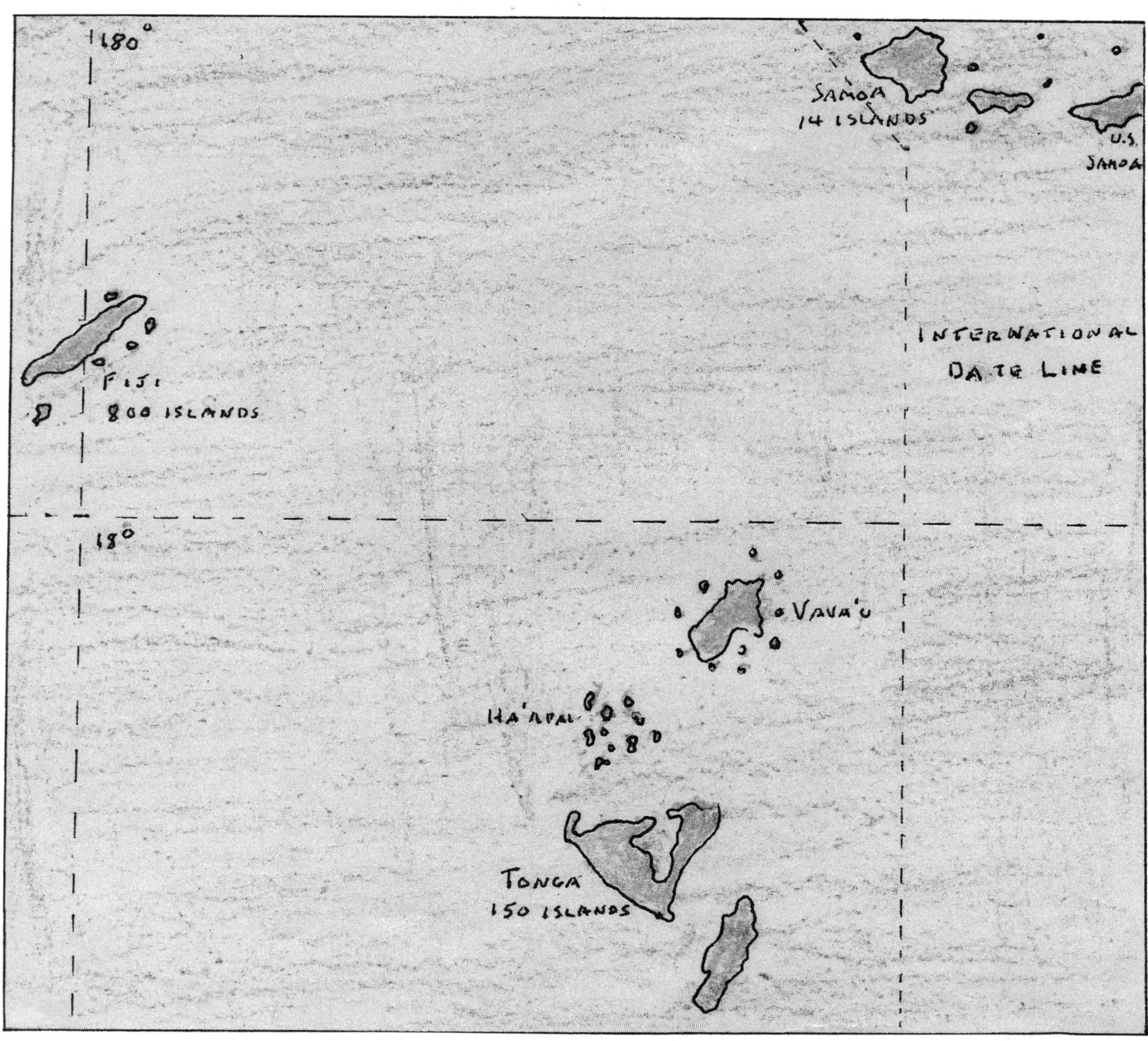

Carbon Copy of the Original Statement

The Tongan episode has been chosen for incorporation because the difference between the opening effort and the final version of what happened is so vast that one can hardly escape seeing the creative process in operation. The first version was pretty bad, the second a bit more spirited. But the first must not be denigrated, because the desideratum here was to get the setting and the story line established, and this effort accomplished that purpose.

I have always felt that in writing the first draft it is obligatory to maintain forward movement, to keep the sequence of ideas firmly established but to follow various tangential inspirations to their logical conclusions. To flounder about in what is popularly known as 'writer's block,' so often seen in the motion pictures about writers or other creative people, is to indulge in self-pity, and when I see the tortured novelist angrily tear up his manuscript, or the painter slash his canvas with black paint, or the composer crash his hands on the piano with frustration, I often wonder how you depict a sculptor expressing his disgust with his block of stone.

Once, while being interviewed on camera, I came up by accident with an appropriate summary of this problem: 'Michelangelo has been painting all week on the ceiling of the Sistine Chapel. He's bone-weary and his eyes no longer focus, so on Friday night he hits the local bistros. On Saturday afternoon he gets drunk with the Pope, and on Sunday he really ties one on. On Monday he's so hung over and so spaced out he'd risk his life if he tried to climb onto that scaffolding. But come Tuesday morning, whether his head is clear or not, whether or not he's feeling inspired, he'd better be up at that ceiling, with his brushes in order and his paint properly mixed, because he is a professional and he cannot indulge himself in prolonged idleness, not for any reason.'

In writing of Tonga my problem was to recall distant events as clearly as I could and, since they were the meat of the story, to present them as interestingly as possible, and this I did, to the limit of my capacity at the moment. But I was hampered by the fact that back in 1945 I had written a detailed account of the incident of the Little Red Truck, but it had been lost in Navy files, and it irritated me not to be able to recall the smaller details that gave the story color and an insight into one aspect of military life. My topic was 'What do soldiers and sailors do in idleness when the fighting war has long passed them by?' This was the problem that Tom Heggen had faced when writing *Mister Roberts*, and as I labored at my typewriter I was fully aware that I was not telling the whole story, but even so I felt compelled to get the framework properly set, so I charged ahead.

My first try appears just as it rolled out of the typewriter, without a word being changed. My typing is poor because a minor stroke has slightly incapacitated my left index finger, but even with this impediment I have been able to type millions of words since. As you will shortly see, I type most material two or three times.

I invite you to study the result of this first attempt and make two judgments: 'Was it worth the effort?' and 'Could it be used as the basis for subsequent improvement?'

Tonga is the fairytale kingdom based on a group of islands some five hundred miles southeast from Fiji, and after I had helped place the eloping priest and his bride on the bomber to Australia, I flew direct from Nadi to Nuku'alofa, capital town of the kingdom where I fell immediately under the spell of the gigamtic Queen of Tonga, six feet eight inches tall and about three hundred pounds, who would cause such a sensation in London some years later when she attended both the burial of King George VI and the coronation of Queen Elizabeth II. That towering bulk and warm gracious smile made her the prkme favorite of the processions came as no surprise to those of us who had known her during thxe war.

She kept on her palace grounds where all could see a gigantic sea turtle reputed to be at least two hundred years old and some said three. Additional highlights in the kingdom were the mystic stone holy places consisting of two massive upright stones across whose tops rested an enormous parallel top---who erected them, when and for what purpose no one could say---and the nightly flight of thousands upon thousands of big bats, so many that they darkened the sky. It was out pleasure to go out at dusk with s otguns and knock a score or so out of the sky as they flew overhead, and we did this not for sport; Tingans dived for the fallen bats, whose flesh they cooked into an excellent stew.

If I have spoken in a somewhat free and easy manner of my extended tour of duty through the islands of my doman the reader must remember that on Bora Bora I worked diligently to compile the record of our military occupation of that island and now on Tonga I was similarly engaged with hour upom hour of research, interview, calculating total figures and trying sometime i vain to answer the quwsrion I had been asked in Noumea before I started out: 'What in hell has been going on donw there in Tonga?'

I spent about three weeks assembling the answer and another week of steady dictation my guess as to what happened, but in doing so I broke down xx so often in raucous laughter that I am not sure I provided a coherent account, and I see no sense in trying to recall the specifics of my report, which ran to many hilarious pages. But a brief summary of what could happen to a group of military men xxx in a tropical paradise when no one was looking will be instructive.

In the early days of the war the Kingdom of Tonga played a role of some importance, because it was feared that thex Japanese attack, which xxxx could strike at any moment, might bypass Fiji, which was better protected, and capture Tonga, whose xxx numerous islands would provided many fine achorages for Japanese warships. Hurried steps were taken to protect the ixslands, and in a corner of the town of Nuku'alofa a very large warehouse was constructed. Crammed with valuavle fighting gear and supplies to help withstand a siege, that warehouse became the focal point of my report, fo everything that happened on Tonga in the period for which I was responsible revolved around that warehouse and its precious content.

Since ~~Tonga was an island~~ the anchorages of Tonga were the targets of importance //The U.S. Navy was naturally placed in control, and in the early days I would suppose that someone like a Rear Admiral or a senior captain was in command, but as the battlefronts moved farther and father north to Guadalcanal, Bougainville and isalnds like Tarawa and Saipan, it was clear that the Japanese fleet was not going to risk the long run to Tonga to do damage there. The danger was over. Experienced admirals and captains were required up in the forward areas, and Tonga was left to fend for itself, which was when I came into the picture.

I am embarrassed to say that although I wrote a rather full account of the affair, I caanot now recall whether the officer left in charge of the island and its extremely valuable warehouse was a Navy doctor or a dentist, but I think it was the latter, although he may have been an osteopath. At any rate, we shall call him Commander Simmons, for although his rank was no higher than mine, a senior lieutenant, he was in charge of the installation and was therefore entitled to a temporary title of commander, and when the Navy put his in charge they picked a winner, for he had probably dreamed as a child of being in command of troops on some distant battlefiel or in charge of a ship in the China Sea during a major engagement against pirates.

Commander Simmons was a tiger who decided during the first days of his command that he would bring some spit-and-polish to his unit, and what that aim constatly in mind he began to issue a chain of orders which disgruntle not only the American military men under his control but also the Tongan workers who up to this time had enjoyed a rathre free-and-easy discipline in their work, for which they were pai d very well indeed. Now hours were to be kept. Tongans were not to drive Navy cars without ~~specific~~ written orders countersigned by Commander Simmons, and Tongan girls, a notablu saucy lot, were to stop lollygagging about the base on one pretext or another.

From what I could learn through careful questioning, sometime after these events, life at the base became rath r unpleasant: 'He treated us natives like cattle. We had handled equipment of great value for the Navy and never lost any of it. //Our Natives who drove the Navy cars and trucks took better care of them than your people did. Our girl typists were much better than the men yeomen, everyone said that. And we had come to think of going to the movies at night as part of our pay. Now all changed, and we don't like.'

As a matter of fact, from what I could learn, nobody liked the changes, with the American/enlisted personnel vying with the Tongan hired hands as to who disliked Commander Simmons most. //At the time it must have been obvious to everyone but Simmons that something was about to explaode.

At this point in the developing trouble in Tonga/three factors became central: a very lovely Tingan girl called Meredith who did not work on the base, her/older brother Tipi who did, and a little red truck, and althpugh I would hear constant stories about that little red truck, I never did learn where it had come from or who owned it, but that it was not Navy property I am sure.

How Meredith received her nickname or how she met Commander Simmons is obscure, but one girl told me that whereas Meredith had a good Tingan name, one of her friends had come upon Meredith in a book and had suggested that the lilting syllables fitted Meredith exactly, and the name stuck. As to the fatal meeting with Simmons, all I learned was that several eager informants, all girls, told me: 'Tipi arrange,' and I suppose he had must have in pursuit of a planned attack, because once Simmons met this/seductive girl a good deal of his military ardor subsided and he began to think more about her than about new rules with which to torment his underlings.

In fact, Warrior Simmons became so preoccupied with Meredith that he moved her into his quarters, showered her with gifts and spent most of his spare time worrying about her rathe than his nominal duties at the base, and many of his men told me: 'Things improved like you wouldn't believe,' and one man voiced the opinion of most: 'Tonga became a good spot for ser ing out your overseas assignment.'

X But I was distressed to learn that it was in this very period of euphoria that the little red truck came ino prominence: ' As soon Tipi satified his sister Meredith keeping Commander Simmons busy, he start runnin' his little red truck.'

'Where did he get it?'

'Where Tipi get anything? He just get it,' and other conspirator said: 'Maybe xx it not red truck. Maybe he paint it, hide it from people.'

It occurred to me that painting a stolen truck red was either a stupid form of camouflage or an extremely clever one, and I began looking more closely into the track record of Tipi. Younger than his sister and the son of parents who had given the Tongan Xpolice a lot of imaginative trouble, he was so clever at handling any problems that arose between the American military and the local population that the Navy employed him to help him keep the locals at ease, though what specifically he did I coudl never learn. He was Tipi and several onformants told me that he was really much smarter than most of the officers he worked for.

At any rate, about eight months before I reached Tonga, a relxd place I will always remember with affection, Tipi established a routine that paid off handsomely: 'I work with him, like you say you already know. Yes, my job watch Commander Simmons headquarters, give signal when him, Tipi's sister take nap. Then TIpi drives red truck down that lane over there, no one can see from here, and go around back.'

I had not yet fathomed what it was that Tipi did with his red truck, for by the time I reached the island he was in jail and I could not get to him, but one of his henchmen who had escaped the police told me: 'We get wircutters, three men, me two others. We go back the big warehouse xxxx nobody can see, we cut xxxx snip, snip, snip'---and his hands opened and closed rapidly as if holding wirecutters---'and we cut twox panels out of warehouse, big enough red truck drive right in.'

'And the purpose?'

'First Tipi load little red truck xxxx full most expensive t ings people want. Radios,. Washingmachines. Little stoves. All what they call G.I. Issue.'

'What xxx could he do with it on this island? We have military police, you know?'

'Very quiet at first. Never take enough make police worry. What he do with it? He give it away, all families get radio, washing machine, set of tools.'

I had seen enough of the South Pacific to realize that the theft of one xxxx small truckload of what was after all trivial stuff not/related to the war effort was not a court-martial affair, especially when the Robin Hood was an alien civilian who distribited xxxx his loot to the Tongan natives, who had been some of our stanchest allies. I was willing to forgive Tipi and even ask the local courtsx to consider leniency in his xxxx case, because from what I had heard of him he seed to be a pretty good sort.

But when I interrogated the islanders further I learned that Tipi had not only made that first haul of little items but that on subsequent/xxxxx when he was sure that Commander Simmons was asleep, he had backed his little red truck boldly into the gaping hole in the rear of warehouse and hauled away some really big items, things the Navy could have used.

'What did he do with things that big?'

'Nobody lookin', he take them to ships in harbor, they go to Ha'apa Group, maybe Vava'u Group, far away, they need things same like us.'

'But why did you always go in the afternoon? You might have been seen.'

'Night time they very careful. Guards. Big dogs too, we not try.'

'And you were never caught?'

'Nobody see us, look, you sit here same Commander Simmons, you not a ble to see back of warehouse, especially you asleep in bed, very happy.'

In order to give my report verisimilitude I knew I had to inspect the big warehouse myself, so with a Tongan policeman, a guard from the nearly disbanded base and my two informants, we went to the big front doors, unlocked the double bolts and stepped into the gloomy grayness of the huge building, but I xxxx received no usable information for it was completely empty. Not a military item was visible, not one carton intended for the PX.

'Where's the gear?' I asked, and the Navy guard said: 'He/stole it all.'

'Who stole it all?'

'The guy in the little red truck.'

'You mean....' I was aghast, for to empty a building that size/Tipi must have made scoe of trips in his little red truck. and his fellow thieves said that he had.

'First time easy, small stuff. Then bigger, still easy. Everything easy, he just keep goin' till all gone.'

'Where did it go?'

'Like before. Small things, P.X. food, like that to people here. Big things take four men to carry, always on little ships to other islands.'

'You mean, everything that was in here...you shipped it all out?'

'Yep. All go.'

'What happened to the littl red truck?'

"Shore police gettin' suspicious, him, me we paint it white.'

'And then?'

'Maybe Ha'apa Grouo, maybe Vava'u, maybe Tipi go fetch it he get out of jail.'

I felt a keen desire to see this mastermind and persuaded the Tongan officer to let me visit the rude jail, where I happened to enter just as an attractive young woman was on her way in to see the prisoner. It was Meredith, Tipi's x sister who had proved so very helpful in her brother's plans. The three of us talked for about an hour, and Tipi satisfied me that carefully laid

his introduction of Meredith to Commander Simmons had not been part of a/plot: 'I see Simmons all tied up, shouting orders here, there, makin' everybody mad, I think: "What slow him down, one pretty gilr."'

'Did you like Simmons?' I asked Meredith, and she said: 'Oh, yes! He very kind to me, very good, he help me fix my house.'

'He gave you many things?'

'Yes, he one good man, got two babies Oklahoma.'

I asked Tipi what he would do when his prison term ended and he said brightly: 'I think maybe go back work Navy. New commander now, Simmons/xin Oklahoma. He need help, maybe.'

go back

'Where did you get the little red truck?'

He considered this for some moments, then said: 'It belong Commander Simmons. Navy blue. Two men, me, we paint it red xx ine night, he never guess.'

'Will you bring it b Where is it now?'

'Vava'u.'

'You bring it back when you get out?'

'Yes. My brother have it, he give it back when I ask.' As I was about to leave the pair, the charming girl, the clever brother, he asked: 'You speak me good, police? Tell them I needed at naval base?'

Our The base was much truncated when I worked berthed there during the writing of my report, but as the Marines said in their famous poster, 'We could use a few good men,' and i made thw recommendation to Queen Salote who towered over me as I spoke and she told me how xxxx gratified everyine on her islands were that the American occupation had gone so smoothly, and she said that without sensible and understanding men like Commander Simmons this would not have been possible. She asked: 'If we pardon this Tipi, would you reemploy him at xxx your base?' and I said a firm: 'Yes.'

Half way through the writing of my report, when I was distressed by the ravages Simmons had created during his bried reign as in charge at Tonga, I had drafted a paragraph which I had intended to use as xxx my final conclusions on this gross miscarriage of military deportment:

> If the Tongan experience rpoves anything constructive, it is that medical doctors just out of civilian life and with a life-long dream of parading as military gen uses must never be placed in command of troops on a isolated base, especially if there are pretty girls about who have cle ver younger brothers.

later

But upon/reflection, especially when Tipi worked in my office/getting my p seeing that my piles of papers papers in good x were kept in order, I concluded that was an intrusive opinion that was not really called for, and I killed it.

Working on the Unsatisfactory Original

I did what I could with the flawed original and was able to recall either new episodes or helpful details to enrich those I already had, but as I ended I had to acknowledge that the real story had eluded me. Events on Tonga had been both hilarious and instructive, and I had missed conveying both aspects.

My second attempt accomplished little, and since I subsequently cut it apart without having had a carbon copy, I cannot display its inadequacy, but pages from my revision shown here indicate how I worked and with what care I went over every sentence before thinking to type it up and send it off to New York for editorial attention.

An obvious question arises: If you don't get it right until the third version, why not try to start with that version when you first sit at your typewriter? The explanation cuts to the heart of creativity: that acceptable third version does not spring full blown from a mind in control of everything. It is slowly uncovered as one does his spadework during the writing of the first two versions.

same
Tongan work force: 'Lieut. Michener, he treated us natives like cattle. We handled equipment of great value for the Navy, and never lost any of it. Our natives who drove the Navy cars and trucks took better care of them than your people did. Our girl typists were much better than the men yeomen, everyone said that. And we had come to think of going to the movies at night as part of our pay. Now all changed, and we don't like.'

PPP/As soon as Tipi heard the first rumors rumbles of discontent, he swing into action with his master plan, and the first step he took was to immobilize Commander Simmons completely with the enthusiastic aide of a prostiture with the lyrical name of Meredith. When I asked her how she had acquired that unusual name, a Tongan girl who worked as secretary at the base told m: 'She has s good proper Tongan name, but one of her friends saw Meredith in a book and tell her: "This sounds pretty, just like you" and the name stuck.' As to the productive meeting with the Commander Simmons, several eager gosspips mongers informed me: 'Tipi fix, and pretty soon Meredith sleeping his cottage, and she sending Navy equipment all kinds...refrigerators, stive ...to her little house next to Tipi's. What she don't need she pass along to him.'

now Tipi had to see that everything worked smoothly, and for a while he was running the base. He told Meredith what to tell the Navy men, and she relayed those orders as if they had come from the commander himself. 'Drill on the base,' one native workman told me, simple. Commander in bed with Meredith. Tipi watching things. Nobody guarding the store.'

It was here that the little red truck became prominent in the history of Tonga, and and although I would hear repeated stories about it, I could not find out where it had come from or who owned it, but that it was not Navy property I felt sure, so for the time being I stopped worrying. about it.

But I was much concerned with an outrageous series of events which came to a violent head on 14 August 1944 and after considerable questioning I lucked upon a native who enabled me to piece together a reasonable account of how it happened: 'I work with Tipi like you already know. My job, watch Commander Simmon's hut be sure he in bed with Meredith, twach the Navy guards, be sue they with their girls off base. I give signal "All O.K." then Tipi drive the little red truck down that lane way over there, nobody see from here, he go around back.'

At that point I had not yet deduced what Tipi did with his red truck, but another of his cohorts enlightened me: '

had escaped the police told me: 'We get wircutters, three men, me two others. We go back the big warehouse nobody can see, we cut snip, snip, snip'---and his hands opened and closed rapidly as if holding wirecutters---'and we cut two panels out of warehouse, big enough red truck drive right in.'

'And the purpose?'

46

stolen from the Navy by Tipi or given to Meredith by Commander Simmons, and I could believe the report that the citizens of Tonga, especially the young women, had profited to the extent of at least one million dollars from the occupation, not counting lawful salaries.

'Did you really like Simmons, Meredith?'

'Oh, yes. Kind man, he help me fix my house.'

'He gave you many things?'

II-50

'Yes. He one good man, got two babies Oklahoma.'

I asked Tipi what he would do when his prison term ended and he said brightly: 'I think maybe go back work Navy. Our commander go, go back Oklahoma. New man need help, maybe.'

'Where did you get the little red truck?'

He considered this for some moments, then said: 'It belong Commander Simmons. Navy blue. Two men, me, we paint it red one night, he never guess.'

'Where is it now?'

'Vava'u.'

'You bring it back when you get out?'

'Yes. My brother have it, he give it back when I ask.' As I was about to leave the pair, the charming girl, the clever brother, he asked: 'You speak me good, police? Tell them I needed at naval base?'

Our base was much truncated when I berthed there during the writing of my report, but as the Marines said in their famous poster, 'We could use a few good men,' and I made this recommendation to Queen Salote who towered over me as I spoke and she told me how gratified everyone on her islands were that the American occupation had gone so smmothly, and she said that without sensible and understanding men like the Commander this would not have been possible.' She asked: 'If we pardon this Tipi fellow, would you reemploy him at your base?' and I said a firm 'Yes.' I needed what only he could tell me.

Halfway through the writing of my report, when I was distresed by the ravages Simmons had created during his brief reign in charge at Tonga, I had drafted a paragraph which I had intended using as the conclusion regarding this gross miscarriage of military deportment:

> If the Tongan adventure proves anything constructive, it is that medical doctors just out of civilian life and with a life-long dream of parading as military geniuses must never be placed in command of troops on an isolared base, especially if there are pretty girls about who have clever younger brothers.

But upon later reflection, especially when Tipi worked in my office seeing that my piles of papers were kept in order, I concluded that this was an intrusive opinion which was not really called for, and I killed it.

47

The Miraculous Surfacing of My Lost Report

In the summer of 1990 I chanced to sail into Tahiti's main harbor at Papeete and a memorable night ensued, for the captain of our Windstar liner had invited to dine with us a notable South Pacific explorer, Bengt Danielsson, who had sailed on the *Kon-Tiki* with Thor Heyerdahl and who, himself, had later explored and reported on various aspects of the South Seas. He was a formidable Swede in his late fifties, a real Viking, tall, heavily bearded, and with a rumbling voice. I had visited with him at his maritime museum in Stockholm, and to find him seated beside me aboard ship in Tahiti was an unexpected pleasure.

In the course of exchanging sea stories he told me: 'Michener, I went to a lot of trouble to scout the little Treasury Islands to see whether there really was the miserable little village on Mono that you said was named Bali-h'ai—the one you used in your book as the name of the place where the French planters sequestered their marriageable daughters in 1942, when American soldiers and sailors began arriving in the islands. I couldn't find it, no one had ever heard of it, and I concluded you were lying. But then one day high in the hills I came upon it, just as you said. Name nailed to the signboard as it was on the day you climbed there. I wrote a report for one of the journals. You were not fraudulent.'

Gratified to be established as truthful at least part of the time, I listened with delight as he continued: 'And when I was researching materials on Bora Bora I came upon a copy of the detailed report you wrote on that island, and it showed me something I hadn't known, that you'd also worked on the other French islands during the bad times of Vichy influence in the region. It was a most interesting document, and proved again that you'd done what you said and visited where you claimed you did. It was a good report.'

I had no comment. The realization that my work still survived was joyous news, for even I had sometimes doubted that what I remembered of those wild and crazy days had ever happened, and as I bowed my head in gratitude I heard the really astonishing news: 'And when I worked with the Tonga material I found your riotous account of what happened there. It was amazing.'

As he spoke there in the captain's cabin, I could see on my desk back in Florida the second version of my Tonga story, the account we've just seen, and I knew that if I could get hold of my 1945 report all gaps could be filled: 'Where is it now?'

'In the Navy archives across the Potomac in Alexandria, Virginia,' he said, and gave me the identification number, F-108-AR-89-74/R#1. Promptly when I returned home I had two photo copies of the two long-missing reports.

Danielsson's memory was incorrect on one significant point: he did not find my original material on either Bora Bora or Tonga; that had long been destroyed. But what he did find was what Owen Laster's men had been seeking earlier: a careful redaction of what I had written—in the Bora Bora report my material was cited repeatedly with my name attached, and I could remember well the phrases I'd written so long ago. I also recalled dramatic events I'd forgotten, but there the verification was, my report in abbreviated form.

For Tonga the situation was quite different. The naval officer who had compiled the history of that island had obliterated my name. At first I was outraged, but as I read his report, the good parts of which were ascribed to an unnamed 'ComSoPac historical officer,' I was pleased to discover that he had quoted almost verbatim those very parts of the Tongan history that I had been most eager to recover and most incapable of remembering. But there they were, the names, the events, the entire history of how a determined medical doctor had snatched command of an island from a totally incompetent island line officer.

I was ashamed when I compared my first two truncated versions with my on-the-spot account of what had actually happened. I had forgotten the nub of the story, the relationship between the ineffective commander and the aggressive doctor. As you can see if you return to my first version, I had lumped the two together as Commander Simmons and had saddled him with many of the misbehaviors of the doctor. How this could have happened I cannot explain, but I trust that even had the missing history not reappeared I would in time have resuscitated the doctor. I think that the gunnery and my accompanying him when he went bat shooting might have reminded me.

The Tongan history, as I retrieved it, is a voluminous affair, 228 pages plus 15 pages of footnotes; I quote below only the passages based on material I wrote and which are essential to my story. In it the names of the two antagonists are given in full, but I have elected to mask them as Commander and Doctor.

I wrote none of the material regarding the unwitting Tongan who had the bad luck to repaint his rusty truck red. It would be poetic justice if this had been written by the man who worked with my material. He borrowed from me and now I borrow from him.

> No native peoples in the South Pacific have such a bad reputation for petty thieving as do those of Tonga. Close runner ups would be the natives of American and Western Somoa.
>
> The native of Tongatabu gave the Navy a great deal of trouble especially in 1944 and 1945 when naval forces were the principal remaining alien force on the island. It is the testimony not only of American service personnel but of European residents as well that for a period of about 18 months personal and public property in Tongatabu knew no safety whatever. For example, in early 1945 the officers' quarters were broken into and robbed for the third time. A considerable quantity of goods was taken. The Commanding Officer, with some of his remaining clothing as evidence, went to the home of an official to protest. While the United States Naval Officer was conferring with the government official in the front room of the latter's home the back room of the house was broken into and the officer lost further items of clothing. ....
>
> Matters came to a head in mid-August 1944. At that time Tongan thieves set a new record for boldness. After a long series of minor pilferings and house breakings they stole a heavy powerful bolt cutter from a Navy warehouse and with it, hacked off the padlock guarding a different Navy warehouse located about a mile from headquarters on the beach near the middle of Nukualofa.
>
> When the warehouse was opened - a Burns Philp South Seas concrete oil and gasoline depository in peace time - the thieves stole large quantities of cigarettes and beer. Then emboldened by their success, they backed a medium sized red truck into the warehouse and

completely cleaned it out. The total monetary loss to the Navy in this haul was approximately $2500.00. When the theft was discovered the anger of American naval personnel was so great that large groups of enlisted men, led by officers, conducted what became known as the "Cigarette Raid."

Ranging over the island most of one night and all of the next day, armed with revolvers and rifles, Navy forces gathered up approximately 40 suspects and lodged them in two improvised Navy brigs at Maufaga. These suspects were, for the most part, Tongan rowdies with bad previous records. After extensive questioning various suspects implicated one another and other Tongans not yet apprehended. In time a prima facie case of breaking in and robbing was made against about 30 of the men. ....

Mr. John Brownlees, the Chief Justice of Tonga, was of the opinion that in spite of the obvious difficulties caused by the raid one had to admit that there was provocation, and that in the long run the Tongans remembered the good that had been done by Americans rather than the ill effects of this startling affair. A New Zealand officer who was stationed in Tonga at the time, and whose formal dance was more or less broken up by the raid said emphatically, "You blokes had every kind of provocation, the raid was a good thing." ....

A naval warehouse owned in peacetime by Burns Philp South Seas Trading Company, was broken into one Thursday night and minor pilferage occurred. Duty chiefs, whose responsibility it was to check this and other warehouses twice nightly and once in the daytime, failed to discover the theft. Therefore on Friday night Tongan roughnecks backed a truck into the building and took out half of the remaining gear. Still the duty chiefs did not discover the breakage. This was probably because almost all of the chiefs then in service on Tongatabu had stopped living in naval quarters, and had rented native shacks from Tongan civilians where they lived with various Tongan girls. ....

On the next night the Tongan thieves, finding the building still open and their breakage still undetected, backed their red truck into the warehouse once more and cleaned the place out. ....

Both the background and the facts of the cigarette raid were unpleasant so far as can be ascertained. After rumor has been discarded and evidence weighed the Commander was a pretty pathetic figure. At this date in Nukualofa almost no one has a kind word for the man. He was personally reprimanded by his local Commanding Officer Major Hardy, a small dour Scottish New Zealander, who upbraided the Commander for living openly with one of Tongatabu's two or three most notorious prostitutes. Each time the Commander replied that he had already discontinued this practice. ....

Considerable amusement was caused among enlisted personnel of both the United States and New Zealand forces because of the fact that the Commander's girl was also consorting with United States Naval enlisted men at the same time and relating choice bits of information to them. The Commander was characterized by three different persons as, "That pathetic old man," "That damned old fool," and "That silly ass." At least two persons on the island wanted to make unofficial representations to some senior United States Naval officer concerning the Commander, but found no opportunity to do so. Almost everyone whom this writer has talked to (enlisted, officer, civilian; American, British, New Zealand) has pointed out that the Commander was never actually the Commanding Officer of the Base, and that an unusual situation had developed in which the able, fiery Doctor actually ran the Base. ....

About this time the earlier practice of setting Tongan girls up with all kinds of naval equipment reached its height. Almost any kind of Navy property could be found in one or more of the various houses maintained by Navy chiefs. In fact one complete house was built on Navy time with Navy property for an attractive girl.

The writer wants to make it entirely clear that he does not necessarily condemn or ridicule this kind of behavior. The Polynesian people are delightful friends. Much of the Navy property given away was of no use to the Navy. Almost every naval officer or enlisted man in Polynesia is the recipient of more kindness, cheer, and entertainment than he could possibly ever repay. In a land where mechanical equipment and consumer goods were at a premium a piece of pipe or an old tire might be a present of such wonderful value that no Polynesian could accept it without complete amazement at, and affection for, his yankee friends. Much of the continued excellent reception given Americans in Polynesia was caused by our generosity with small items, many of which it is true, belonged to the United States Navy. It is probable that the friendships thus created (in the entire area) have cost the Navy up to a million dollars in property which would otherwise have rusted or have been given away on lend lease. It is, however, even more probable that America has thereby won a lasting regard in the South Pacific which will ultimately be valued at many many times one million dollars.

As examples of this high-handed generosity in Tonga, civilians who entertained troops, who invited men and officers from visiting warships into their homes, and who frequently acted as hosts to visiting dignitaries, received Navy property of one kind or another. It was noted by several people that whenever a unit had a catholic officer in command local Catholic schools and missions were showered with gifts whose titles were not always clear. Protestants also aided missionaries of their faith. As a matter of fact civilian equipment such as generators and carburetors, radios, and ice boxes could be repaired and maintained only by service personnel using service tools and service equipment. The same should be said for medical skill and supplies whose proper use in the South Pacific has done much to make America seem like a nation of friendly helpers in all matters.

The above observations are made for the following reasons: Nowhere, apparently, was Navy property more lavishly given away than at Tongatabu. Major Hardy, the Commanding Officer of the island, protested twice to the Commander about the excessive amount of property that was being distributed, especially to the families of girls who were living with American navy personnel. New Zealanders in general, whose army has a much more niggardly system of personal accounting for public property, were astonished at the largesse distributed by Americans. It was the opinion of most responsible civilian personnel in Tongatabu that the general decline of honesty among the Tongan people must be attributed to the United States Army and Navy, and especially the Navy. The writer cannot evaluate this statement, but it is so widely held in Tongatabu that there may be some truth in it. At any rate the Tongans' reputation for flagrant, open thievery seems to have been a very recent acquisition. ....

Without a single exception everyone this writer has talked with in Tongatabu says: "The United States Navy had provocation when they made the cigarette raid, but the Navy brought that provocation on itself." It is an interesting fact that two of the officers and chiefs who participated most vigorously in the raid subsequently lived with Tongan girls whom they showered with gifts; one of the officers who participated subsequently had an attractive baby girl; and one of the enlisted men whose outraged virtue led him to storm houses, kick down doors, and manhandle people in searching for stolen goods, was himself later court-martialled for trading stolen Navy property to Tongans for whiskey.

The cigarette raid was an astonishing affair. An armed body of naval personnel, led by a staff officer brandishing a revolver, toured unchecked through the island for two days. The Commander broke his men out at 2300 on the night of 14 August 1944 and turned them over to the Doctor, who from that point took over. From then on the Commander was no more seen. ....

At about 0300 in the morning some especially vigorous units of Task Force Doctor burst into the home of the Tongan Premier. Brandishing revolvers and firing once, they roused the Prime Minister's wife and family out of bed, lined them up against the wall, and searched the place for contraband. This action was subsequently explained and excused by British residents on the island as a regrettable mistake. Subsequently when the Premier wished to have an explanation of this and similar actions from the United States Navy and the Commanding Officer of the Tongan Defense Force, the meeting was thrown into consternation by the late arrival of the American officers carrying loaded revolvers and taking control of the meeting.

Task Force Doctor also achieved a star on its operational ribbon by sweeping into various houses containing old people, (and possibly young thieves) shooting off pistols in the yards, lining up women and children, and kicking in doors. ....

At least one officer, Lt. P.G. Polowniak, protested the above actions of Task Force Doctor. For doing so he was threatened by the Commander with "removal from office for insubordination."

Shortly after making this threat to Lt. Polowniak the Commander called on the British Consul and informed that official that he (the Commander) was considering the establishment of military law. Mr. Johnson promptly inform the Commander that he (the Commander) was incompetent to do such a thing, and that military law could be pronounced only by Major Hardy, who had no intention of doing so. This information rather surprised the Commander and no more was ever heard about this violent effort to declare war on the Government of Tonga.

There were some astonishing results of this search. Certain vindicative enlisted men wanted to search the house of their Commanding Officer's girlfriend. She, however, wisely disappeared with her belongings and the search revealed nothing. One officer who felt ashamed of the entire proceedings went into Nukualofa with his own task force, stopped the automobile of a prominent and extremely upright European and took therefrom two new Navy tires which had recently been given to that European by a friendly naval officer. Numerous houses in Maufaga which had been furnished by previous naval personnel were stripped of their "gifts" above loud protests that, "So and so gave me that!" It was noted by impartial observers that the homes of current favorites were not molested.

The story of the cigarette raid would not be complete without two further comments. Protests were subsequently made that the Doctor ought to stop "so much shooting at night." He apparently used to shoot out into the night whenever he suspected that natives might be approaching his quarters. It should be observed, however, that no one ridicules the professional or personal ability of the Doctor. No one accuses him of anything more than liking to play with firearms. ....

(At this point my official report on Tongan high jinks is interrupted by the details of a tragi-comic affair which happend after I had left the island. An elderly Tongan busybody named Supileo 'Uhatafe owned a little white truck so rusted that it needed a paint job. Seeking variety he had the colossal bad luck to paint it red, and I will let you guess what transpired when alert Navy personnel spotted what was obviously the infamous 'Little Red Truck.' Snippets from a score of official reports provide the flavor of what occurred on the night of 14 August 1944.)

'I was arrested on the roadside by the Americans, they rushed at me with guns, pulled me down and questioned me about cigarettes said to be stolen on a truck painted with red paint. I own a lorry which is also painted red, but it is different altogether from the lorry they referred to...

'I was again ordered to get on my lorry or else I would be shot, so I did... But then out came the Doctor, he took his pistol out and hit me with it, it landed on the back of my head. He did hit me and also kick me. I begged the constable to assist me, but the Doctor again slapped my face, I showed him the blood from my injury but he again slapped my face in return, we came back and I was placed in their lock-up. The Doctor swore in return when I asked him to treat my injury...'

When the U.S. Navy refused to compensate Supileo for his false arrest, the Premier of Tonga, on 12 March 1945, intervened on his behalf: 'You will have noted that his claim was for cash, but he is now agreeable to receiving some compensation in kind. There seems no doubt whatsoever that he was completely innocent in the cigarette robberies, and was only brought into the matter on account of his unfortunately possessing a red lorry similar to the one that was being searched for.'

The Navy having rejected this appeal, the matter was forwarded on 3 May 1945 to His British Majesty, Consul in Tonga, who threatened to lodge Supileo's appeal with the British Governor-General in Fiji, so very belately, on 25 July 1945, eleven months after his arrest, Supileo was offered compensation amounting to 'one dollar in cash and 'other valuable considerations.' The official report on the affair, which runs to six closely-typed pages, ends with this thoughtful summation:

'For this release he received the sum of one dollar, a length of pipe, six sheets of ramp wire, and some lumber. All of this was to have been delivered by a Navy truck to Supileo's home. Two months later this same Supileo was claiming "he didn't get everything he was promised," but it was the general belief that having gotten so much good Navy equipment for such a little thing as a mauling around, Supileo felt that he might be able to squeeze out a little more. A fellow Tongan observed that that was the kind of a trick Supileo would try to pull.' NOW BACK TO MY ACCOUNT.

There are numerous American babies on the island, and these children are among the most prized in all Tonga. Some naval personnel have allotted small payments to Tongan mothers for the care of these children. There is little evidence that American military personnel debauched the island or changed in any fundamental way its moral principles. Drinking was never a very serious problem except among certain military personnel and this problem, too, has subsided. ....

Even by the wildest stretch of imagination one cannot claim that the Navy sent first-rate men to Tonga in this period. The lieutenant commanders who served as commanding officers were at best only adequate, and at worst ridiculous. The two junior officers who closed out the base were excellent and responsible young men, but it was obvious to everyone in Tonga that they had been sent to the island merely to close up affairs. It is a shame that men of their general ability holding the rank of commander or lieutenant commander did not appear earlier in the war. ....

In another war, however, with Guadalcanal and Espiritu Santo in the hands of an enemy power (or even seriously threatened by an enemy power) Tonga would lie athwart the normal United States - New Zealand supply line and would be of critical importance. In such a case the broad level plains of the island would provide airfields and airfield parking spaces almost unlimited in size. The harbor would never be a first-rate harbor but could provide protection for even major units of the fleet. It is therefore important that amicable relations with the Tongan Government be maintained. To this end it would be desirable to have occasional visits from units of the fleet. As in most other South Pacific islands the United States now needs merely to retain and build upon the affection and respect already in existence.

Editing the Lost Data

The task in fitting the recovered story into the structure as already set—imperfectly by me since I had not been willing to trust my memory—was threefold: to bring the gun-happy doctor into the action; to strengthen the behavior of Tipi; and to introduce, if possible, the high comedy of the second little red truck. I succeeded in the first two but failed in the third because space was not available. I'm glad to see the story revived in the preceding notes.

In the early days of the wab the Kingdom of Tonga played a role of some importance, II-49A

becauae it was feared that the Japanese attack, which could strike at any moment, might

would

bypass Fiji, which was better protected, and capture Tonga, whose numerous islands/pro-

in peacetime

vided many fine achorages for Japanese warships. Hurried steps were taken to protect the

which had belonged to the trading firm of Burns Philp, was converted into a huge Navy warehous.

islands, and in a corner of the town of Nuku'alofa a very large warehouse was constructed.

Crammed with valuable fighting gear and supplies to help withstand a siege, that warehouse

became the focal point of my report, for everything that happened on Tonga in the period for

which I was responsible revolved around that warehouse and its precious contents.

Since the anchorages of Tonga were the targets of

importance/The U.S. Navy was naturally placed in control, and in the early days I would suppose

HAD BEEN

that someone liie a Rear Admiral or a senior captain was in command, but as the battlefronts

moved farther north to Guadalcanal, Bougainville and perilous islands like Tarawa and

WAS CLEAR THE

Saipan, it became obvious that that the Japanese fleet was not going to risk a long run

south to do minor damage to Tonga. The danger was over. Experienced admirals and captains

SO

were required in forward areas. sp Tonga was left to fend for itself, and that was when I

CAME INTO

entered the picture.

Only Gilbert and Sullivan could do justice to what happened next, and even they would

DOUBLE

have required a couple of shots of brandy prepare themselves to grapple

with real folly. Principal comedian was a weak-chinned, inept, frightened Naval officer

of moderate rank who found himself commanding officer of the island and whom I shall

The

call simply/Commander. He had several memorable characteristics.

From seeing too many movies he had acquired the idea that naval commanders navy captains

RASP OUT

ought to bluster and shout commands, but at the same time he was absolutely terrified of

HANDLED

any emergency and confronted it by disappearing. In one incident after another, when I tried

to learn how he handled it, I was invariably told: 'He disappesred. We didn't see him

for three days. Couldn't find him, and when I asked:

No PP 'Where did he disappear to?' my informants would say: 'He just vanished. Maybe

did

hiding in bed.' In not one crisis about which I shall speak was The Commander ever partic-

ipate.

He was a totally average man, indistinguishable in any way from a herd of a thousand

sweating men

AFTER

/hurrying home to work at five o'clock in the afternoon of a sultry day in New York or

Los Angeles: about forty, overweight, thinning hair, wobbly voice, knock knees, watery eyes

and a kind of permanent half-smile on flabby lips. He did have one peculiarity which

many of his men commenred upon: from any group of women he had a penchant

for picking out the prostitute and moving her into his quarters...on the Navy base.

OPERATION

No PP It should be clear that our base on Tonga was going to have problems. 48

lived in Nuku'alofa about the Naval base carried theft to a degree of profiency that would have awed Fagin or Al Capone, and the presence of what they saw as wealthy American troops in their midst made their mouths water.

Chief of the thieves in my time was a sly young fellow named Tipi, twenty-six or seven, wiry, all smiles, light tan in coloring with jet-black hair and very white teeth which he flashed at me whenever I interrogated him, and a capacity for lying and covering his tracks that would have done justice to a lynx trying to steal a chicken. Had he continued with school, which he quit after the third grade, he would pretty surely have been brilliant in a business career or as a salesman for some reputable firm. As it was, all his gamin aptitude went into thieving, and to pit a young man of his restless skill against The Commander was unfair, but when he went up against the gun-toting Doctor, he met his match.

It started, so far as I could reconstruct, shortly after The Commander surrendered control and allowed The Doctor to assume domination. Thirsty to taste the fruits of power, the belligerent Doctor issued a machine-gun battery of orders calculated to bring discipline under control, but this caused irritation among both the sailors and the Tongan work force: 'Lieut. Michener, he treated us natives same as cattle. We handled equipment of great value for Navy, never lose nothin'. Natives drive Navy cars, trucks take better care your people do. Girl typists mo bettah men yeomen, everyone say that. Goin' movies at night part of our pay. Now all changed, we don't like.'

As soon as Tipi heard the first rumbles of discontent, he swung into action with his master plan, and the first step he took was to immobilize The Commander completely with the enthusiastic aid of a prostitute with the lyrical name of Meredith. When I asked her how she had acquired it, a Tongan girl who

I was about to leave the pair, the charming girl, the clever brother, he asked: 'You speak me good, police? Tell them I needed at naval base?'

Our base was much truncated when I berthed there during the writing of my report, but as the Marines say in their famous poster, 'We could use a few good men,' and I made the recommendation to Queen Salote who towered over me as I spoke and she told me how gratified everyone on her islands were that the American occupation had gone so smoothly and she said that without sensible and understanding men like The Commander this would not have been possible. She asked: 'If we pardon this Tipi fellow, would you reemploy him at your base?' and I said a firm 'Yes.' I needed what only he could tell me.

Halfway through the writing of my report, when I was distressed by the ravages The Commander and The Doctor had visited upon our friendly ally Tonga, I drafted a paragraph which I intended to use as my evaluation of this gross miscarriage of military deportment:

> If the Tongan experience proves anything constructive it is that incompetent base commanders must be identified early and moved out quick. But they should not be replaced by medical doctors just out of civilian life who love revolvers and have dreams of military glory, especially if there are attractive girls about who have larcenous friends.

But upon later reflection, especially when Tipi worked in my office seeing that my piles of paper were kept in order, I had a much happier thought which came closer to the truth about such situations:

> When these two lovable clowns were finally removed from Tonga, their place was taken by a fine young lieutenant in the Naval Reserve named P.G. Polowniak whose wise administration had the place back on track within three weeks. They should have sent him two years earlier.

My last stop was Matareva and if I reported now what I thought when I first landed on that island, the reader would be justified

50

The Printout of the Enriched Version

After many efforts and much travail my various efforts were merged into what became a rounded portrait of two naval officers running wild, each in his own way, and of an entire barracks 'going ape,' as the current phrase was. There was, however, a saving touch of harmless comedy to the affair, and this was intentional—indeed, had been worked upon, and for good reason.

As I was struggling with Tonga I always kept in the back of my mind the far more serious affair on the imaginary island of Matareva, a name invented to mask a real-life military tragedy. On Tonga the nonsense involved a warehouse, a little red truck and a gang of essentially lovable natives mixing it up with a group of essentially decent young Americans far from home and forgotten in the war that had passed them by. On Matareva about the same number of young Americans, Marines this time, were also led by a fanatic who had usurped command, this time an enlisted man wresting it away from an incompetent officer. It happened that the usurper was a homosexual in those far-off days when the military shuddered at the word and adopted terrible measures to stamp out sexual behavior that it found unacceptable. On isolated Matareva the same rebellious principles that had made Tonga a comedy conspired to make it a tragedy, ending in mass court-martial and possible murder.

So if I wrote and rewrote to try to catch the hilarity of Tonga it was for a purpose: to play its comic history against the tragic one of Matareva. I believe the segments shown below capture that lighter spirit. Words screened indicate where the original copy survived the various cuts.

A COMMANDER IN PARADISE

In the early days of the war the kingdom of Tonga played a role of some importance, because it was feared that the Japanese attack, which could strike at any moment, might bypass Fiji, which was better protected, and capture Tonga, whose numerous islands would provide many fine anchorages for Japanese warships. Hurried steps were taken to defend against this, and in a corner of the town of Nuku'alofa a very large warehouse which had in peacetime belonged to the trading firm of Burns Philp, was converted into a huge Navy warehouse. Crammed with valuable fighting gear and supplies to help withstand a siege, that warehouse became the focal point of my report, for everything that happened on Tonga in the period for which I was responsible revolved around that warehouse and its precious contents.

Since the anchorages of Tonga were the targets of importance the U.S. Navy was naturally placed in control, and in the early days I would suppose that someone like a rear admiral had been in command, but as the battlefronts moved farther and farther north to Guadalcanal, Bougainville and islands like Tarawa and Saipan, it was clear that the Japanese fleet could no longer risk the long run to Tonga to do minor damage. The danger was over. Experienced admirals and captains were required in the forward areas, and Tonga was left to fend for itself, which was when I came into the picture.

Only Gilbert and Sullivan could do justice to what happened next, and even they would have required double shots of brandy. The principal comedian was a weak-chinned, inept, frightened Naval officer of moderate rank who found himself commanding officer of the island and whom I shall call simply The Commander. He had several memorable characteristics. From seeing too many movies he had acquired the idea that navy captains ought to bluster and rasp out commands, but at the same time he was terrified of any emergency and handled it simply by disappearing. In one incident after another, when I tried to find out how The Commander handled it, I was told: 'He disappeared. We didn't see him for three days. Couldn't find him,' and when I asked: 'Where did he disappear to?' my informants would say: 'He just vanished. Maybe hiding in bed.' In not one crisis about which I shall speak did The Commander ever participate.

He was a totally average man, indistinguishable in any way from a herd of a thousand sweating men hurrying home after work at five in the afternoon of a sultry day in New York or Los Angeles:

THE REAL COMMANDER

Chief of the thieves in my time was a sly young fellow named Tipi, twenty-six or seven, wiry, all smiles, light tan in coloring with jet black hair and very white teeth which he flashed at me whenever I interrogated him, and a capacity for lying and covering his tracks that would have done justice to a lynx trying to steal a chicken. Had he continued with school, which he quit after the third grade, he would pretty surely have been brilliant in a business career or as a salesman for some reputable firm. As it was, all his gamin aptitude went into thieving, and to pit a young man of his restless skill against The Commander was unfair, but when he went up against the gun-toting Doctor, he met his match.

It started, so far as I could reconstruct, shortly after The Commander surrendered control and allowed The Doctor to assume domination. Thirsty to taste the fruits of power, the belligerent Doctor issued a machine-gun battery of orders calculated to bring discipline under control, but this caused irritation among both the sailors and the Tongan work force: 'Lieut. Michener, he treated us natives same as cattle. We handled equipment of great value for Navy, never lose nothin'. Natives drive Navy cars, trucks take better care your people do. Girl typists mo bettah men yeomen, everyone say that. Goin' movies at night part of our pay. Now all changed, we don't like.'

As soon as Tipi heard the first rumbles of discontent, he swung into action with his master plan, and the first step he took was to immobilize The Commander completely with the enthusiastic aid of a prostitute with the lyrical name of Meredith. When I asked her how she had acquired it, a Tongan girl who worked as a secretary on the base told me: 'She has a proper Tongan name, but one of her friends came upon Meredith in a book and said: "This sound pretty, just like you," and the name stuck.' As to the productive meeting with The Commander, several eager gossipmongers informed me: 'Tipi arrange, and pretty soon Meredith sleeping on base and fixing for Navy equipment all kinds...refrigerators, stoves...to go to her little house next to Tipi's, and things she got extra, it goes to Tipi.'

Men on the base rarely saw The Commander after Meredith moved in, but now Tipi had to neutralize The Doctor, and he did this in a charming way. He had Tongan workmen build a small pistol range far removed from the big warehouse, and there the warlike Doctor conducted target practice hours at a time. The drill on the base became: 'Commander in bed with Meredith, Doctor busy at the range, nobody guardin' the store.'

THE LITTLE RED TRUCK

But I was much concerned with an outrageous series of events which came to a violent head on 14 August 1944 and I lucked upon a native who enabled me after considerable questioning to piece together a reasonable account of how it happened: 'I work with Tipi like you already know. My job, watch the Commander's shack be sure he in bed with Meredith, watch the pistol range be sure The Doctor over there. I give signal "All O.K." then Tipi drive Little Red Truck down that lane way over there, nobody see from here, he go around back.'

At that point I had not deduced what Tipi did with his red truck, but another of his cohorts enlightened me: 'We get wirecutters, three men, me two others. We go back the big warehouse nobody can see, we cut snip, snip, snip'---and his hands opened and closed rapidly as if holding wirecutters---'and we cut two panels out of warehouse, big enough Red Truck drive right in.'

'And the purpose?'

'First time Tipi drive his truck in, he take only cigarettes, canned food, things native people like, all what you call P.X. stuff.'

'How could he sell it? We have military police, you know.'

'Not sell! Give away!'

'Surely somebody must have discovered the big hole in the back of the warehouse?'

'Commander asleep, Captain firing gun. Navy chiefs all home their Tongan girls.'

'So what happened next?'

'Tipi never take enough make police catch on. Next trip radios, washing machines, fine set of tools.'

That was how things stood on the evening before the fourteenth of August, but on that morning the Doctor, who was now in complete charge, found that a gasoline can had been stolen from his jeep, and he went to an official of the Tongan government to lodge a formal complaint, but while he was outside the office, thieves jacked up his jeep and stole the four tires, and when everyone ran out front to inspect the car with no tires, a different set of thieves sneaked in through the back of the office and stole most of the furniture, including the Doctor's briefcase.

THE PEACEFUL CONCLUSION

'Yes. My brother have it, he give it back when I ask.' As I was about to leave the pair, the charming girl, the clever brother, he asked: 'You speak me good, police? Tell them I needed at naval base?'

Our base was much truncated when I berthed there during the writing of my report, but as the Marines say in their famous poster, 'We could use a few good men,' and I made the recommendation to Queen Salote who towered over me as I spoke and she told me how gratified everyone on her islands were that the American occupation had gone so smoothly, and she said that without sensible and understanding men like The Commander this would not have been possible. She asked: 'If we pardon this Tipi fellow, would you reemploy him at your base?' and I said a firm 'Yes.' I needed what only he could tell me.

Halfway through the writing of my report, when I was distressed by the ravages The Commander and The Doctor had visited upon our friendly ally Tonga, I drafted a paragraph which I intended to use as my evaluation of this gross miscarriage of military deportment:

> If the Tongan experience proves anything constructive it is that incompetent base commanders must be identified early and moved out quick. But they should not be replaced by medical doctors just out of civilian life who love revolvers and have dreams of military glory, especially if there are attractive girls about who have larcenous friends.

But upon later reflection, especially when Tipi worked in my office seeing that my piles of paper were kept in order, I had a much happier thought which came closer to the truth about such situations:

> When these two lovable clowns were finally removed from Tonga, their place was taken by a fine young lieutenant in the Naval Reserve named P.G. Polowniak whose wise administration had the place back on track within three weeks. They should have sent him two years earlier.

My last stop was Matareva and if I reported now what I thought when I first landed on that island, the reader would be justified in protesting: 'Wait! You just said the same sentences about the situation that faced you on your arrival at Tonga!' and the complaint would be justified. Matareva had been vitally important in the early days of war, as had Tonga. When the threat of

Corrections in Galleys

One would think that with the amount of work done on the manuscript there could be nothing left that required correction in the galleys. That is never the case, and often a book is saved from grievous error by a sharp-eyed proofreader, or sometimes by the author herself or himself, who catches something at the last possible moment.

As before, the copy editor, in this case a learned veteran who has attended to the final stages of several hundred manuscripts, finds at the last minute many small errors she wishes to correct or spots at which the flow of words could be improved. She can also, as shown here, give an exact quotation rather than a colloquial approximation.

The cryptic circled letters *ea* stand for editor's alteration, which means that this correction was made by the editor and will not be charged against the royalty of the author.

issued a battery of orders calculated to ensure discipline to the island, but this action caused irritation among both the sailors and the Tongan work force: 'Lieutenant Michener, he treated us natives same as cattle. We handled valuable equipment for Navy, never lose nothing'. Natives drive Navy cars, trucks, take better care your people do. Girl typists mo bettah than yeomen, everyone say that. Goin' movies at night part of our pay. Now all changed, we don't like.'

As soon as Tipi heard the first rumbles of discontent, he swung into action with his master plan, and the first step he took was to immobilize The Commander completely, with the enthusiastic aid of a prostitute with the unlikely name of Meredith. When I asked how she had acquired it, a Tongan girl who worked as a secretary on the base told me: 'She has a Tongan name, but one of her friends saw Meredith in a book and said: "This sound pretty, just like you," and the name stuck.' As to the productive meeting with The Commander, several eager gossipmongers informed me: 'Tipi arrange, and pretty soon Meredith sleeping on base and fixing for Navy equipment all kinds—refrigerators, stoves—to go to her little house next to Tipi's, and things she got extra, it goes to Tipi.'

Men on the base rarely saw The Commander after Meredith moved in, but now Tipi had to neutralize The Doctor, and he did this in an ingenious way. He had Tongan workmen build a small pistol range far removed from the big warehouse, and there the Doctor conducted target practice for hours at a time. The drill on the base became: 'Commander in bed with Meredith, Doctor busy at the range, nobody guardin' the store.'

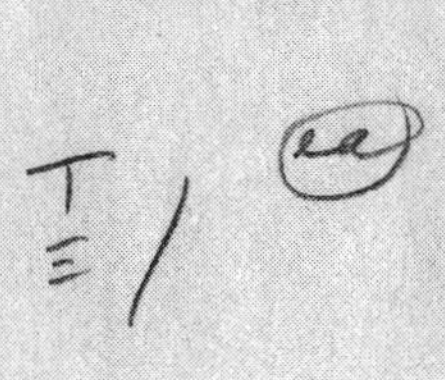

It was here that the little red truck became a major part of the story of Tonga because it was involved in an outrageous series of events that came to a violent head on August 14, 1944, before I reached the island. A native enabled me after considerable questioning to piece together a reasonable account of what happened: 'I work with Tipi like you already know. My job, watch The Commander's shack be sure he in bed with Meredith, watch the pistol range be sure The Doctor over there. I give signal "All O.K." then Tipi drive little red truck down that lane way over there, nobody see from here, he go around back.' Another of Tipi's cohorts enlightened me: 'We get wire cutters, three men, me two others. We go back the big warehouse nobody can see, we cut snip, snip, snip'—his hands opened and closed rapidly as if holding wire cutters—'and we cut two panels out of warehouse, big enough red truck drive right in.'

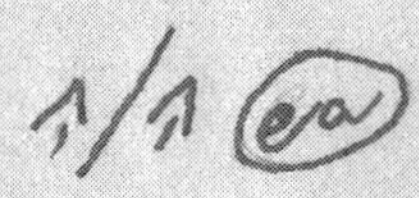

'For what purpose?'

'Yes. My brother have it, he give it back when I ask.' As I was about to leave the pair he asked: 'You speak me good, police? Tell them I needed at naval base?'

Our base was much reduced when I berthed there during the writing of my report, but as the Marines say in their famous poster, 'We could use a few good men,' and I made the recommendation to Queen Salote, who towered over me as I spoke. She told me how gratified everyone on her islands was that the American occupation had gone so smoothly, and that without sensible and understanding men like The Commander this would not have been possible. She asked: 'If we pardon this Tipi fellow, would you reemploy him at your base? and I said a firm 'Yes.' I needed what only he could tell me.

Halfway through the writing of my report, when I was distressed by the ravages The Commander and The Doctor had visited upon our friendly ally Tonga, I drafted a paragraph that was intended as an evaluation of this gross miscarriage of military deportment:

> If the Tongan experience proves anything constructive, it is that incompetent base commanders must be identified early and moved out quickly. But they should not be replaced by medical doctors just out of civilian life who love revolvers and have dreams of military glory, especially if there are attractive girls about who have larcenous friends.

But later my attitude was somewhat softened:

> When these two lovable clowns were finally removed from Tonga, their place was taken by a fine young lieutenant in the Naval Reserve named P.G. Polowniak whose wise administration had the place back on track within three weeks. They should have sent him two years earlier.

My last stop was Matareva. Just as with Tonga, Matareva had been vitally important in the early days of the war. When the threat of Japanese invasion waned, the real fighting men were moved north. A cadre was left behind to guard the place, and an officer not qualified for the job was left in charge, a mirror image of the Commander at Tonga.

But there the similarities end: Tonga was manned by happy-go-lucky sailors, Matareva by a company of sharply trained Marines; and where events on a bypassed and forgotten tropical base at Tonga led to comedy, on Matareva they would end in tragedy.

The Published Version

A staff officer who in no way was entitled to command, The Doctor, everyone agreed, proved himself to be an almost ideal Navy line officer. He was not afraid to issue orders, and they were usually the right ones. Nor was he loath to keep his men in line, for when necessary he could be stern.

He looked the part he liked to play: trim, with a firm jaw, eyes that missed little, a crisp voice suited to command and a handsome bearing. After spending a few days observing the pitiful performance of The Commander, he moved in and took control.

Like even the best men, he did have one weakness: he simply loved to discharge his heavy .45 revolver, for its powerful snap made him feel as if he were commanding not a backwater naval base on a peaceful island but a four-master fighting pirates on the open seas. Men who had enjoyed serving under him told me: 'Doc just loved to fire that cannon of his.' He'd hear a noise at night and come out blazing. In the afternoon a bird of some kind would fly near his quarters, and out would come the .45. At other times, we would see him standing on the sick-bay porch just firing away at a coconut palm as if he were determined to cut it down with bullets, just for the hell of it. He was one gun-happy man, and we used to say: 'Stay around him long enough and you'll lose a leg.'

But the base on Tonga might easily have operated without trouble, for The Commander never made waves and the captain was basically a responsible man, but they had the misfortune to operate in the midst of an unusual population, described in the official history in this blunt way: 'No native people in the South Pacific have such a bad reputation for petty thieving as do those of Tonga.' That judgment is mild, because the Tongans who lived around the naval base in Nuku'alofa carried theft to a degree of proficiency that would have awed Fagin or even an Al Capone, and the presence of what they saw as wealthy American troops in their midst made their mouths water.

Chief of the thieves in my time was a siy young fellow named Tipi, in his mid-twenties, wiry, light tan in coloring with jet-black hair, very white teeth, which he flashed at me whenever I interrogated him, and an awesome capacity for lying and covering his tracks. Had he continued with school, which he quit after the third grade, he would almost certainly have had a brilliant career in business or as a salesman for some reputable firm. As it was, all his aptitude for wheeling and dealing went into thieving, and when he came up against the gun-toting doctor, he surpassed himself in his acts of cunning.

It started, so far as I could reconstruct the episode, shortly after The Commander surrendered control and allowed The Doctor to assume command. Thirsting to taste the fruits of power, the belligerent doctor issued a battery of orders calculated to ensure discipline on the island, but this action caused irritation among both the sailors and the Tongan work force: 'Lieutenant Michener, he treated us natives same as cattle. We handled valuable equipment for Navy, never lose nothin'. Natives drive Navy cars, trucks, take better care your people do. Girl typists mo bettah than yeomen, everyone say that. Goin' movies at night part of our pay. Now all changed, we don't like.'

As soon as Tipi heard the first rumbles of discontent, he swung into action with his master plan, and the first step he took was to immobilize The Commander completely, with the enthusiastic aid of a prostitute with the unlikely name of Meredith. When I asked how she had acquired it, a Tongan girl who worked as a secretary on the base told me: 'She has a Tongan name, but one of her friends saw Meredith in a book and said: "This sound pretty, just like you," and the name stuck.' As to the productive meeting with The Commander, several eager gossipmongers informed me: 'Tipi arrange, and pretty soon Meredith sleeping on base and fixing for Navy equipment all kinds—refrigerators, stoves—to go to her little house next to Tipi's, and things she got extra, it goes to Tipi.'

Men on the base rarely saw The Commander after Meredith moved in, but now Tipi had to neutralize The Doctor, and he did this in an ingenious way. He had Tongan workmen build a small pistol range far removed from the big warehouse, and there The Doctor conducted target practice for hours at a time. The drill on the base became: 'Commander in bed with Meredith, Doctor busy at the range, nobody guardin' the store.'

It was here that the little red truck became a major part of the story of Tonga because it was involved in an outrageous series of events that came to a violent head on August 14, 1944, before I reached the island. A native enabled me after considerable questioning to piece together a reasonable account of what happened: 'I work with Tipi like you already know. My job, watch The Commander's shack be sure he in bed with Meredith, watch the pistol range be sure The Doctor over there. I give signal "All O.K." then Tipi drive little red truck down that lane way over there, nobody see from here, he go around back.' Another of Tipi's cohorts enlightened me: 'We get wire cutters, three men, me, two others. We go back the big warehouse nobody can see, we cut snip, snip, snip'—his hands opened and closed rapidly as if holding wire cutters—'and we cut two panels out of warehouse, big enough red truck drive right in.'

scores of trips in his truck, and his fellow thieves confirmed what he said.

'First time easy, small stuff. Then bigger, still easy. Everything easy, he just keep goin' till all gone.'

'Where did it go?'

'Like before. Small things, PX food, like that to people here. Big things take four men to carry, always on little ships to other islands.'

'You mean, *everything* that was in here—you shipped it all out?'

'Yep. All go.'

'What happened to the little red truck?'

'Shore police gettin' suspicious. Him, me, we paint it white.'

'And then?'

'Maybe ship to Ha'apa Group, maybe Vava'u, maybe Tipi go fetch when he get out of jail.'

I felt a keen desire to see this mastermind and persuaded the Tongan officer to let me visit the rude jail. I happened to be entering just as an attractive young woman was on her way in to see the prisoner. It was Meredith, Tipi's friend, who had proved so helpful in Tipi's plans. We talked for about an hour, and I deduced that Tipi had propelled Meredith into The Commander's bed not primarily to provide cover while he emptied the warehouse but rather to enable each of them to cadge a newly built house from the Navy. Everything in Meredith's house and his, including walls, ceilings and roofs, had been either stolen from the Navy by Tipi or given to Meredith by The Commander, and I could believe the report that the citizens of Tonga, especially the young women, had profited to the extent of at least one million dollars from the occupation, not counting lawful salaries.

'Did you really like The Commander, Meredith?'

'Oh, yes. Kind man, he help me fix my house.'

'He gave you many things?'

'Yes. He one good man, got two babies Oklahoma.'

I asked Tipi what he would do when his prison term ended and he said brightly: 'I think maybe go back work Navy. Old commander go, new man maybe need help.'

'Where did you get the little red truck?'

He considered this for some moments, then said: 'It belong Commander. Navy blue. Two men, me, we paint it red one night, he never guess.'

'Where is it now?'

'Vava'u.'

'You bring it back when you get out?'

'Yes. My brother have it, he give it back when I ask.' As I was about to leave the pair he asked: 'You speak me good, police? Tell them I needed at naval base?'

Our base was much reduced when I berthed there during the writing of my report, but as the Marines say in their famous poster, 'We're looking for a few good men,' and I made the recommendation to Queen Salote, who towered over me as I spoke. She told me how gratified everyone on her islands was that the American occupation had gone so smoothly, and that without sensible and understanding men like The Commander this would not have been possible. She asked: 'If we pardon this Tipi fellow, would you reemploy him at your base? and I said a firm 'Yes.' I needed what only he could tell me.

Halfway through the writing of my report, when I was distressed by the ravages The Commander and The Doctor had visited upon our friendly ally Tonga, I drafted a paragraph that was intended as an evaluation of this gross miscarriage of military deportment:

> If the Tongan experience proves anything constructive, it is that incompetent base commanders must be identified early and moved out quickly. But they should not be replaced by medical doctors just out of civilian life who love revolvers and have dreams of military glory, especially if there are attractive girls about who have larcenous friends.

But later my attitude was somewhat softened:

> When these two lovable clowns were finally removed from Tonga, their place was taken by a fine young lieutenant in the Naval Reserve named P.G. Polowniak whose wise administration had the place back on track within three weeks. They should have sent him two years earlier.

My last stop was Matareva. Just as with Tonga, Matareva had been vitally important in the early days of the war. When the threat of Japanese invasion waned, the real fighting men were moved north. A cadre was left behind to guard the place, and an officer not qualified for the job was left in charge, a mirror image of The Commander at Tonga.

But there the similarities end: Tonga was manned by happy-go-lucky sailors, Matareva by a company of sharply trained Marines; and where events on a bypassed and forgotten tropical base at Tonga led to comedy, on Matareva they would end in tragedy.

When I first landed on Matareva and was driven from the airstrip to

A Horrendous Error

During my years in the South Pacific I was privileged to know two gifted Americans, each a writer of distinction. James Norman Hall, of Iowa, was world-famous not only for his coauthorship of the *Bounty* Trilogy and the motion pictures made from his novels but also for his gallantry in World War I, when, as an American citizen, he volunteered to serve as a fighter pilot in France's Escadrille Lafayette. In Tahiti he was a formidable figure, idolized by both American tourists and the local French government, for he had truly been a hero.

Robert Dean Frisbie, of Cleveland and California, was a writer with a talent equal to Hall's but without the benefit of the latter's consistent good fortune. He too lived on islands more or less associated with Tahiti, and I was a great admirer of his writing, which appeared regularly in the prestigious *Atlantic Monthly*, as did Hall's.

The men knew each other and between them developed a bond of affection and respect, for they were figures of some importance in the South Pacific, but there the similarity ended. Hall, keeping always to the established society of Tahiti, married Sarah Winchester, the radiant daughter of an English sea captain and his Polynesian wife. Lala, as Sarah was called, was a kind of queen of the islands, beautiful, lively, humorous, and the mother of two fine children—a boy, Conrad, who would win an Oscar as a Hollywood cameraman, and Nancy, a charmer who would marry the heir to the Rutgers (of New Jersey) fortunes. James Norman and Sarah Winchester Hall lived in splendor on the royalties he earned on his famous books and the fees paid him by the movies. They proved that white men—her English father and her American husband—could find stability and happiness in the tropics.

Frisbie sampled Tahitian society but found its heavy socializing and settled culture oppressive. He was a man of the lonely islands, the atolls whose highest elevation above sea level might be a mere dozen feet, making them prey to any hurricane that stormed in. He married a beautiful island girl with whom he had five children. Incredibly, he took his family from one isolated island to another, always stopping long enough to write some exquisite essay about his day-to-day experiences in the lagoons, the storms, the ever-present allure. At intervals he would find employment as an island storekeeper for the famous South Pacific merchant chain, Burns Philp, whose storm-beaten trading ships would periodically bring fresh stores to the islands and haul away the copra that the natives collected from their palm trees. But most of the time he was strapped for money, borrowing here and there, waiting nervously for one more check from the *Atlantic Monthly*. How he survived remains a mystery, but he did, and always he kept his children with him.

In summary, Hall had money and land; Frisbie had neither. Hall wrote books that sold enormously; Frisbie wrote essays that brought him little. Hall stayed put in Tahiti; Frisbie roamed the low atolls. And what struck me most significantly was that Hall wrote a fine book about an imaginary hurricane and watched it made into a stunning movie, while Frisbie lived through a real hurricane and survived only by tying himself and his children high in trees.

When my wartime duties took me into the Tahiti area I was delighted that I would be meeting Hall but was stunned when directed to fly far to the north to rescue Robert Dean Frisbie, who seemed to be dying on Penrhyn, one of his remote islands. It would be a journey of bittersweet associations about which I would report in *The World Is My Home*, which would appear in 1991, forty-seven years later.

In the book I focused more on Frisbie than on Hall, explaining how I helped the crew of a navy C-47 rescue Frisbie from an isolated island, leaving his children behind as we took off with their father, and delivered him at last to a Navy hospital in Pago Pago, capital of tiny American Samoa. I painted a portrait of the archetypal beachcomber, a man who had come to the end of his rope in the remote atolls, and told not only of his death but also of the rescue of his children and their introduction into American life. It was a heroic yarn, and I found pleasure in reviving interest in Robert Dean and in watching his children miraculously finding a vibrant new life. I had paid Frisbie the respect he deserved.

But in Tahiti, prior to rescuing Robert Dean, I had also established contact with his alter ego, James Norman Hall, and the respect I felt for him appears in the passage reproduced below.

In the meantime, through the good offices of Lew Hirshorn I was meeting an exciting array of Tahiti residents. T ere were nglish remittance men living well on allowances which would have been niggardly had they fled to Southern France, American sons of important industrial families who had gone native, Europeans of all sorts, and out on the edge of town the island's most famous son, James Norman Hall with his delightful English-Polynesian wife, Lala Winchester, daughter of an English sea captain and a Tahiti princess. They were a grand couple, he stately and reserved, she a bubbing cauldron of funny stories and outrageous rumors about the ridivulous behavior of island couples. Hall was famous even then for his Bounty trilogy which I liked everyone else had liked, but I was especially fond of his Hurricane, which seemed to me to capture better than anything else I had read the quality of life on a small island, and I told him so. Of course everytone on Tahiti knew that Hall's collaborator, Charles Nordhoff, had shared at least the responsibility for the books, and some said that Nordhoff supplied the poetic portions, Hall the pedestrian working out of plot and scene, but I gave no credit to that rumor.

I never met Nordhoff and am not sure he was living in Tahiti during the various trips when I visited the island, and I never head Hall speake even one word about him; I judged that he was fed up with visitors to the famous island who wanted to discuss aspects of their collaboration, one of the most famous in history, but he did rusprise me by talking freely about another American writer, the Robert Dean Frisbie whom I was supposed to look after when I flew north from Bora Bora.

He was most excited by the possibility that I might help Frisbie: 'Oh Michener! He knows the South Seas the way few of us do. Far better than me,' and waxed eloquent as he told of Frisbie's entry into the area, an almost penniless writer with a meager background of success who married a native girl and settled first on one lonely atoll, then another. 'He has four or five children, you know, and the grand thing about him, the noble thing really, is that he will never abandon them. They must be a dreadful burden, him with os little money, but wherever he goes, from one lonely spot to another, he takes his island wife and her four or fice children with him.'

He spoke of the fact that Frisbie was a difficult man: 'For me, with the good luck I've had with my books and a wife when had an estalished place in island society...higher than mine I can tell you...it was easy. Look at this house on the side of a beautiful hill looking down into that bay with its reef and palm trees. I've known the paradise of the South Pacific. Frisbie's known the hell.'

'Hell?'

'Yes. Last we heard here he was dying...alone...on a tiny atoll.'

'His children?'

'I believe they're with him. They always were when I knew him.'

I had never met Frisbie but I had read one of his books which had been recommended to me by an Australian who had given it the same high praise as Hall. It was a lovely, relaxed account of life in the area I was coming to know so well, and it was obvious to me, as an editor, that if Fresbie got hold of himself he could write a fine novel about the kind of adventures he'd had. To learn that he was dying was a shock.

But I could wait till I reached Puka Puka to grapple with that sad problem. Now I was immersed in the Ratchett Kimbrell matter and the more I saw of this delightful man the more I liked him, for he was a kinf of elf, a person with wit but no guile. If he allowed Reri to handle his secret code books it was because he felt that she would gain pleasure from an exercise which bored him, and if he was willing to allow Lieut. McClintock to woo Reri during the early hours of the evening it was probably because it gave her a feeling of the old days in Paris to have such a young and gallant admirer, for he knew that when the young man was gone back to his hotel afire with dreams of the South Pacific, Reri would be coming home to him. Me? I was enraptured with one of Reri's younger sisters or cousins, but I was forlorn as McClintock, for she was in love with someone else.

But I was enjoying myself in Papeete, for in the early part of the evening we all went

Hall's Daughter Corrects My Error

Pleased with what I had accomplished in saluting these two remarkable Americans, I flew off to Hawaii, where, as I was lolling in a Venetian gondola at one of the new hotels, I heard a joyous shout from the prow of a passing gondola: 'Michener! What are you doing here?' It was Nancy Rutgers, Hall's daughter, and I shouted back: 'Call me at this hotel,' and when she did, she and her husband, Nick, arranged a meeting with my wife and me.

How fortunate it was that we met! For when I told Nancy about my report of meeting her father in Tahiti in 1944, she astounded me: 'But Jim, Father was in Iowa all during the war!'

'But I talked with him—at the beach house east of Papeete. I met Lala, I met you—don't you remember?'

'Sure, I remember. Dad liked you because you knew all his movies. But that was when you came back after the war. No way you could have seen him during the war, because he simply was not there,' and Nick confirmed this.

There was nothing to do but rewrite the Tahiti scene in which I learned of Frisbie's travail on his little islands. It must have been Lew Hirshorn, the wealthy expatriate from Long Island and owner of the interisland steamer *Hiro,* who had told me. As a lad out of college sometime in the thirties he had stepped off a tramp steamer and remained in Tahiti the rest of his life. A major citizen of the island, he was an invaluable guide.

I was astounded to learn that Hall had not been in Tahiti during the war, but I could not refute the evidence. The pages that follow show how a writer reacts to a devastating blow. He kills the erroneous text and substitutes a better. But if you were to ask me today who told me about Frisbie in Tahiti in 1944, I would still say: 'James Norman Hall. I can see him sitting by the lagoon when he told me.' Of course, the lagoon was still there when I visited Hall in 1950, but I'm still convinced I saw him there in 1944.

Theresa: Hall's son-in-law has just reminded me that James Norman was not in Tahiti during WWII. I had met on two subsequent trips. Make this correction on 59-9* And thanks. J.N.

I was especially sorry to have missed Hall because I'd heard that he'd been a supporter of this man Frisbie I was supposed to look after when I flew north from Bora Bora. But my friend Lew Hirshon was able to help fill that gap: 'Everyone in Tahiti is familiar with the Frisbie story, young American writer of great promise, came out here penniless and went native. Hall spoke of him in glowing terms. "Great talent, but doomed." The American colony in the island regularly discusses what we can do to help Frisbie. He has four or five children, you know, and even though we deplore the way he's livdd, we have to admire the fact that he will not abandon those kids. Where he goes, they go. But he's a cantankerous son-of-a-bitch, and even though you have the best intentions in the world, you can't do anything to help him. He won't allow it.'

'His native wife?'

'Dead. So he drags his kids from one lonely atoll to another, pitiful case. Hall told me once: "I often think of Frisbie. He knows far more about the islands than I ever will. But because I've found a steady life I've known the paradise that the South Pacific can be. Frisbie's known the hell."'

'What's he doing on Pukapuka?'

'Dying.'

A Later Correction

the islands than I ever will, but self-destructive. Doomed." Americans in Tahiti often discuss what we can do to help Frisbie. He has four or five children, you know, and even though we feel sorry for the way he has to live, we do admire him for refusing to abanodon the kids. Where he goes, they go. But he's a cantankerous son-of-a-bitch. Won't let you help him, so we've prtty much written him off.'

'His wife?'

'Dead.'

'If I am able to help him, then what?'

'He'll go on dragging his kids ffom one lonely atoll to another, pitiful case. Hall told me once: "Because I've found a steady life I've known the paradise that the South Pafcific can be. Frisbie knows the hell."'

'What's he doing on Pukapuka?'

'Dying.'

Still Later Correction by Hall

'Michener, you must keep the names straight. There are two Pukapukas, a little one in the Tuamotus east of here. Frisbie never went there, so far as I know. The other is well north of here. Same name, Pukapuka, but its official name is Danger Island. He lived there and wrote about it. But when you picked him up that time he was on Penrhyn Atoll, which is properly known as Tongareva. Can you keep that straight?'

54

Editing at Its Best

When I was searching through this part of the manuscript for an example of constructive editing, I found no page with enough comment to justify inclusion, but at the very end when I was leaving Hall and Frisbie I found a page containing eight examples of problems met and solved by good editors. I have numbered the passages:

1. It is helpful for editors or copy editors to identify places in the text where further elaboration might be needed to clarify.

2. I do not handle pronouns effectively in the first draft and welcome suggestions as to clarifying antecedents. But here it seems fruitless to repeat Ratchett.

3. Every writer can profit from having someone with a good eye suggest deletion of short phrases, which, though they might add a little color, take too much space or sidetrack the forward movement. I surrendered the phrase, but not happily.

4. Three years into my writing career I dropped any attempt to differentiate between *that* and *which*. As a former teacher of grammar I had once known the rules, but I have now forgotten them and to keep in mind the multiple ramifications and niggling niceties is beyond me. I therefore appreciate the help of copy editors who have strong opinions on the matter and encourage them to enforce their rules. For myself, I am guided mostly by the sound of the sentence, and so are many other writers.

5. Editors are helpful in spotting places where authors or their typists have dropped a word. More important at this point is the clarification asked for regarding who was in love with whom and when.

6. This is the most interesting query, in that it deals with clarity of expression, and in this instance there was in the original a confusion as to which situation the word *interesting* applied. The confusion could be clarified only by the insertion of the two words *an* and *title*.

7. This is one of the more instructive queries on this page. When I wrote that south of Pago Pago there was nothing but the South Pole, I relied on two implied conditions: *South* meant directly south, *South Pole* covered the entire polar region. Given those two reasonable suppositions, what I wrote is accurate, and I believe that most mariners would interpret my statement that way. But an editor must suspect everything and anticipate the reactions of the ordinary reader, who may take words literally. Strictly speaking, a huge percentage of the Southern Hemisphere is south of American Samoa, but that's carrying ordinary reasoning a bit far. I appreciate such minute examination of what I write. Additionally, I have been especially grateful to sharp-eyed editors who detect the most egregious sexual readings in ordinary prose. I once wrote and printed: 'This is the story of an attractive young girl from Wyoming laid in Greenwich Village.' My woman editor noted: 'You're probably right both ways.'

8. And last, the most difficult annotation of all. Here my editor says clearly: 'This passage could be cut because it impedes the flow of the story.' To few current writers could this criticism be more frequently applied than to me. I love the rich embellishment of a statement, the marshaling of arcane data, the retelling of illustrative incident, and the hammering down of the point I seek to make. Readers have constantly thanked me for that approach to storytelling; editors have properly warned me against redundancy. I have tried to follow a rule of reason and have profited from editorial advice. In this instance I wanted to refer to that delightful actor Gene Lockhart because I had recently acted on an informal stage in Belgium with his daughter, June. The passage could be cut. Sorry, June.

was obvious to me, as a book editor, that if Frisbie got hold of himself he could write a fine novel about the kind of adventures he'd had. To learn that he was dying was a shock.

But I would wait till I reached Pukapuka to grapple with that sad problem. Now I was immersed in the Ratchett Kimbrell matter and the more I saw of this relaxed Pickwick of a man the more I liked him, for he was a kind of elf, a person with wit but no guile. If he allowed Reri to handle his secret code books it was because he felt that she would gain pleasure from an exercise which bored him, and if he was willing to allow Lieutenant-Commander McClintock to woo Reri during the early hours of the evening it was probably because it gave her a feeling of the old days in Paris to have such a young and gallant admirer, for Ratchett knew that when the young man was gone back to his hotel afire with the dreams of the South Pacific, Reri would be coming home with him. Me? I was enraptured with one of Reri's younger sisters or cousins, but I was forlorn as McClintock, for she was in love with someone else.

But I was enjoying myself in Papeete, for in the early part of the evening we all went to the movie house, which was a lively scene with young people all over the place and a level of noisy involvement that I had not seen elsewhere. The island had only one film, a colossal disaster called South of Pago Pago, which was interesting, because if you look on the map there is absolutely nothing south of that tiny island but the South Pole. This did not deter the movie makers, who offered the exquisite but doomed Francis Farmer, one of the most serene of all stars but an incurable addict of alcohol and drugs, in a concoction featuring sharks, buried treasure, palm trees and two of the most conniving villains ever, Gene Lockhart and Douglas Dumbrille: to see them was to hate them.

56

Planning a Summary Chapter

I do not outline in traditional ways, in notebooks or on filing cards, the data for either an entire book or a chapter. But as the facing page from my working notebooks shows, when I tackle an individual chapter I do keep at my elbow for constant reference a blank page headed with only one word—in this case, *Meaning*, the title of the last chapter in *The World Is My Home*. On it I write down notes as they occur to me, reminders of important facts, lists of things to be done, and proposed developments of topics.

Such chapter pages for nonfiction and fiction cannot be differentiated. The process is the same: untidy, arbitrary, provisional, and extremely useful. If I did not jot down my thoughts as they evolve I would be hopelessly lost or, what would be worse, confused. I don't recommend this process for others, but for me it works.

In studying the various entries so long after they were made and used, I cannot always decipher what problems they pretended to solve, but in its day each was significant. The boldly printed name in the dead center of the page, Hugh McNair Kahler, is there because he was a man who played an important role in my education as a professional writer, and I have trouble remembering his name. When needed, it does not come; when I'm thinking of something else, up it pops—on one such occasion I hurried to my page and wrote it large.

The page is relevant in that it faithfully represents the hesitancy, the stumbling along of a writer who is attempting to compose a summary of his experience in which concepts, fugitive ideas, and facts are the heart of what he wants to say. Each little block of ideas was of salient importance, but they did not reach me in orderly fashion like European military men who parade in dazzling lockstep, arms swinging in rhythm, eyes straight ahead. My ideas have never been so precise, but they have been remarkably persistent, like a gang of Daniel Boones probing through the wilderness.

Special attention should be paid to the list of subjects in the lower-right corner. This was compiled bit by bit as I worked on the chapter and represents those ideas that I knew I would have to come back to, either to insert new material or to improve what had already been touched upon. Later, when I edited the rough first version, I would check off each reminder as it was dealt with.

What seems significant about this page of scrambled notes is that each entry deals with some aspect of an intellectual life, some turning point that made the difference. This page should be studied in conjunction with the nine short excerpts of editorial work illustrated shortly. Taken together, they show how difficult it sometimes is to express an idea accurately, and how it has to be slaved over until it is expressed in acceptable language. And again, I would stress that if this page dealt with fiction, the laboriousness shown to hone a passage properly would be the same.

As I typed this page in April 1991 my wife called from the television room: 'Cookie! President Bush is about to quote you!' and as I listened he ended the celebration of victory in the Gulf War by reciting a crucial line from my short novel *The Bridges at Toko-Ri*. The elderly admiral, who has just lost a treasured pilot over Korea, asks: 'Where did we get such men?' The words seem so appropriate as a comment on war and bravery that President Reagan quoted them frequently. Admirals and generals have done the same, and that fine actor Fredric March, who played the admiral in the motion picture, told my wife shortly before he died: 'Of all the speeches I had to memorize during a long life in the theater, that's the one that comes back to me most often.' And without hesitating, he recited the entire passage. Now President Bush was quoting the key line again in an emotional moment.

I wrote that ending eight times before I got it right. If I'd been satisfied with the first version, neither Reagan nor March or Bush would have paid attention, nor any reader, either.

A

MEANING

JOHN PAUL II
NEHRU
HALSEY
STANTON
BUCKLEY

HANNAH
MABEL
ARTHUR
ROBERT
LAURA
SAINTED SON?

MICHENER
1. PASSPORT
2 NAVAL OFFICER
3. LAWYER JAMES (JOHN B.???)

KIDS
LITWACK, HARRY
DOROTHY
ELEANOR
VIRGINIA
ESTHER
TOM

MICHENERS
SHADDINGER
1, 2, 3
J.A.M.'s
MARINE
HAWAII
ASIA
PIPERSVILLE
FBI
DENVERZAND
THE AUNT
The Cornerp
BETTER TOO CONGRESS
PULITZER

TRAVEL
14
18-22
EUROPE
SHIPS
P+O
WAR
ASIA

KNUT HAMSUN (PEDERSEN)
1859-1952
PAN 1894 - NOBEL 1920
IW 1945 - AGE 86

GEORGE MURRAY
BOYS' BRIGADE
1909 SCOUTS
BASKETBALL

19
DECISION
BOOTS
GOD
WELCOME {BUCK
HAMMERSTEIN

1888
-1807
81

CRITICS
L-A
O. PRESCOTT
J.H. BROWN
DRIFTERS
FIRST 3 CB
AEGEAN NAVY
PREP WASH-ON
JET/FIGHTER

SWARTHMORE
SPILLER
BRANSHARD
{LYSENKO
MENDEL
SORITES
PLAYS
{HAMBURG SHOW
PANTOMIME

COMPLAIN
EXPLAIN
DISDAIN

GEORGE MURRAY
FRANK SCHEIBLEY

HUGH McNAIR KAHLER

NOBEL
HAMSON
MISHMA
CONRAD ERNEST
T. WILDER
R.P. WARREN
SAUL BELLOW
JAMES BALDWIN
MAILER
CAPOTE
J.C. GATES

HARDY-ZOLA-PROUST
JAMES-GORKY
VS.
EUCKEN-HAMSUN-ASTURIAS

BUT I'D BE PROUD
UNDSET, MANN, ONEILL
YEATS

FINAL
POLAND
BORA BORA
MODAL FREEDOM

TERM PAPER POETRY
MODAL FREEDOM
~~MR. MAXWELL, $40~~
~~DRAKE'S DRUM~~
~~JESUS SAVE~~
~~MISS ANERSON~~ (12)
~~CRIMINALITY~~
KYAKHTA
CALIFORNIA
~~MINNESOTA~~
~~HARVARD HAMLET~~
13 TH THE BATES
CHROMO RESEARCH
~~BORN AS ART~~
SCHOLAR'S INSTRUCTION
~~DAME SHERNING~~
~~JAM - THE TWIN CORRECT~~
TROFIM LYSENKO
ANTAEUS FACTOR
MR. MAXWELL
HAMMOCKS / VIN ROSÉ
EXUPERY
SYLLOGISM

LIFE OF WRITER
PEOPLE
EDUCATOR TO WORLD
(PRES. OF BROWN)
{MARACAIBO
SHERIDAN
SUBJECTS ±
HOTELS
LIBRARIES
ORDINARY SUBJECTS

RECIDIVISM

SUMMARY
POLITICAL AMB.
PSYCHOL
MANNERISMS

57

Rough Draft of Concluding Pages

Below is the start of a verbatim retyping of the carbon copy of my first attempt at summarizing the final chapter in the book. My ideas stand just as they came from my typewriter and illustrate precisely the tentative way in which I attack a passage that I recognize as important to the whole. If you study even a few of these pages carefully, you will see that a slight impediment in my left hand, the result of an extremely minor stroke, makes me type poorly when I'm in a hurry, but this does not hold me back, for my errors can be easily corrected by pen. I also strike out passages and insert afterthoughts.

Look at the third paragraph from the end, where I say 'two examples of misguided comment come to mind.' I then give the first, which deals with my device of introducing the narrator in a three-step plan. But in my zeal to finish that day's work I had forgotten my second example, the one dealing with the absent Afghanistan navy. This oversight will be corrected later. This rough draft comprises 7.5 manuscript pages; the next version, 24.5; the final, 21 pages. Thus a manuscript experiences neap and spring tides, then neap again.

SUMMARIZING A BOOK AND A LIFE

My savage comment on Knut Hamsun needs elaboration for it illustrates rater
The son of a
precisely my attitude toward writing. Hexwasxa/Norwegian peasant family, he
knocked about Norway and the United States as a casual laborer, then
returned tomexto to the literary world where he wrote some ofx excellent
works which received respectful notices. At forty he astinished Norway and
Europe with a powerful novel Hunger, which broke new ground with its
z
Nietschean overtones and lyrical, impressionistic prose. It deserved the
Nobel Prize, which he won as a mature literary gian in 1920 ate the age of
sixty-one. THe prize seems to have gone to his head, for he became the
spokesman for strange ideas and when, in t9x Aorld War II the German Nazis
invaded Norway he becamextheirxsqx saw Adolf Hitler as the savior of Europe
and the world. His behavior was appalling, the negation of everything writ-
When the Nazis were defeated, he was into
ing if supposed to creat and support. /Rejected by his peopleand,thrown xx
jail as a known traitor and saved from angry punishment only because his extreme age, eight-six allowed them government forces to dismiss him as a
having brought his
silly old man. Feed, lived seven more years, xx embarrassment to thexgreatx
a
prize hexhadxmade, ax shame to his nation and sx disgrace to himself.

All my professional life I have faced, one way or another, this dif
ficult problem of what a writer owes to his homeland. I have never been a

flag-waving patriot nor have I written that way, but at times of testing I seem always to have come down xxxxthe in defense of my nation. As a Quaker pacifist I could have pleaded non-combatant service in World War II, but in Europe I had seen the madness of Hitler and in my studies I realized what a fearful enemy Japan could be, so I went into the Navy instead. During long spells of my working years writers would be excuse from taxes if they stayed out of the United States for 501 days in succession, and many tried to reorganize their lives to do and once by accident I qualified, but I was ashamed and never did it again. It was also much to a writet's advantage to live in Ireland, and pay no taxes to anyone, but those who did saved a little money and damged their careers, especially the actors who missed all the good acting roles at home and had to content with one cheap European quickie after another.

rying again until Monday morning, and this day-to-day attitude lasted unchal lenged until I was nearly forty

people and make them extraordinary, and I have done it repeatedly.

Furthermore, in an age xs when the calm of classic writing seems to be xxx pushed off the stage by wild sex, savage violence, bizarre inhuman em phases and the destruction of traditional values, I have been able to write long/books and keep people attached to them without resorting to the/xxxxxxx popular fashions exemplified by Friday night videos. With an unruffled and at times even stately indifference to fashion, I have continued to write books the way I want them to be. The miracle is that I have been able to keep so many readers with me, and I think the ex lanation must be that Ithey know they can trust me to talk write of important matters in a manner which invites the reader to stay with it in assurance that rewards of delight and enlightenment will be forthcoming. Whatever it is I do, I do it very well.

and sometimes tedious

destructive

Critics have had a difficult time with me. They would like to condemn me for writing for money, but they know that is not true, because I have given most of what I received away. They would like to say that I direct my writing to low or even base interests, but in view of what I said in the preceding paragrah, that would be laighable. They sometimes claim that I write easy books for people who cannot handle anything more difficult, but msny of my correspondents are among the brightest people in the cluntry. And they would like to intimate that no one should bother with my books be cause they are not written in approved styles, but the books go one and on, and only only at home.

The man who runs the excellent program in Great Britain in which xxxxxxx the government collects data on who reads what in public libraries throughout the nation and then pays the authors of the books taken out, did me the honor some while back of sending me a report of what the British sys tem <u>would</u> have paid me xxx if they paid similar fees to foreign authors, which they should not, and my books stood near the top of the list for foreign authors and quite high even among the local writers. The same would be true, I judge, for certain of my books, not all of them by any means, in countries like The Netherlandsa and Germany.

Chauncey Made,

Typical criticism of my work was well voiced recently by/the Books Columnist of the Fort Lauderdale , Florida <u>News Sin-Sentinel:</u>

> Sometime in the late '60s or early '70s, James Mi ener ceased to be a serious writer, at least in the literary sense and became some thing else---a indisrty, his typewriter a factory upin whivh, with two fingers pecking, he took history and processed it into bestpsell ing novels that could also be used as door-stops and further processed into movies or, betterx yet, TV miniseries.*

the which came with
*Inxhis covering letter/xwhenxsendingxme his review, Mapes wrote: 'While I do not think you are a great writer, I do see you as a great American whose life and ideals provide one of the few examples worthy of admiration and imitation in our troubled age.'

The lastx review is witty x, well phrased, witty and legitimate in its content, and I receive many such attacks, to none of which do I ever respond, for xIxwasxtaught at the beginning of my career I was indoctrinated by old-timers into the/sacrosanct rules of the true professions xknots on sofar as criticism is concerned: 'Never complain. Never explain. Never dis dain.' The veteran who first advised me to conduct myself that way said: 'It looks petty and little juvenile o complain. Make sure the publisher sends you a check for/xallxthatxisxsux what you've hinestly earned, and go on to the next one. It's useless to explain, for if you've spent three hundred pages putting your thoughts on paper and haven't succeeded, what makes you think you can xxxxxxxxxxxxxxx make it more clear in/one-page letter which the editor will cut to a quarter page? And as for disdaining your critics, remember that they are probably brighter than you are, have t ought more deeply about iterature than you have, and could probably write a damned sight better than you can, if they put their minds to it. Never fight with a critic, because you will lose. Be sides being superior to you on every way, they have that big, forty-sheet newspaper behind them.'

I read far more criticism than the average citizenx: what movies are best, what shows to go to, what music is worth buying x in compact discs, what restaurants are worth the effort. I prize their opinions and am guided
but I never, never read criticism of my own work.
by theirxxxxxxxxx recommendations,/xxxxx I summarize the problem this way: 'Critics are invaluable in xxdvis advising you how to spend your money. They have no merit at all in telling you how to spend your talent.'

At ine period in my life numerous critics, when writing of other writers, were fond of comparing them to me, and always the other fellow came off best: 'He is a xbi better storyteller than Michener' or 'His novel moves mor honestly than a Michener.' For a while I kept a list of such comparisons because I wanted to know what happened to all these peop;le who were better than I was, but it came to naught because most of them were never heard from again, and those that were had only feeble lasting power.

well-known
Two xgreat critics were of inestimable help to me when I started, Orville Prescott of the <u>New York Times</u> and John Mason Brown of the literary clubs; they lifted me from obscurity and I shall always been indebted to them, but I often wonder when I read later critics if they have any idea of
unceasing
what the life of a writer like me is, the/letters of thanks xthat for the
e
books that xwx changed lives, the almost tarful pleas that I write about other places of merit, the starlinv experience of walking to the rear end of an airplane on and intercintinetal flight and finding that seven or eight people are reading your novel and often one ;ublished a quarter of a century ago, the constant contact xf with people who love books and who are endeavoring to get their children to read,too, by giving them one of mine.

I hope that anyone rwading this book will carry away two portraits of me, because I thinxkthat they, better than any other imagery, convey the picture of a writer. I have told earlier of being burned lut of Maracaibo and smuggled across the alke in dead of night, but and that was exciting but what followedwas more so, because the radio told of my escape to x the headquarters of an oil-drilling company, and in succeeding days some hundred people streamed kj from as far as a hundred miles away with copies of my books for me to autograph. Most, of course, were American oilfield workers stationed in remote areas where books were essential for sanity, and mine perhaps because they so long ad gave such good return for the money in vested; but a surprising number were Venezolanos who had bought the books because their white co-workers had recommended them as a rewarding ay to learn English, xxx others were ordinar citizens of half a dozen different nationalities, and of course, as in all countries wherever I go, afew qer Hungarians who I had xxxxxxxxxxx helped many led to safety across the bridge at Andau. Every person whose book I signed in that informal literary festival had a special story, and taken altogether they explained something about books that even professional connected with industry forget: books are bridges bet wee people, and when the author is deemed to be asomeone who has made a spe cial contibut on to a life, the bridge can be both fragile and extremely poignant, covering as it must a considerable disance between a station in the Venezuelan jungle and an oil field near Maracaibo.

More dramatic in a way was the day in Sheridan, Wyoming when at ten in the morning I leanred that a plane I had expected would not arrive and that I would xxxxxxxxxxxx have to remain where I was overnight. The town librarian, hearing of my en- forced stay, aksed whether I would meet/with xxxx that evening a few local people whi liked books, and when I agreed, she hopped onto the telephone and radio to alert people in far distant town that I would be in her library that night a seven. Free from respinsibilities till then, I spent the afernoon visitng tye Little Big Horn to see where Gwneral Custer had xxxxx led his cavalry into disaster and when we returned after sunset we found tthe lybrary ab solutely jammed with families that had driven tremendous disatnces if response to radio messages into their little towns advising them of the im provised meeting. Carloads of enthusiasts hads driven down from Billings, ???? miles away; others had come two by two from remote settlements, and a surprising number had brought their children to chare in an experience that would not often be repeated. XX was an amazing audience that night, because under the circumstances anyone who was present was there because she or he

at
liked books, and as always xin such xinstancesx occasions we talked not about my books but about books in general: How difficult would it be for a young woman in Billings to find a New York publisher? Do you have a big staff that does your reswrach for you? Is there still a market for children's books? Do you go to Hollywood then they make a picture from one of yorur stories?

The metting lasted two hour ; it xmigx could hae lasted xfour and with some of us, xall nightx till dawn, because books are terribly important in some lives, and people who write them somtimes acquire a significanceto which they are not entitled but which, in a sense, they have earned. When I die I shall be reme,bered by a tomstone which will read the eiptaph I have composed myself and which Ix insist on: 'Here lies a man who never shoed home movies or served vin rose'and,three fine/libraries in wildly scattered parts of the world, and two Michiner art galleries. There could have been several other buildings, but I would not allow it. If one is gling to work in the arts let him or her aspire to tru professional stanrads; I love professionals and have tried to be a tested professional write; and

The epitaph is not irrelevant. //If one is going to drink wine let it be a clear white or an honest red, not a soggy mix of half- and-handx, but

As to critics, two examples of well intentioned but misguided comment and relevant come to mind. One very knowedgable man /xwrotexof pointed out that in The Drifters 'Mr. Michener absnet-mindedly carelessly shifts the point of vew in his narration in each of his first three chapters, forgetting that many of his readers will have rememberd Henry James' dictum that pooint of view is everything.' He was quite correct in his facts; the pint of view did shift in a most un-Jamesian riot, but what he did not know was that the publisher and I had studied the problem with care and xx prolonged discussions to see if my plan would sork; to have the narrator slowly rev al himself after two epislde in which he was peripherally involved. I liked the idea, one of my editors did not, and obviouslt thecritici didn't either, and maybe he was right. But to assume that it was through overisght was quite wrong. Here the presence of superior knowledge in the citic's mind tempts him, not the writer, into error.

During a long lifetime of writing I never once defended either my style or my books, but I believe a time for honest assessment has come without any intention to break the first rule and tryto xsolvx answer commentators and critics. I have been a phenomenon, off to one side living by my own rules and obedient o my purposes. I have written a series of books which, without bizarre efforts, have captured the minds and attentions of many readers who have found in them substantial rewards. ithin the quiet limits I have set myself I have been able to write a sequence of books, calm xxxxx in tone xxx but if not inflammable always pressing forward with something important/to say. I have brought hope and new insights to hundreds of thousands of readers, and I have done so without excessive fanfare, alwasy preferrings to remain in the baxkground.

I have been very good at what I did, and I have remained at my self-appointed xthroughx tasks long after scores of my colleagues have retired from the effort, and I have persevered xxxxxx in considerable pain and potential mental distress. My chain of successes has ben unparalleled in recent decades, for wherever I stop in my journeys about the world I find clusters of people who have read my books and understood them, for with my pen I have earned myself a warrant of citizenship in all/corners xpartsx of the xworldx earth. The world has been my home, and I have striven to be a worthy citizen of it.

27 February 1988
Coral Gables Fla.

End of manuscript
But two chapters to come

Nine Segments Edited

When it came time to end the manuscript I found myself in a curious position. I was writing the last pages of the final chapter and striving to finish it off properly without being mindful that it would also be the conclusion of the entire book. Thus, what I was working on with only a limited aim in mind required a much broader vision: whether I wanted it to or not it would summarize an entire life.

On 27 February 1988 I completed the rough draft of the conclusion as shown in the preceding reproduction of that version. It consisted only of the basic materials expressed in pedestrian fashion, and even as I was writing it I realized that this was at best no more than an aide-mémoire and that the real work remained to be tackled. But I had come up with one happy phrase that did epitomize my life's work: 'For with my pen I have earned a warrant of citizenship in all corners of the earth.' You will see that in later versions I improved on the rhythm of the statement, but through all changes it would persist as the effective summary.

A few days later, 3 March 1988, as Item 1 shows, I was back at my typewriter for another try. The chopped-up result contains some phrases of significance, but they seem tacked on and do not lead properly to the conclusion, which is in no way improved over its first version. So as I ended this attempt I realized that I had much more work to do.

After working to make the concluding passages appropriate, I recalled an incident from the previous year that seemed to tie wandering bits into a neat package. As Item 2 shows, it dealt with a tradition about which few are informed: the gathering in the White House of certain citizens who have served the nation in various capacities. There they are greeted by the president and handed an award testifying to their worthy citizenship.

The next five items, 3 through 7, provide brief glimpses of what a rewriting job consists of but the exact wording has not yet been achieved. However, work of this type helps bind the manuscript together and is of considerable value, even though not much of it can be used in the final version.

Since each of the five excerpts deals with a topic of some importance to my work, the question naturally arises: 'Why didn't he get it right the first time?' Fair question, for if I were a noted stylist one might expect the golden words to flow forth in perfect order, weight, and harmony. That dream may be realized by certain fortunate writers, but not by me, for I can affirm that I am unable even to write an important one-page business letter composed of three or four different ideas without first drafting it, then correcting it, and then polishing it before I pass it along to my skilled secretary, who may suggest her own corrections if she detects a gaffe. It is not uncommon for me to hand her a short three-paragraph letter on a single sheet of paper with my second try at the top but crossed out to make way for my third effort at the bottom.

The examples that follow show rather effectively the sort of rewriting and revising I do, for almost nothing that leaves my desk for hers is without its eight or ten emendations in heavy black ink. For me writing is a cruelly difficult task.

Item 8 shows how I will often rewrite an entire paragraph immediately after finishing a first draft. Halfway through the first time, I realize that I'm not saying what I wanted or how I wanted to say it, so I junk it instantly. More often, however, I go back later.

Item 9 illustrates my attempts to give the reader maximum information and assurance. Anyone attempting a book like this is concerned about the veracity of what he is reporting, and often the only verification he can provide is: 'This is how I remember it.' Substantiating papers have been lost. Witnesses have died. Official reports are buried under mountains of more important documents, and memory itself plays one false, as demonstrated in my insistence that I had met James Norman Hall during the war and not on later trips to Tahiti. One longs for substantial verification. This item demonstrates the point, but it did not survive into the final version.

1. All my professional life I have faced, one way or another, this difficult problem of what a writer owes to his homeland. I have never been a flag-waving patriot nor have I written that way, but at times of testing I seem always to have come down in defense of my nation. As a Quaker/pacifist I could have pleaded non-combatant service in World War II, but in Europe I had seen the madness of Hitler and in my studies of ASIA I LEARNED what a fearful enemy Japan could be, so I went into the Navy instead. During long spells of my working years writers would be excused from taxes if they stayed out of the United States for 501 SUCCESSIVE days, and many tried to reorganize their lives to do so, and once by accident I qualified, but I was ashamed and never ALLOWED it again. It was also much to a writer's advantage to TAKE RESIDENCE in Ireland, and pay no taxes to anyone, but those who did saved a little money and damged their careers, especially the actors who missed the good acting roles at home and had TO SETTLE FOR one cheap European quickie after another. They paid a heavy price for their flight. Even more defrauded, I always thought, were the writers who moved to Europe to save taxes; far removed from their roots, they wrote trivial stuff and slowly slid down the ladder. I KNEW several of them and they were AN unhappy lot for I THINK KNEW THEY HAD ENTERED A PACT WITH THE DEVIL.

I preferred to keep my legal address at home, pay my taxes and feel myself engaged in the problems of my native land. I do not mean super-patriotism, and I certainly leave the door open for any writer to print savage attacks on his country's msibehaviors, ~~and~~ or to lampoon ~~its~~ the follies of its leaders, but I do feel that a writer does best when he clings to his homeland and does not dodge the taxes or other obligations ~~which~~ it imposes.

How do I reconcile this belief with the fact that I worked overseas so much? People have often asked that question ~~me why I wrote about foreign places, [illegible] sandwiched in between the times I wrote about the United States~~, and I have answered by ~~pi~~ pointing out that our greatest novelist, Herman Melville, wrote principally about the South Seas and that two of our Nobel ~~Prize~~ novelists, ~~mx~~ Pearl Buck and Ernest Hemingway, wrote about China and Spain respectively, while one of our most American writers, Jack London, ~~[illegible]~~ used the South Seas and the Canadian~~xAlaska~~ Klondike for his ~~most famous~~ settings. Washington Irving wrote about Spain and a host of mid-Nineteenth Century wriers chose Italian themes, while in recent times two of our ~~two~~ best writers, Henry James and T.S. Eliot, lived in and concentrated upon ~~wrote principally about~~ Europe and Great Britain, finally renouncing their American citizenship to become Englishmen. Obvuiusly a ~~man~~ writer can contribute to his native literature while dealing with foreign themes or even taking perm anent residence in alien ~~foreign~~ lands.

When purists ask: 'Why don't you write American novels within the academic traditopn?' I reply: 'From an early age I made the entife world my home, and every corner of it has become as important to me, and sometimes as familiar, as any locale in Iowa or Vermont.' The novel I always wantwd to write---had I had a chance to inspect its location---~~would~~ has been one dealing with Ulan Bator in Outer Mongolia. I would focus ~~center~~ upon its legendary fur market at Kyakhta on the border with Siberia and not far from Lake Baikal. Considering the work I've done on this region I think I might be able to write something signoficant, for its setting is one of my homes.

STET → ~~I have worked hard to excel in writing strong, solid books and have remained at my self-defined tasks long after scores of my~~ contemporaries ~~colleagues have retired from theirs.~~ Wherever I halt in my journeys ~~hournies~~ about the world I find clusters of people who have read my books and cherished them, for with my pen I have earned a warrant of citizenship in all corners of the earth. The world has been my home and I have wanted no more than to be a worthy citizen of it.

Coral Gables
3 Myach 1988

End of Manuscript
But two other chapters not finished

2.

SPACE

On a day of blizzards in January 1977 I was invited to the White House for a the conclus

REACHED A CONCLUSION

to my desire to be a good citizen. President Ford, to my surprise and upon the advise

INVITED ME TO THE WHITE HOUSE

from his counselors, had decided to award me our nation's highest civilian honor, The

RECOGNITION OF A FEW LATER

Medal of Freedom in appreciation for my services in various fields. That evening my wif

AT THE HOME OF RUSSELL TRAIN

and I had dinned with the British ambassador who excited Mari by saying: 'What happened

by saying: 'What happened in the White House the other day is the American equivalent

ANNOUNCED EACH

of our Queen's New Year's honors list. In our country it would mean that your husband

ANOTHER ENGLISHMAN

now Sir James and you are Lady Mari.' While she was preening in her new title he real

such lists, now and then, there may be

stunned her: 'In eachxhimxthemxwhichxhemxxxxx a knight or two who will be

awarded lorships and several times they've been given to people in the arts like Lord

Olivier and Alfred, Lord Tennyson. One of our men heard that your hisband stood very

IF YOU WISH

high on the list, so you can make believe that he's now James, Lord Michener.'

'And what would my title have been?' she asked and he replied: 'Still Lady Mari.

THROUGH

With women that covers wives all the way up to Earls,' and she said: 'Discrimination at

its worst,' and I thoight Dreams of Glory.'

Coral Gables, 10 March 1988

End of manuscript
But two segments to come

59

3.

away. They would like to say that I direct my writing to low or even base interests, but in view of what I said in the preceding paragrah, that would be laighable. They sometimes claim that I write easy books for people who cannot handle anything more difficult, but many Of my correspondents are among the brightest people in the country. A national magazine recently interrogated a large sampling of mature men who run the nation's largest industries as to their reading habits and many responded: 'We are simply to busy to read much outside our field,' but those who knew they ought to keep reading said overwhelmingly: 'If I find time, I read a Michener book. He has substance.' Another inquiry among young military men in training to be fighter pilots revealed their reading tastes: 'Only Exupery and Michener,' and I thought: If a writer can keep the old lions with him and the young tiger, he must be doing something right.

Some critics also like to intimate that no one should bother with my books because they are not written in approved styles, but the boooks continue to live and not only at home. The man in charge of the excellent program in Great Britain by which the goverment

4.

and living by my own rules, and obedient to my own purposes. I have written a series of books which, without bizarre deviations, have captured the minds and loyalties of many readers who have found substantial rewards in them. Within the limits I have set myself I have written an unmatched series of works which have brought pleasure and new insights to hundreds of thousands of readers, and I have done so without excessive fanfare, always preferring, because of my peculiar history, to remain outside the mainstream.

Furthermore, in an age when the calm of classic writing seems to be pushed off the stage by wild sex, savage violence, bizarre inhuman emphases and the destruction of traditional values, I have been able to write long and sometimes tedious books and keep people attached to them without resorting to the destructive popular fashions exemplified by Friday night videos. With an unruffled and at times even stately indifference to fashion, I have continued to write books the way I want them to be. The miracle is that I have been able to keep so many readers with me, and I think the explanation must be that they know they can trust me to write of important matters in a manner which invites the reader to stay with it in assurance that rewards of delight and enlightenment will be forthcoming. Whatever it is I do, I do

5. In Canada and Poland I have refused royalties on my books, preferring that the money go to help young writers in those countries. I HAVE DONE SOMEWHAT THE SAME FOR CARIBBEAN WRITERS. And best of all, I helped turn that jail into an art museum.

My years of travel have been remembered generously by three hotels in which I did some of my best work: Aggie Grey's in Samoa, the historic Raffles in Singapore, and in the one judged by many to be the best in the world, the Oriental in Bangkok. In each a room has been designated by a plaque to mark where in my wandering years I worked and listened to local sages. In the next century young travelers such as I was then may visit those rooms and hear someone explain the texts: 'Years ago an American much like you came to this room, fell in love with our land, and heard the stories which he later put into a book.'*

* The Oriental has a cluster of four elegant suites honoring writers who worked there, the three others being Joseph Conrad, Somerset Maugham, Noel Coward.

6. ~~I have composed myself and which I prefer insist on: 'Here lies a man who never showed home movies or served vin rosé'~~ and, three fine Michener libraries in wildly scattered parts of the world, and two Michener art galleries. There could have been several other buildings, but I would not allow it.

The epitaph is not irrelevant. If one is going to work in the arts let him or her aspire to professional standards; I love professionals and have tried to be a professional writer; and If one is going to drink wine let it not be a clear white or an honest red, not a soggy mix of half-and-half, but and relevant

As to critics, two examples of well intentioned but misguided comment come to mind. One very knowledgeable man pointed out that in The Drifters 'Mr. Michener carelessly absent-mindedly shifts the point of

7. I prefer not to discuss the other critic who was mean enough to point out that in The Bridges at Toko-ri I had my hero, who flew a jet fighter, creating a problem with his propellor wash. (SINCE FIGHTER JETS HAVE NO PROPELLERS) I spent some time trying to contrive a logical explanation of how this could happen but gave up. For sometimes critics are right, but if I feel honor bound not to quarrel with them, my wife is not so constrained. She makes a little wax model of any one who bad-mouths one of my books and attacks it with red-hot needles, and I can tell you that certain critics are walking about in far more peril than they realize.

During my years of writing I have never once defended either my style or my books, and because I have quietly agreed with any criticism lodged against me I have probably

8.

One amusing experience illustrates professional standards. A young writer of consieradble promise, Paul Dietz, published a wild and furious historical novel calle Goliath which several critics compared favorably to work I had done. Because of the notoriety his novel attracted, he was invited by a major publication to review my next work, and had he been a propr professional he would have recused himself, that is, refused to review my book since he was, in a sense, in competition with me. Instead he seems to have grabbed at the invitation as an opportunity to slaughter my work in an implied comparison with his own. He used offensiv inuendos, outright attacks on my judgment as a story-teller and even personal ridicule.

The attack was so devastating that friends asked: 'What are you gping to do about it?' and I explained that the professional ethics had been that I say nothing: 'And not stopp to his level.'

Half a year later, as I browsed in the bookstore, I came upon a new historical novel The Phoenician back cover proclaimed: contains even more sex and violence than Paul Goliath.' Closing the new novel and replacing it on the shelf, I thought: That codifies and evaluates his credentials as a critic.

One amusing experience illustrates the pitfalls one stumbles into when professional traditions are ignored. A young writer of considerable promise, Paul Dagan, published a wild and furious historical novel called Goliath which several critics said excelled my work in a similar vein. Because of the notoriety his novel attracted he was invited by a major pub;ication to review my next book, and had he been a proper professional he would have recused, that is, refused to review my novel lest he appear either to praise or condemn a competitor. Instead he grabbed at the invitation as a chance to slaughter my work in an implied comparison with his own. He used offensive innuendos, attacks on my judgment as a story-teller and even personal ridicule.

His attacks were so devastating that friends asked: 'What are you going to do about it?' and I explained that the professional credo to which I adhered forbade me to do anything: 'And common sense warns me not to stoop to his level.'

Half a year later, as I browsed in a bookstore I came upon an historical novel by a new writer. The Phoenician, it was called, and its back cover proclaimed: 'Contains even more wild sex and violence than Paul Dagan's Goliath.' Closing the new novel and replacing it on its shelf, I thought: That codifies Dagan and evaluates his credentials as a critic.

I have never felt or expressed resentment over what professional critics have said about me or my books. They have their job to do, I have mine and never the twain shall meet, but they have not prevented me from enjoying success and gaining a multiude of readers. But certain amateur critics have been irritaing.

9.

One
~~Excxxxx~~ day in 1988, as I was working in Florida, a Mrs. Schroeder of Fayetville, Arakansas, sent me a xerox of a letter from me which she had found among her husband's papers. I had mailed it on 14 July 1946, forty-two years earlier, in response to an inquiry from him about ~~the kind of man~~ ~~married~~ how I had helped a friend of his, x Lt. Comdr. JASON Barslag, ~~to~~ escape a court-martial for gross misbehavior in wartime Fiji. I was glad to supply details.

~~I had known~~ During my frequent trips to Fiji I had known Barslag well and favorably. and I was surprised when word filtered back to headquarters in Noumea that 'Lt. Cmdr. Barslag has gone completely Asiatic, tearing up the place. Send someone immediately to ~~stxx~~ subdue him.' I got the job, and listened as a British officer sationed in Fiji summarized the situation:

> I'm afraid your chap Barslag has really soiled his copy book. ~~I~~ Staggered onto the Governor-General s tennis court at the height of a gala party and passed out cold while playing doubles with three members of the diplomatic corps. When two chaps and I lugged him back to his room, he whipped out his .45 and shot up the place. I summoned the New Zealand military police who disarmed him. This outraged him, threw him ~~around frenzyx~~ into a titanic rampage which I reported to headquarets this way: 'Unable to get his car started, he spayred the engine block with gasoline and set it on fire to warm it up.' His wild actions continued until suddenly he fell aound asleep, and when he awakened ~~he had no~~m the last thing he could remember was that he was supposed to be playing tennis with the Governor-General.'

Taking all facts into considerateoon I recommended to the U.S. high command: 'It was TRULY an epic binge, but the Fijians are ~~dismissing~~ TAKING it as an ~~evidence~~ EXAMPLE of American tomfoolery. It makes them feel SOCIALLY superior to us and does little harm. Since no one was hurt and not much government propety destroyed, I recommend no further action.'

I then ~~told~~ WROTE Schroeder IN 1946: 'End of the story? No. Some weeks later while I was working in Tonga on the Little Red Truck case a Major Costigan flew in from headquarters, blazing mad: "In Fiji Lt. Cmdr. Barslag went ~~Asiatic~~ APE and really shot up the place. Halsey sent some stupid son of a bitch out from headquarters to report ~~and~~ on the case and what do you think this ~~xxxsex~~ horse's ass did? Sent back a report clearing Barslag and the tone was so ~~vafirable~~ FAIR that Barslag was promoted to full commander and shipped home from Honolulu with special priority." Major Costigan told me he'd like to find out who that horse's ass was, but I felt it best not to tell ~~him~~.

63

Fumbling Efforts at a Summation

If a would-be writer or a layman interested in books and their authors sought the heart of this workbook, he or she could do no better than to compare a few of these next provisional pages with the final entry where part of the finished essay is printed. The first two explain how I see myself, the next three show how I have responded to criticism, and the last one summarizes the entire self-evaluation. They demonstrate the balance between original composition and later emendations. They show also the exploration and the groping for meaning that characterize the final stages of a manuscript. This improvement did not come easily.

Highlighted with a benday screen are words and passages that survived from the first version, and how few they were.

PORTRAIT OF A WRITER

I know of no finer portrait of a writer than one offered some years ago by a young black aspirant from one of the small Caribbean islands: 'When I finally reached New York City my heart expanded and in sheer joy I cried: "To think that I am in the same town with James Baldwin and that when I turn the next corner I might meet him."'

I hope that anyone reading this book will carry away two portraits of me, because I think that they, better than any other imagery, convey the picture of a writer. I have told earlier of being burned out of Maracaibo and being smuggled across the lake in the dead of night, and that was exciting but what followed was more so, because the radio told of my seeking refuge at the headquarters of an oil-drilling company. In succeeding days some hundred people streamed in from as far as a hundred miles away with copies of my books for autographs. Most, of course, were American oil field workers stationed in remote areas where books were essential for sanity, and mine were present perhaps because they were so long and gave such good return for their cost; but a surprising number were Venezolanos who had bought the books because their North American co-workers had recommended them as a good way to learn English, others were ordinary citizens of half a dozen different nationalities, and of course, as in all countries wherever I go, a few were Hungarians whom I had led to safety across the bridge at Andau. Every person whose book I signed in that informal literary festival had a special story, and taken together they explained something about books that even professionals connected with the industry forget: books are bridges between people, and when the author is respected as someone who has made a valued contribution to one's life, a journey of a hundred miles from a jungle station in Venezuela to an oil field near Maracaibo is not unreasonable. It took me a long time to sign those books, because I wanted to hear the story of everyone who stood before my writing desk.

More dramatic in some ways was the day in Sheridan, Wyoming when at ten in the morning I learned that a plane I had expected would not arrive and that I would have to stay where I was. The town librarian, hearing of my plight, asked whether I would meet that evening with a few local people who liked books, and when I agreed, she hopped onto the telephone and radio to alert people in far distant towns that I would be in her library that night at seven. Free from responsibilities till then, I spent the afternoon visiting the Little Big Horn to see where General Custer had led his cavalry into disaster and when we returned after sunset we found the library absolutely jammed with families that had driven tremendous distances in response to the radio messages in their little towns advising them of the improvised meeting. Carloads of enthusiasts had driven down from Billings, 128 miles away; others had come two by two from remote settlements, and a surprising number had brought their children to share in an experience that would not often be repeated. It was an amazing audience that night, because under the circumstances anyone who was present was there because he or she liked books, and as always at such occasions we talked not about my books but about books in general: Which is more important, character, theme or plot? How difficult would it be for a young woman in Billings to find a New York publisher? Does a writer have to have a big staff to do research? Is there still a market for children's books? Do you go to Hollywood when they make a picture from one of your stories? Is the writer obligated to provide a psychological profile of each character? The meeting lasted two hours and for an excited few it could have continued till dawn, because in some lives books are important, and those fortunate ones who write them are sometimes accorded a significance to which they are not entitled, but which, in another sense, they have earned.

There remains a major mystery about my selection of subjects. Why, if I had such a deprived childhood, and such a dramatic adolescence, with hitch-hike trips up and down the continent and work in the amusement park, followed by the grave dislocation about my parentage, my adventures with radical ideas in Europe and then two painful divorces, why have I not treated that kind of material in my novels, and how can I possibly be what so many have called me: 'The incorruptible optimist?' The question is relevant and the answer three-fold. First, as a boy I read Balzac and as a young man Dostoevsky and Strindberg and concluded that I did not see my own experiences in those harsh lights. Second, looking at the way in which good luck

WRITERS AND CRITICS

And now to the most delicate question of all. How do I see myself as a writer? First let me comment briefly and in good humor about how critics see me. Academic critics dismiss me completely, for like Beckmesser in Die Meistersinger they have fairly rigid rules as to what constitutes literature and what I write is not included. I am sorry, for I think they are wrong and so do many reader.

Public critics have a difficult time with me. They sometimes condemn me for writing for money, but as I demonstrated in the preceding section, that is patently absurd. Others say that I direct my writing only to middle-brow or even lower interests, but two recent studies have disproved that. In the first, a national magazine interrogated a large sampling of the well-educated mature men who run the nation's largest industries as to their reading habits, and while many said honestly that they were too busy to read anything but reports relevant to their jobs, many others said they knew they ought to keep reading and when they found time they habitually read a book by Michener because they knew it would be readable and reward them with something of substance. The second inquiry was directed to the young military men in training to be fighter pilots and they said: 'Only Exupery and Michener. Those two knew what flying was,' and I thought: If a writer can keep the old lions and the young tigers with him he must know something about narration.

Other critics intimate that no one should bother with my books because they are not written in approved styles, but the books continue to live and not only at home. The Englishman in charge of Britain's excellent program by which the government collects data on reading tastes in public libraries throughout the nation and then pays cash awards to the authors of the books taken out most frequently did me the honor of sending me a report of what the British system would have paid me had they paid similar fees to foreign authors, which they should not. My books stood close to the top of the list for foreign authors and quite high even among local writers. The same would be true, I judge, for certain of my books, not all of them by any mean, in countries like the Netherlands and Germany.

Typical criticism of my work was well voiced recently by Chauncey Mabe, Books columnist of the Fort Lauderdale, Florida News Sun-Sentinel:

> Sometime in the late 60s or early 70s James Michener ceased to be a serious writer, at least in the literary sense and became something else--an industry, his typewriter a

factory upon which, with two fingers pecking, he took history and processed it into bestselling novels that could also be used as door-stops and further processed into movies or, better yet, TV miniseries.

The rest of the review was well phrased, witty and laced with legitimate content, but in the covering letter Mabe illustrated the ambivalence which some critics feel about me.*

Christopher Lehmann-Haupt, most cerebral of the New York Times reviewers, makes somewhat the same point as Mabe in his review: 'Rice Krispies happens to be one of my favorite junk foods, just as I regard Michener as superior among junk writers.' That is a clever juxtaposition of ideas, to which I take no offense, for it is an honest opinion amusingly delivered, but I suspect that some of my readers will be surprised to learn that the books which have meant so much to them were only junk.

A writer is well advised never to respond to negative criticism, a tenet which was hammered into me by prudent editors and publicists when I worked at Macmillan and by several grizzled veterans of the writing wars when I joined their ranks. The rules were laid down by my trusted mentor, Kahler: 'The Old and New Testaments regarding criticism: "Never complain. Never Explain. Never disdain." To complain makes you look petty and juvenile. Make sure that your publisher sends you a check for whatever you've honestly earned, and keep your mouth shut. Put your full attention on the next job, because to complain is fruitless. And don't try to explain. If you've spent three hundred pages putting your thoughts down and haven't succeeded, what makes you think you can clarify them in a one-page letter? Anyway, the editor will cut you to a quarter page. And as for disdaining your critics, remember, never make a joke at their expense. They're probably brighter than you, have thought more deeply about literature, and could probably write a damned sight better than you, if they put their mind to it. If you fight with such a talented man you will lose. Besides being superior to you in every way, he will have that big, forty-eight page newspaper in which to blast you for the next six months.'

I read far more criticism than the average citizen: what movies are best, what shows to go to, what music is worth buying in compact disc, what restaurants are worth the effort. I prize their

----

*'While I do not think you are a great writer, I see you as a great American whose ideals and whose life provide one of the few examples worthy of admiration in our troubled age.'

opinions and am guided by their recommendations but I never, never read criticism of my own work. I summarize the problem this way: 'Critics are invaluable in advising me how to spend my money. They are not qualified to tell me how to spend my talent.'

At one period in my life numerous critics, when writing of other writers, were fond of comparing them to me, and always the other fellow came off best: 'He is a lot better storyteller than Michener,' or 'His novel moves more honestly than a Michener.' For a while I kept a list of such comparisons because I wanted to know what happened to all those people who were so much better than me*, but it came to naught because most of them were never heard from again, and those that were had only feeble lasting power.

Obedient to Rule Three of the professional writer's code, I have never tried to rebut any critic, and in general I had no cause to, because so many greeted my books with an enthusiasm that enabled publishers to garner as many encomiums as they had space for in their paperback editions and no critic, so far as I can remember, ever treated me unfairly. Those who did not like what I had written, or the style I used, usually had ample quotations to back their judgments, but it is a solemn fact that for the past eighteen or twenty years I have refused to read even one review of anything I have written. (The Mabe review arrived in a personal letter and I could not discard the first paragraph.) I find praise distasteful, harsh criticism irrelevant; I am not saying that I ignore criticism or denigrate it; I just don't read it. My wife does and chortles over good notices, moans over bad ones, but down the long years of any productive life what critics say has only limited relevance to a career, because it will all be re-evaluated some decades hence.

It would ill behoove me to speak poorly of critics, since two played major roles in my writing life. When my first book was published Orville Prescott of <u>The New York Times</u> wrote a glowing comment, one of his most enthusiastic, in which he predicted that I was a writer from whom more might be heard; and John Mason Brown, that gallant, polished master of the lecture circuit spent an entire season reading excerpts from my first book, thus bringing me to the attention of thousands of people who were interested in books and who bought them. My debt to those two experts is incalculable, and in their lifetimes I told them so.

I know that the proper pronoun in this usage is <u>than I was</u>, but like many other contemporary writers I find that cumbersome. We use <u>me</u> in conversation in our books, and I am testing it in non-conversational situations.

FINAL COMMENT

It is rewarding to know that one's books rest on library shelves throughout the world. They are alas, not printed on that fine durable paper contained in the books of the 1860's and 70's which enthralled me when I first became aware of how handsome an ordinary book could be; mine and all those of my generation have been printed on a cheap, self-degrading paper which will simply disintegrate in less than a century. But it was fun having them available while they lasted.

In obedience to the dictate of St. Paul which has governed me, I have endeavored to keep my life pure--that is, simplified--and have directed that my tombstone bear this inscription: 'Here lies a man who never showed home movies or served vin rose.' My writing may not get me into heaven, but that epitaph will. It summarizes what I would say to anyone wanting to become a writer: 'Be a professional. If you take wine, let it not be an insipid mix of half-this, half-that but a clear white or an honest red.'

During my years as a writer I have never once defended either myself or my books, and because I have quietly nodded when criticism was lodged against me, I have provided interviewers with justification for writing that 'Mr. Michener, who acknowledges that he is not a very good writer, said modestly...' Such reporters have misconstrued courteousness and indifference as acquiescence in their pre-formed opinions. The time has come to register a correction.

I am enormously proud of that long shelf of books which bear my name and consider myself one of the ablest writers of my generation. Surely I am one of the best story-tellers. I have been a quiet phenomenon off to one side, living by my own rules, obedient to my own purposes. I have written a series of books which, without bizarre excesses, wild sex or savage violence have captured the minds and loyalties of many readers who have found in them substantial reward. Within the guidelines I developed for myself and with an unruffled equanimity I have dedicated myself to the task of writing books the way I wanted them to be; the miracle is that in all countries readers have stayed with me. The explanation must be that they trusted me to write of important matters in a manner which promised delight and instruction. The director of one of the world's premier libraries said the other day: 'You've been educator to the world.'

I have been more, a working resident of that world, one who labored to describe it with understanding and affection . With my pen I have engraved warrants of citizenship in the most remote corners, for truly the world has been my home.

Editorial Work on Revised Pages

These pages illustrate the careful work done on the closing pages of the book. The first, 'Granting a Prize,' deals with a literary problem which I thought fascinating but which the editors considered a distraction, and since I try to maintain the forward thrust of any manuscript, I had to agree. Good story lost, but space was too valuable to waste on problematic material. Since I have shown numerous instances in which I agreed with editorial suggestions for cutting or changing parts of the manuscript, I should point out that perhaps 10 percent of the time I reject such suggestions. Editors submit a recommendation in pencil on the manuscript, and when I cannot accept it I quietly erase it and the matter is forgotten. The editors didn't like the segment and sent their carefully weighed opinion: 'While the story of the movement to reward you with a prize is a good idea, it and the story of the traitor Hamsun go on too long, sidetrack us too much in a chapter that we believe should stick to essentials.' When I studied the matter I had to agree, but an interesting story was lost.

XIII-75 deals with a most difficult problem, money, and I tried various approaches. Editors suggested another, and a compromise was reached.

XIV-83 shows how good editors are not afraid to suggest drastic cuts. The first cut was no problem, the second kills a fine story, which I'll use somewhere later.

XIV-84 at bottom left, shows the number of different times my secretary had to type out this page, and it still wasn't right. I wanted to state the summary with precision and failed repeatedly. But the last two lines, dated from the earliest effort, did survive and they're what count.

GRANTING A PRIZE

One group of letters has caused embarrassment; they come from readers who think I should by now have received the Nobel Prize, and a movement was started some years ago to attain that goal for me, but I put a stop to it. I wrote to Ernest Cuneo, a delightful, free-wheeling man who'd been commissioned to lead the campaign:

> You must stop instantly any such effort, for I have not written in the manner that attracts such a prize, nor do I aspire to it. I can think of some eight or ten other American writers who would be eligible, and lest you think this is mere verbalism I will name them: Thornton Wilder, and why he hasn't gotten it already I'll never know; Robert Penn Warren who has a wide scatter of books in different fields; Saul Bellow who writes the heavy kind of book the Nobel people like; James Baldwin who is almost sure to win if he can turn out one good, solid book; Norman Mailer whose breadth is impressive if he can knuckle down and do the big one; Joyce Carol Oates if she can get more lift into her work; and maybe Truman Capote just for the hell of it. I have others in mind, that's enough.
>
> Other enthusiastic friends have wanted to nominate me for the Peace Prize on the grounds that my books have shown millions in all countries the merits of brotherhood. Do not redirect your efforts in that direction for I have always been embarrassed when I read of how writers like Proust and O'Hara campaigned for Nobel prizes, and there is one writer right now who is shamelessly politicking, to the amusement and scorn of his fellows.

> I do not wish to stumble into that pathetic category. I've received all the awards to which I was entitled, and the best are those a writer engraves with his own pen.

But to the ordinary readers who wrote, ignorant of the politics of international awards, I drafted an entirely different kind of letter which I kept on file to send to anyone who raised the subject. After an opening paragraph in which I listed my nominees as cited above, my significant paragraphs said:

> When I consider the great writers who have been eligible for the Nobel Prize but were denied it---Thomas Hardy, Emile Zola, Marcel Proust, Henry James and Maksim Gorky among them---and then think of the clowns who did---the dreadful Rudolf Eucken, that blot upon the writing profession Knut Hamsum, plus a whole chain of nonentities I had better not specify, the laughable Miguel Angel Asturias will represent them nicely---I would much rather stand with the former than lie down with the latter.
>
> Writers earn their awards in the hearts of their readers and external laurels mean little, but I must be honest. I would be proud to be affiliated in any way with some of the other winners like Sigrid Undset, Thomas Mann, Eugene O'Neill and William Butler Yeats.

I had a trivial but revealing contact with the Nobel awards. During an interminable flight from Copenhagen to Hong Kong a distinguished Swedish diplomat asked if he could sit and consult with me, and as we talked he confided: 'The Nobel people have given me a commission in Japan. They feel the time is ripe to make an award there, but they don't know any Japanese writer to give it to. You've been there a lot. Do you know any,' and I strongly recommended Yukio Mishima---this was before his dramatic hara-kiri---but when the announcement was made I saw that they had tapped Yasunari Kawabata, and I have often wondered if later they had regretted not giving it to Mishima, who today seems by far the more important.

America including writing, their inquiries led to me. I knew nothing of how I was chosen, but when the group gathered in the White House, corporate givers mostly, the President's staff revealed that their research showed that my wife and I had given widely to assist beginning writers. Since then we have divested ourselves of our art windfalls, and it

In a previous draft, and exact dollar amount , proving your generosity in the most unquestionalbe way, was given. Why the decision to cut figure? O.T.

Olga: This has become a question of propriety, and I must now leave its resolution to you, Kate and Sono. You're right. Original copy read: 'The Presidents staff revealed that their resarch showed that my wife and I had given to various projects relatung to writing a total of eight million dollars. Since then we have divested ourselves of the art bonanzas, ampunting an additional eighteen million, and it....'

The up-to-date copy that you suggested reinstating would now read as above, but with this correction: 'writing a total of eight million dollars. Since then the figure has risen to forty-three million, and it must be obvious...' The sum has grown so, that it seems/preposterous that I feared readers might see it such. But there the figures are, all demonstrable, and I leave their handling to you.

must be obvious that when I die I shall will the legally required half of what's left to my wife and the balance to colleges and universities. Of course, when she dies, she will distribute her residue in comparable fashion, but to which institutions she will not tell me.

By what seems a series of fortunate accidents I shall have earned a great deal of money from writing and will have given it all away. With my background I could have done no other.

Sono: Concerning my wish to drop great before deal, it's a countryism with which I grew up. And the RH Dict. approves as an idiosyncrasy. To us it meant not a huge amount, like great deal, but not an insoiderabl amount either, just so-so. I'd like keep the plain deal if that doesn't offend you. J.M. (I've taken it out three times but secretaries, to be helpful, keep putting it back in.)

James A. Michener
Rough Draft
Coral Gables, Florida
6 March 1989
Revised 1 August 1989

TMP 5/30/89
8/1/89

XIV - 83

Samoa, historic Raffles in Singapore, and the one judged by many to be the best in the world, the Oriental in Bangkok. In the next century young travelers such as I was when I occupied those rooms will hear someone explain: 'Years ago an American much like you came to this room, fell in love with our land, and heard the stories which he later put into a book,'* and that might give them encouragement.

*The Oriental has a cluster of elegant suites honoring writers who worked there, the three others: Joseph Conrad, Somerset Maugham, Noel Coward.

But mostly I would want to be remembered by that row of solid books which rest on library shelves throughout the world. They are, alas, not printed on that fine durable paper contained in the books of the 1860's and 70's which enthralled me when I first became aware of how handsome an ordinary book could be; mine and all those of my generation have been printed on a cheap, self-degrading paper which will simply disintegrate in less than a century. But it was fun having them available while they lasted.

In obedience to the dictate of St. Paul which has governed me, I have endeavored to keep my life pure---that is, simplified---and have directed that my tombstone bear this inscription: 'Here lies a man who never showed home movies or served vin rose.' My writing may not get me into heaven, but that epitaph will. It summarizes what I would say to anyone wanting to become a writer: 'Be a professional. If you take wine, let it not be an insipid mix of half-this, half-that but a clear white or an

moving toward conclusion perhaps best not to get sidetracked now.

This is amusing, but a little light, deflating for concluding moments of a moving, important book.

I also think the flippant touch jars a bit

MY GOD! I HAVE AN EDITOR WHO LIKES VIN ROSE. CUT

65

criticism was lodged against me, ~~I have provided interviewers with justification for writing that 'Mr. Michener, who acknowledges that he is not a very good writer, said modestly...' Such reporters have misconstrued courteousness and indifference as acquiescence in their pre-formed opinions. The time has come to register a correction.~~

I am enormously proud of that long shelf of books which bear my name and consider myself one of the ablest ~~writers~~ of my generation. ~~Surely I am one of the best~~ story-tellers. I have been a quiet phenomen off to one side, living by my own rules, obedient to my own purposes. I have written a series of books which, without bizarre excesses, wild sex or savage violence have captured the minds and loyalties of many readers who have found in them substantial reward. Within the guidelines I developed for myself and with an unruffled equanimity I have dedicated myself to the task of writing books the way I wanted them to be; the miracle is that in all countries readers have stayed with me. The explanation must be that they trusted me to write of important matters in a manner which promised delight and instruction. The director of one of the world's premier libraries said the other day: 'You've been educator to the world.'

Kate: I have labored over this passage and want to get it just right. Please give it your eye, too.

I have been more, a working resident of that world, one who labored to describe it with understanding and affection. With my pen I have engraved warrants of citizenship in the most remote corners, for truly the world has been my home.

James A. Michener
Rough outline
Coral Gables, Florida
14 March 1988
Revised 28 March 1988
Revised 27 August 1988
Revised 31 March 1989
Revised 29 July 1989
Revised 6 September 1989
Revised 11 September 1989

TMP - 5/24/89
7/29/89
9/06/89
9/11/89

Valued Advice from a Libel Lawyer

When the manuscript has been edited, especially if it is a nonfiction book dealing with real people, the publisher will often send it to a lawyer who specializes in libel. Sometimes this lawyer is not a member of the company publishing the book but an expert who serves many publishers. His or her counsel is invaluable, especially since in recent years the law of libel seems to be swinging sharply against the writer. Publishers must protect themselves against costly suits. In the chapters dealing with my experiences in World War II, my publisher used an in-house expert, Mallory Rintoul, who raised the following points, among others. My responses follow.

Q. Draft board: 'The necessary chairman of the local draft board, who despised the author, may still be living. Statement needs corroboration or toninq down.' **A.** He was more unsavory than I said. Dead. (This latter fact was all-important, since one cannot libel a dead person.)

Q. Heroic ship captain: 'Captain Reid is probably dead. If not, we should confirm that he had three ships sunk under him and survived every time while a lot of the ships' crews went down.' **A.** Captain Reid was a close friend, a little fireball. I heard reports on his performance in my old ship, and others, from a crewman and have reason to believe they were accurate. If he is still alive I hope he reads of my reactions.

Q. Southern gentleman: 'If your friend Bill Collins is still alive we assume that he would not be troubled by the account of his smuggling Southern Comfort aboard ship and his forging orders to enable the author to travel throughout the South Pacific.' **A.** He would applaud.

Q. A language problem: 'Fact query. In the penultimate line, "up tight" may be an anachronism. The Random dictionaries attribute its first use to the '60s.' **A.** I will kill the up tight and thank you.

Q. When was it said?: 'Fact query. I can't track down "Wha Hoppen?", but I have a vague feeling it came during or after WWII.' **A.** I can see the paper clearly becasue it was such a shock to all of us, the outcome of the election, I mean. Will keep.

Q. Who was to blame for the crash: 'The implication is that the pilot did not fly the plane properly. Is he identifiable?' **A.** This query surprised me, but I see its merit. I've corrected the text. Field at fault.

Corrections on Galleys

I appreciate it when an editor cuts the superfluous last words of one of my sentences, as in the case of *as I did*. I add them automatically when I write, in order to complete sentences or thoughts, but quite often they are not needed.

The insert at the top of the second page is an admirable one, for adding the name *Laurence* improves the parallelism of the three names. I did not like the lower-casing of *Sir* and *Earl*, but that was house policy, and I did not complain. As for *glasnost*, I never know when a foreign word requiring italic has become an English word requiring none. Editors do.

30016 15 24 2314 0 0 08/23/91 15:21:29 500

MS. P. 934; FF 5 30016

. . .

Having escaped the personal degradation or even criminality that could have been the consequences of my deprived childhood, I have been driven in later years to reflect on the plight of the average black boy in modern American society. Raised with no man in the family, often unable to determine who his father is, rejected by white society, demeaned by almost every agency of government and cheated by his teachers, who routinely pass him along instead of trying to teach him, he is the outcast of our society, doomed from birth.

I have, understandably, compared his lot with my own and tried to explain why I, as a fatherless boy in a household headed by an unmarried woman, could make my way in American life while the black boy of comparable character and skills cannot. The answer seems simple. All the black boy needs is a mother like Mrs. Michener, who has the moral support of her brothers and the assistance of her sisters, all of whom have good jobs; the support of her church; the moral support of his entire community; the counsel of older men who tell him: 'Get out of this pool room and stay out!'; the ennobling aid of an inspired friend to the young like George Murray; instruction from dedicated teachers who insist that he learn; and a fees-paid scholarship to a great college like Swarthmore.

The unceasing support that I encountered is not available to the black boy, and the mistreatment he suffers is one of our national disgraces, which, if continued, will do irreparable damage to the country itself. The tragedy gnaws at me, for whereas I had the Boys' Brigade, the black boy has a gang. I had Coach Grady, who preached: 'Don't eat greasy foods'; he has the man in the corner saying: 'Here, kid. Try this new one, crack.' And while my opportunity of going to college was backed by that good night job at the hotel, he can find no work of any kind that can support him.

I am appalled at the difference, at the waste of human talent. Of course, every boy is better off if he grows up in a family where a wage-earner father is present, but if that is not possible, society ought to help mothers provide constructive alternatives. The black boy faces mainly destructive options, and my heart grieves for him.

Now, toward the end of a long and lively run, how do I see myself as a man and a writer? I see myself as a standard American with a usable I.Q. and a strong education drilled into me by dedicated professors. Throughout my life I have been able to work more diligently than most and to keep my wits about me ~~as I did~~. I was deficient in the standard

like Lord Olivier or Alfred, Lord Tennyson. One of your men heard that your husband stood high on the list, so if you wish you can make believe he's now James, Lord Michener.'

'And what would my title be?' Mari asked, and he replied: 'Still Lady Mari. With women that covers everything from plain Sir up to Earl,' and she said: 'Discrimination at its worst,' and I thought: 'Dreams of glory.'

I have always wanted the areas, nations and states about which I have written to receive my books dispassionately and to acknowledge that I had written with fairness if not total accuracy, but that has rarely happened. Hungary, Spain and South Africa banned my work; Indonesian and Afghan officials threatened to beat me up if I ever again set foot in their territories; Israel, Hawaii and Texas abused my work. But I was especially grieved when Poland, a land in which I had toiled with diligence and affection not only banned my novel but also let it be known that I would not be allowed back in the country. I must admit, however, that my castigation of Communist rule in Poland did give its leaders ample cause to reject me. But in late 1988, when the spirit of glasnost was emanating from the Soviet Union, I received cryptic word that I would be granted a visa if I wished to return to renew my acquaintance with the brave members of the writers' union I had known in the old days.

Eager to see a land I loved, I slipped into Warsaw, and on my second night in the city it was arranged that I would meet the writers. It was a snowy, sleety night, the kind I remembered well as we drove to the meeting hall, but as we approached it I thought: Mistake. This has got to be Warsaw Castle. But before I could query what was happening I was whisked inside, down corridors and into a meeting room.

It was not the writers' union hall. It was the grand ballroom of the castle, a great gold-and-silver reception hall filled with flowers and some five hundred leading Polish artists and government officials. Before I could catch my breath, Mieczyslaw Rakowski, the prime minister of the country, with the prior approval of General Jaruzelski, the Communist dictator who had banned the book, came forward, embraced me and pinned on my chest the highest medal that Poland can award a citizen. Later I was told: 'We still don't like certain passages in your book, but we realize that people throughout the world are reading about our nation in a way they never did before. You have proved you were an honest friend.'

The Published Version

tions of ambition and once said, accurately: 'I've been content if I could reach Friday in one piece. And I never start worrying again till Monday.' I do not think of myself as a romantic dreamer; my life has been too hard for that indulgence. But when I have suffered my physical setbacks I have muttered a saying I heard once but whose source I have not been able to identify: 'I will lay me down and bleed awhile, then rise and fight again.' I have been persistent.

But I have never set goals for myself save one: I insist on being a reliable citizen who works to help society hold itself together.

Viewing myself as a writer, let me first comment briefly and in good humor about how critics see me. Academic critics dismiss me completely because, like Beckmesser in *Die Meistersinger,* they have fairly rigid rules as to what constitutes literature and it does not include what I write. I am sorry, because I think they are wrong, and so do many readers.

Literary critics have a difficult time with me. They sometimes condemn me for writing for money, but as I demonstrated in the preceding section, that is patently absurd. Others say that I direct my writing only to middle-brow or even lower tastes, but two recent studies have disproved that. In the first, a national magazine interrogated a large sampling of the well-educated mature men who run the nation's largest industries as to their reading habits, and while many said honestly that they were too busy to read anything but reports relating to their jobs, many others said they knew they ought to keep reading and when they found time they habitually read a book by Michener because they knew it would be readable and reward them with knowledge of value. The second inquiry was directed to the young military men in training to be fighter pilots and they said: 'Only Saint-Exupéry and Michener. Those two knew what flying was,' and I thought: If a writer can keep the old lions and the young tigers with him, he must know something about narration.

Other critics intimate that no one should bother with my books because they are not written in approved styles, but the books continue to live and not only at home. The Englishman in charge of Britain's excellent program by which the government collects data on reading tastes in public libraries throughout the nation and then pays cash awards to the authors of the books taken out most frequently did me the honor of sending me a report of what the British system would have paid me had they paid similar fees to foreign authors (which they should not). My books stood close to the top of the list for foreign authors and quite high even among local writers. The same would be true, I judge,

that I have the fictional junior senator of some state play the role that a real senior senator in a real state had played. Good idea, but when you're working in a known time period when there was a known junior senator from that state holding the office, and you have your man acting up, the real senator can rightly claim that whatever you say about your fictional character has to represent him; his claim for damages would be valid on the face of it, and lawyers know this. So they advise writers to create a fictional state—in *Space* I chose the State of Franklin—which gave me an imaginary junior senator who could misbehave as either he or the author wished. A lot of lawsuits are avoided by such a device.

Sometimes critics are devastatingly right. In *The Bridges at Toko-Ri* I have my hero flying a jet fighter and creating a wash with his propeller. One critic, a pilot himself, wrote: 'Miraculous! I wish Mr. Michener had explained how he did it.' I spent one afternoon trying to devise an answer but gave up; jet fighters don't have propellers. But if I feel honor-bound never to quarrel with a critic, my wife is not so constrained, and if anyone bad-mouths one of my books she makes a little wax effigy of him and attacks it with red-hot needles. I can tell you that certain critics are walking about in far more peril than they realize.*

I sometimes wonder when I read what even knowledgeable people say about writers and writing if they have any conception of what the life of a writer is like, especially if his or her books achieve wide circulation in many languages. What they don't know might include: a visit to the dentist when people from six surrounding offices come with their books to be signed; the letters that arrive daily thanking you for books that changed the letter-writers' lives; the startling experience of walking to the rear of an airplane to exercise your bad legs and finding six or seven people reading your novels, and often ones published a quarter of a century ago; the warming contact with people who love books and who are endeavoring to entice their children to read, too, by testing them with one of yours; and the knock on the door from a group of neighbors: 'We heard you were in town. We have almost all your books—would you please sign them?'

I know of no finer portrait of a writer than one offered some years ago by a young black aspirant from one of the small Caribbean islands:

*If I never read criticism, how did I learn about the three just cited? My publisher asked me how I had made such embarrassing errors.

quite painful, Mr. Michener, to be a Turkish intellectual and realize that when you go to Paris to address an international group and stand before the audience, not one person in that well-educated group has ever read any book about Turkey except *The Forty Days of Musa Dagh.* Come and do for us what you did for Israel.'

The correspondence that has meant most to me has been with great scholars in various countries who write to me about something I have said regarding their fields, and often they tell me further things I did not know when I wrote but should have. They form a network of active minds throughout the world, and when, as sometimes happens, they point to errors in what I have said or important aspects that I have overlooked, I feel ashamed at having let them down.

In 1968 I was in Venezuela as a cultural ambassador to the university in Caracas, but the Communist student body threatened to shoot me if I stepped on campus, so I was whisked far west to Maracaibo to address students there. My speech, which I had carefully prepared, was to have been delivered at eleven in the morning, but at ten the local Communists burned down the assembly hall, and for the rest of that eventful day my wife and I were spirited about the city from one safe hiding place to another. When night fell we were hustled to a forbidding dock on the shore of Lake Maracaibo, where a small boat waited to ferry us to the eastern shore. It was a dramatic ride—when the moon appeared we could see above us, rising from the middle of the lake, the derricks of great oil wells.

When the radio told of my seeking refuge at the headquarters of an oil-drilling company, in succeeding days some hundred people streamed in from as far as a hundred miles away with copies of my books to ask for autographs. Most, of course, were American oilfield workers stationed in remote areas where books were essential for sanity, and mine were there perhaps because they were so long and gave such good return for their cost. But a surprising number were Venezuelans who had bought the books because their North American co-workers had recommended them as a good way to learn English, others were ordinary citizens of half a dozen different nationalities, and as in all countries wherever I go, a few were Hungarians whom I had led to safety across the bridge at Andau. Every person whose book I signed in that informal literary festival had a special story, and taken together they explained something about books that even professionals connected with the industry forget: books are bridges between people, and when the author is respected as someone who has made a valued contribution to one's life, a journey of a hundred miles from a jungle station in Venezuela to

generation. Unobtrusively I have lived by my own rules, obedient to my own purposes. I have written a series of books which, without bizarre excesses, wild sex or savage violence, have captured the minds and loyalties of many readers who have found them richly rewarding. Within the guidelines I developed for myself and with an unruffled equanimity, I have dedicated myself to the task of writing books the way I want them to be; the miracle is that in all countries readers have ringingly endorsed what I have produced. The explanation must be that they trusted me to write of important matters in a manner that promised both delight and instruction. The director of one of the world's premier libraries said the other day: 'You've been educator to the world.'

I have been more: a working resident of that world, one who has labored to describe it with understanding and affection and share it with others. With my pen I have engraved warrants of citizenship in the most remote corners, for truly the world has been my home.

Questions Most Frequently Asked by Would-be Writers

Some Basic Questions

Since this workbook may fall into the hands of young people aspiring to be writers—to belong to one of the world's noble professions—it might prove helpful if I share the answers I give to the questions I am most often asked about writing. These queries have come from three sources: letters I receive; the question-and-answer sessions I often conduct; and the seminars in which I assist younger professors of writing in Florida and Texas. Unfortunately, the first questions deal with publishing, not writing.

Will a publisher read my manuscript if I mail it in unannounced? Probably not. Many publishers have found that they waste their time plowing through mountains of unsolicited manuscripts, 'over-the-transom junk' it used to be called. One publisher said: 'We found that only one manuscript in nine hundred proved worth the search, and the cost of identifying it was excessive.' Today publishers want their manuscripts weeded out by agents, by teachers of writing, by established writers, or by trusted acquaintances. However, my publisher still inspects all submissions, and so do a few others.

If a publisher will not read my unsolicited manuscript, how can I attract his attention? It is considerably more difficult today than when I started in the 1940s. Then it was simple. If you published three good short stories, several book publishers would invite you to write a novel. And if you wrote a good novel, all the magazines invited you to write short stories, which paid the rent. And when you had written a handful of good stories and two or three successful novels, Hollywood beckoned with its golden enticements. Today the commercial magazines that once published short stories no longer exist, and Hollywood no longer uses novels as its main source for stories to film. Gifted film people write their own scripts. So today's beginning writer has it far more difficult than I did. However, there is still a royal road to finding a publisher.

Remember that you have two tremendous advantages. First, the great publishing houses do not have the option of sitting out a publishing season. They have up to a hundred salesmen on the road who must be given something to sell. They have commitments with printing houses and paper manufacturers and warehouses. A major house must find scores of manuscripts every year, and if their established writers fail to produce them they must look elsewhere. Every publisher is desperately seeking good manuscripts; it's just that the rules of the search have changed.

The second advantage the beginner has is that every day the established writers grow older. John Updike, Joyce Carol Oates, and Saul Bellow cannot go on writing forever, and their places must be taken by someone. Each year another golden opportunity, or maybe a dozen, opens up and someone has to fill it. So the pathways to acceptance should be recognized and followed. My rules, culled from years of watching publishing, first as an editor myself and then as a writer, are these.

1. Assuming that you have no third party to intercede for you (agent, professor, writer, or friend), you must write to a publisher or a group of publishers to say that you have a manuscript well under way: 'It deals with the interesting subject of ——, and may I have permission to send you a copy of the outline and three sample chapters?' You should then add one or two paragraphs in which you establish your credentials as a serious writer: education, courses taken in writing, and, especially, a fairly complete list of writings actually published—anything, that is, that will lift you out of the ordinary and encourage the publisher (the editor, of course) to think that it may be worth the trouble of looking at your material. In a surprising number of cases, if you are a real writer, you will make your letter so enticing that the editor will write back: 'Yes, please send it along and we'll take a look.' I must stress that this letter of inquiry could be one of the most important letters you will ever write, so spend time drafting it to make your manuscript and yourself sound solid and worth the trouble.

Excuse the interruption, if my letter of inquiry is so important, what should it say?

Sample Letter of Inquiry

Kinetic Press
Madison Avenue
New York, New York

Gentlemen:

I am a professional writer with a modest track record of publication. I seek permission to send you a proposal—a complete outline and three sample chapters—of a nonfiction book that I believe might be of considerable interest to the general public.

It is titled *Doomed at Birth* and deals with a problem that is growing in all parts of the country: babies born to teenage mothers unable to care for them and the cost to society. The first chapter epitomizes the horrendous situation. Baby Diana is the premature child of sixteen-year-old Laura, a big-city roamer with no fixed abode, an alcoholic, a cocaine user and an AIDS carrier. She has infected her fetus with the last three afflictions and the opening chapter shows how society does all it can to save her baby and fails. We see the mother, the daughter, the doctors in the charity ward, the nurses who try to save preemies, the physical effects of the three addictions inherited by Baby Diana, and the hopelessness of her situation. The chapter is not morbid, but it is a harrowing one.

Subsequent chapters deal with all aspects of this problem, such as the profligate alcoholic husband, church efforts to help pregnant women, minimum health regimes for pregnant women, the probable adult characteristics of the baby if it survives; recent court cases regarding responsibilities of pregnant women. I will be using case histories when appropriate and calling upon respected experts for counsel. The final chapter proposes safeguards and solutions.

I believe I'm qualified to write this book because I've worked in hospitals as a lay assistant; I've studied widely; I've consulted with scores of experts; and I know the field.

I was an honors graduate at Rutgers, spent one year in Columbia's school of writing, and attended three different summer writing seminars at the universities of Iowa and Houston and Wellesley College. I have a modest portfolio of my published work—articles, three short stories, a chapter in a symposium on industrial health-care programs—and would be prepared to bring it to New York for you to inspect.

I hope you will allow me to submit this prospectus.

Sincerely,

John Weller
31 Gold Gateway
Ratison, Nebraska 68882

If there is any way possible to address your letter to a specific editor, the opening sentence might read: 'Professor Tim Doherty, of Columbia's advanced course on writing, suggested that I send you this letter, with his endorsement.' You can dig deep to find a possible reference, but be scrupulously honest. The recipient of your letter will probably call Doherty: 'Can this kid really write, or is he just whis-

tling Dixie?' Your effort is wasted if you do not enclose a self-addressed, stamped envelope and, as is shown in my sample, you should also include your address in your letter because papers do get lost.

Now back to your other rules. 2. I have known several beginning writers who have gone to New York with no preliminary arrangements and pounded the pavement from one publishing house to the next trying to peddle a finished manuscript or one partly completed. When I was an editor at Macmillan I used to have the job of interviewing such aspirants, and it made all the difference if the young person could place before me a portfolio containing eight or ten articles that had actually been published in various magazines or newspapers. Such displays cried aloud: 'Look! I'm a writer who knows the language and the rules.' Such a practical approach was much more effective than saying: 'I went to Smith College and got an A in English.' Anyone ought to be able to get an A in English. To have learned what to do with that A is a different matter. The portfolio is obviously the same as the letter of inquiry, except that it's delivered in person. I advise the letter, but I have known young people whose portfolio gained attention and a contract.

3. The most effective approach is one in which the publishers come to you rather than you to them. This is accomplished by your publishing first-rate stories in the little magazines that pay nothing but do confer reputation. I can assure you that if you do achieve publication in these journals, New York will hear about it, because every publisher has some editor or scout whose job it is to know what's happening in the prestigious journals. I know of a score of young writers who have followed this route with such success that publishers have written to them, asking them to stop by when in the city or to submit a manuscript or even a plan for a manuscript. Of all the routes I am suggesting, I believe this is the one I would follow if I were in my twenties and had the skill to break into the world of the literary magazines.

4. The approach that seems to produce the maximum number of published books, especially those of merit, is for the graduate of a college that takes writing seriously to move on to a two- or three-year graduate writing course at one of the highly regarded universities. There the young writer meets dedicated professionals familiar with the problems of establishing a foothold in the serious business of writing. Older writers not on the academic faculty may also be in residence and serving as part-time consultants or even participants in one-term seminars. In addition, publishing experts from the big houses and the big agencies will be stopping by to share their experiences. But the most rewarding aspect of the course might be the daily contact with the two dozen or so other young aspirants, some with an obviously superior writing skill. Out of this creative mix surprising things can happen. A professor can spot a student of exceptional talent and arrange for a publisher to take a look. An agent visiting the school learns of a young woman with a powerful novel half completed and accepts the writer as a client. Or the course inspires a young person to take writing more seriously than before, and a book results. I am impressed by what the good writing schools can accomplish and consider the two or three years spent there a worthwhile investment. Even the mediocre schools occasionally produce miracles.

5. I am always surprised when I hear that one of the many summer writing festivals has helped a writer bring his or her talents to the fore, because the ones with which I was acquainted produced little of consequence. But the imposing record is there and cannot be refuted: people in their thirties do attend these seminars, they do become dedicated writers, and they become professionals—not many, but it does happen. In recent years the faculties at some of these summer seminars have been of such high quality that learning can take place and professional friendships can be cultivated. If you cannot afford either time or money for a two-year course at a university, a two-week seminar with good teachers could prove a rewarding substitute. Barnaby Conrad out in Santa Barbara operates one of the best.

6. Recently I have watched the development of a new way for writers outside New York to gain the attention of New York publishers. The writer, often a young woman, lands a job as columnist for a regional newspaper or one of the big-city magazines; she or he writes such exceptional columns about social and political subjects and her fame spreads so widely that she comes to the attention of national publishers. Then a New York editor telephones: 'We've been reading your work. We'd like you to do a book for us.' This route is open to any young

person with writing skills and an intuitive sense of what subjects interest readers.

7. When all else fails, one can follow what might be called the rogue-elephant approach. This involves dragooning a personal friend who happens by chance to know a publisher, an editor, an agent, or an established writer—anyone who functions in the writing profession—who will look at your manuscript and perhaps sponsor it. I hesitate to suggest this publicly because I already receive a plethora of manuscripts, the majority of them dreadful, but I have heard of so many instances in which older writers have helped younger ones that I know it can happen. But without exception, so far as I know, the relationship has been a long-standing personal one and not an acquaintanceship launched by the mailing of an unsolicited manuscript to a writer one does not know. However, the frustration of trying in vain to get a publisher to at least read one's manuscript can be so oppressive that almost any intrusive behavior can be excused, even the trumpeting of a rogue elephant.

Those are the approaches I recommend to my students, but I have been disarmed by one would-be writer who said that my last one sounded like the Hungarian recipe for a ham omelet: 'If your neighbor will give you an end of ham, steal three large eggs,' and I agree that there is a similarity.

How many good publishers are there in America? I looked into this some years back and concluded that while it would be reassuring to be published by Random House, Knopf, Simon and Schuster, Little, Brown, or Doubleday, there are another sixty that would know what to do with a good manuscript if one fell into their hands. They would know how to edit it, design it, print it, and merchandise it, and every year three or four of those lesser-known houses come up with blockbusters. The young writer is not restricted to the famous houses. There are five dozen out there begging for good manuscripts. The big houses seem to attract more of the big books, but some of those little houses are on their way to bigness, and I'd be honored to be published by any of them.

Are there reputable publishers outside New York? Houghton Mifflin and Little, Brown did spectacularly well in Boston, and Lippincott did the same in Philadelphia, although all three houses maintained editorial branches in New York. Regional presses in California and Texas prosper and Henry Regnery does well in Chicago. Also, smaller presses that specialize in regional publishing like Caxton Press for Western themes, and Gulf Publishing in Houston for Southern topics. Many writers launch their careers by writing first for the regional presses and then branching out into the national arena. I would be content to start that way, or even end with the smaller presses.

Would you consider publishing with a vanity press? No. The traditional vanity press charges too much to publish your book, usually does a poor job, sells almost no copies, and in the end asks you to buy back the unsold copies at your expense, even though you've already paid for publishing them. However, if I were determined to see my manuscript in print and had the money to spare, I might pay the $6,000 to satisfy my vanity (hence the name of the system). And every year some professor publishes his own book, sees it catch on with students in other universities and ends up transferring the publishing rights to an established publisher. That is truly entering the profession through the back door, and it is an honorable path to pursue. I have helped pay for the publication of three of my books that were subsequently translated into various foreign languages with considerable success. But that was not vanity publishing: I worked with a reliable house; I knew there would be a market among scholars; I understood the gamble I was taking.

Should I consider one of the university presses? If you're lucky enough to have your manuscript accepted by one of the good university presses, you're fortunate indeed. In recent decades some of these presses have made spectacular advances in publishing major books with major successes. It is true that they generally limit themselves to nonfiction titles, but in that field they often rival the best work done by the bigger commercial houses. And in specialized fields they often excel. I could not have written my Western stories without the great books published by the University of Nebraska Press, whose original books on the West and reprints of older classics proved invaluable. I've had two of my books published by the University of Texas Press, and in editorial assistance, design, printing quality, and skill in distribution, their people equaled the best work done elsewhere. And one of the books was sold to several foreign publishers, and at home became a book club selection. One of my graduate assistants had his first book published by Yale University, his second by Nebraska, and his academic career was launched. Today a gifted writer who specializes in nonfiction books of high quality can build a solid career with university presses.

Do I need an agent? Street wisdom in the profession used to say: 'You don't need an agent until you reach the point in your career at which you don't need an agent.' In the past, very few beginning writers sold their first novels through an agent, but after they proved they could write and sell their novel, four or five agents would offer to take them on as clients. I had none until my third book; today I find my agent invaluable because he takes care of many business matters: he may send me three or four letters a week concerning foreign editions, sudden interest in a book written half a century ago, crazy propositions, and appeals for forewords to other people's books. Without his help I would be completely inundated. I am told that today quite a few first novels are circulated to publishers by agents.

How do I find an agent? When I started, it was easier to find a publisher than an agent. And if you'd published nothing, it was almost impossible. Agents could not afford to invest their time and office expenses in young people who only vaguely 'wanted to write.' They had to conserve their energy for young people with proven talent. The sovereign way to get yourself an agent was to write a good book. The other basic rule was that not even a good agent could help you much on your first book, but on your third he or she could perform miracles. In recent years, however, agents have been helping young writers earn substantial advances for first novels, so the talented beginner now has opportunities that I did not have when I started. A good place to look for names of agents is the *Literary Market Place*, which is available in most libraries.

Can my agent get me an advance on royalties? Yes, but even without an agent most publishers upon issuing a contract to a writer, especially to one who has already published a book, will pay a modest advance to lend encouragement. It is generally not recoverable even if the contract turns sour and no publishable manuscript results, but the publisher accepts that risk in order to cultivate new talent. It might be in the five- to ten-thousand-dollar range. An established writer with a growing reputation might receive a sum in the fifties, but any announced advance beyond that should be greeted with the skepticism one accords the announcement of the latest lottery winner: 'Jane Doe wins ten million.' What she really wins is the interest on ten million spread over many years. The lottery management retains the ten million and doles out only some of the interest that investment earns. The writer who is announced as having received a million-dollar advance is sometimes in a similar situation: he gets the money if each of seven or eight conditions are met, such as bestsellerdom, book club sales, paperback sales, sale of foreign rights, etc., etc. The catch is that by the time all the conditions have been fulfilled, he has earned the million, and if the conditions are not met, and quite often they aren't, he receives only the portion that he has rightfully earned. And even so, if payment is deferred, as it may be for tax reasons, the writer is in exactly the same position as the lottery winner: what he receives is the interest on money that is already his or hers. I have tried to steer away from advances, because they place more pressure on the writer than is wise, and when my contract has contained numerous caveats I have rarely satisfied all of them. The prudent advice to beginners is: 'Accept only the advance you need to live on till the manuscript is finished. You'll sleep more easily.' Cynics preach: 'Grab the maximum advance possible, for if the publisher has a lot of money tied up, he'll have to make an extra effort to sell your book when it comes out.' I would be mortified if my publisher lost money on one of my books, and so would most sensible writers.

If I am lucky enough to find a publisher, should I work on the royalty system or sell my manuscript outright? Go wash your mouth with soap for asking such a question! The history of literature is replete with tragic stories of men and women who sold their manuscripts for pennies only to watch the buyers reap fortunes, and in music such theft has been common. It seems to me there are only two honorable procedures for a writer: you can spend your own hard-earned money with a vanity publisher, who will see that your book is published in hardcover, or you can give your manuscript to an established publisher—if you can find one who will take it—retain the copyright yourself, and take a royalty on each copy sold. Any arrangement in between seems immoral to me and often pathetically unfair. Never sell all rights to your manuscript; writing is an honorable gamble of your talent against the world, and if you're afraid to risk everything on sales to the public, you're not ready to become a professional. I advocate this tremendous gamble without hesitation or qualification. Because my long novels were so expensive to research in far places, and required so much secretarial help, I often had more than a hundred thousand dollars spent before a single page of manuscript was mailed to the editors. If the finished manuscript proved a bust and did not become a published book, the loss was mine, but this did not deter me. I would rather surrender two fingers on my left hand than sell all my rights to a manuscript prior to publication. My right hand, with fingers intact, would refuse to sign the contract. Of course, when one sells a short story to a magazine, there is no arrangement by which a royalty can be paid; that is an outright sale, but you retain the copyright with permission to reprint the story later in a collection of your stories. Or you are free to sell rights to radio, television, or the movies. You also retain rights to sell abroad, for a book that has been well received in the United States could be picked up by four or five foreign-language publishers. Permanent rights are like spare buckets of blood plasma for the writer; they have the capacity to suddenly infuse life into a long-dead manuscript, and if you allow anyone to steal them, you are out of your mind and not ready to be a professional.

Do editors like Maxwell Perkins who aided Hemingway and Thomas Wolfe still exist? Yes. I had two at Random House and I've heard of others like Alex Campbell and Hiram Hayden. But with American publishing falling increasingly into the hands of business conglomerates, editors are becoming acquisition specialists rather than manuscript editors, and writers are the losers, for a sensitive editor can accomplish wonders with even top-flight writers and an occasional miracle with the basically untalented. I would not want to publish without the guidance of a skilled editor, and I listen to what she or he says.

Should a writer cooperate in the publicizing of her or his book? I have found this distasteful, and at my age can determine how much I will do and where, for the traditional tour in which I used to hit five media stations in a single city—five minutes' maximum at each stop with the interviewer not having read the book—was murderous duty, which I now avoid. But if I were a beginning writer you could get me to your store with a postcard. Let me illustrate my high standards. Bob Bernstein, then president of Random House, called me in Maryland: 'Jim? Can you drop over to Washington and hold an autographing session for a bookseller who likes your books?' I replied: 'Bob, you know our deal. One city, three days, and that's it,' and he said: 'You fulfilled every promise and we thank you.' But the next day he called again: 'Jim, it would mean a great deal to me if you'd do the Washington bit,' and again I said I'd completed my obligation and again he agreed. But the next day during his third call he said: 'Jim, I'm afraid I haven't explained the Washington thing. This man, if he likes your performance, has the authority to order thirty-five thousand copies of your book at one shot,' and I said: 'I'll be there.' The beginning writer should do everything within the rules of decency and his or her physical limits to cooperate with the publisher's publicity department in hopes of establishing an identity as a proven writer who intends to be around for a long time.

Does it help if the would-be author is a stunning young woman or a handsome man who looks great in a tweed jacket and smoking a pipe? Yes. One of the principal detriments to my life as a writer has been the regrettable fact that I don't look like one.

Now the Real Questions

So much for the mechanical questions. It has not been illogical to deal with them first, because in every session I conduct—often with mature people who should know better—the first query will be 'How do I find an agent?' as if the manuscript has mysteriously written itself. This has caused me to think: He doesn't want to write a book, he just wants the excitement of having published it. I recall the Arkansas boy, thirteen years old, who unsolicited, sent me his novel of twenty-three pages with the following neatly typed on the cover:

Warning!
This Novel Has Been
Copyrighted

First North American
Serial Rights Only

Like most beginners, he had placed the cart of gratification before the horse of hard work. Let us real writers now concentrate on the writing.

What is the essence of being a writer? It's an act of incredible arrogance for a young girl of sixteen to proclaim: 'I'm going to be an actress.' Consider the odds against her: the competition, the dreary chase after roles, the disappointments, the constant threat of failure. And yet every year some young women succeed in that dream and become glowing stars, bright as any in the heavens. Think how arrogant it is for a young fellow of sixteen to say: 'I'm going to be a sculptor.' How in the world does one become a sculptor? How can he afford the materials? How can he find a teacher? How does he locate a spot at which to exhibit his work if he does succeed in finishing a piece? It seems absolutely impossible for a young man to become a sculptor, yet each year some do. And how about writing an opera and getting it produced? The odds against that are monumental, and yet operas are written and staged and enjoyed. To write and publish a book is infinitely easier than any of the three comparisons I've made, but even so, the young man or woman who aspires will fail unless he or she has what I've come to think of as divine arrogance, an I-can-do-it conviction; that despite all the negatives, it can be done. I advise every young person who aspires to be a writer to cultivate that divine arrogance, because without it I doubt you will succeed. I do not mean bravado or exhibitionism or fatuous display of dress or manner. I mean that assurance I've had even when a manuscript was not going well and doubt assailed me (and with the amount of work I've done I've had those doubts more than most), but as I've risen from bed and gone back to the typewriter I've taken comfort in the thought Well, there's nobody on this block better qualified to lick this problem than me. I'm not sure I believe it, but I'm willing to act on that faith in myself. I recommend that you cultivate such an attitude, but keep it to yourself, and keep it low-key. Think what an arrogant act it is to sit down at a typewriter some morning to start a job that will require three years, and six hundred thousand words typed out three times, and the expenditure of most of your savings. I've done it ten or fifteen times and it would have been impossible had I not been fortified with the divine arrogance of the sixteen-year-old girl who says: 'I can be an actress,' or the boy who tells himself: 'I can write an opera.'

Can writing be taught? No, not unless there is a basic verbal skill to begin with. But if a young person does have the minimal skills required, such as an appreciation of words, a delight in storytelling, a curiosity about human behavior, and a sense of the dramatic, an inspired teacher can accomplish wonders. I believe that almost everything a human being does can be done better with the help of skilled instruction. We have seen that young people with dramatic talent have learned to perfect it at Yale. Young would-be filmmakers have profited from their work at U.C.L.A. And would-be writers have become professionals at Iowa. I could cite at least a dozen similar examples, but I can also point to other schools in which attendance has been largely a waste of time. If you have reasonable cause to think you have the basic skills, take the chance, and enroll in a reputable school.

Suppose I have the arrogance to be a writer, what specific skills do I need? If you answer a lusty affirmative to each of these ten questions, you may be qualified to make the effort. Do I love to tell stories to my friends? Do I see what motivates them in various situations? Am I beginning to understand why men react so differently to certain situations than women—and vice versa? Can I imagine myself a member of the opposite sex? Do I have a sense of the changes that overtake a man or woman during each decade of a life that lasts seventy years? Can I imagine how a baby girl of three sees the seven other children in her kindergarten class? Can I place myself on death row in my last six hours? Can I imagine what it would be like to be a United States senator being reprimanded by the entire Senate for my misconduct? Can I make-believe that I am a female pelican weaving a complicated nest with sticks that my mate brings me? Can I describe five o'clock in the morning on a July day on a Nebraska prairie? There are your first nine questions, and now the most important of all: Do you *want* to do such things? That longing to put dreams into words is the beginning of writing.

When I said 'skills,' I meant things like spelling and typing. What about them? If a young person wants to find the kind of job that writers my age used to seek as an entry to writing, they simply must learn word processing, and the basic skill for that is the ability to type on the keyboard of the ordinary Qwerty typewriter. If you do not already have this skill, learn it immediately, for you will need it in college, in a writing course, or in any job you might take relating to publishing. You will also require it if you want to be a writer.* For a reasonable price you can buy for your word processor a program that will correct your spelling, provide six or seven alternatives to any word you're using, give you a wealth of commonly needed data like the size and population of all the nations of the world, and will also warn you if your sentences are running too long, if you've already used that word, and if you always use clauses in the same dull sequence. By the time you read this, some new genius will have produced a machine that will be able to do not only all that but a great deal more. With a good word processor, a printer, and a set of those new programs, you will have infinitely more aids than I ever had, and you will escape much of the drudgery.† But to enjoy this bonanza you must master Qwerty (the first six letters on the next-to-the-top-line on the typewriter).

What college courses should I take to enhance my prospects as a writer? I assume that you have already acquired a broad vocabulary, that you have a feel for language, and that in high school and college you've learned what sentences and paragraphs are, and I further assume that throughout the rest of your life you will occasionally read books dealing with current theories of language and contemporary rules of usage. What should you do to lift yourself to higher levels of understanding? If I had a daughter or son who truly aspired to be a writer in the most serious sense of that word, I would advise two courses that would jolt her or him out of complacency and reveal whole new compartments of comprehension. First, I would advocate a course in rhythmic dancing to encourage the body and the mind to break loose and glory in the freedom of movement to encourage the sensation of being a free spirit moving in bold new directions. Second, I would strongly advise a course in ceramics, in which the young practitioner at the potter's wheel can feel the mass of inanimate clay mysteriously take form. I believe an inherent sense of form, especially emergent form, is essential to a writer, but I suppose one could also attain this through a well-taught course in introductory architecture, where the sense of great forms uniting and interacting to create a pleasing whole would be nurtured. I acquired much of my sense of form through self-administered courses in geography. You might attain yours through the analysis of the sonata form in classical symphonies and string quartets, or the best popular music of the past thirty years. As to specific subject matter, courses at the college level would be useful: psychology, world history to feel the great movements of people and nations, analyses of contemporary social patterns, and perhaps the study of one other national literature, such as the French, German, or Japanese. Of course one must, in one's spare time, read widely in contemporary literature so as to know what the good writers of one's own day are accomplishing and thus avoid doing what they're already doing. I have long had the suspicion that no young person can become a writer who does not wear glasses by the age of twenty-three; failure to do so would mean that you hadn't done enough reading, and without ample reading I cannot see how one can ever become a writer.

What reading would help me be a better writer of fiction? My mind was blown wide open by Erich Auerbach's *Mimesis,* the study of mimetic writing, storytelling, through the centuries. It taught me what a novel was, although I must admit I did not understand the last two chapters. On the art of the novel I profited from various standard texts, especially Janet Burroway's *Writing Fiction: A Guide to*

*In the seminars at which I assist, we professional writers will not accept any student paper unless it is typed—or word-processed—with the spacing, margins, and neatness one would have if submitting it to a magazine. And it has to be in a dozen or so copies, one for each professor and fellow student. A word processor is almost obligatory.

†A local computer store assures me: 'We can provide a student with a complete machine—processor, advanced software for writers, and a good printer—for a little over fifteen hundred dollars.'

Narrative Craft. I used Fowler's *Modern English Usage* to remind me of what our language really was, but I found many of his strictures overly pedantic and have ignored them in my own writing. I have gained usable insights from my constant reading of literary biographies, always the latest available to check changes in evaluations: Dickens, Balzac, Dostoyevsky, Flaubert, Hugo, Hardy, Hawthorne, Melville, Mark Twain, Dreiser, Hemingway, Fitzgerald, Virginia Woolf, Mrs. Gaskell, De Maupassant, and Goethe—more or less in the order in which I read them. Note that my early education was only in European material and I would have profited from a university writing-school course on the American novelists, for I missed Faulkner and Thomas Wolfe.

What do you consider the main components of a novel? Since I favor storytelling, I stress character, setting theme and plot, plus another factor well exemplified in this story which I have told before, about Alexandre Dumas, *Père*. A brash young man came to him saying: 'Monsieur Dumas, I've studied your novels and know how you do it. I'm going to take your design and write a novel that will surpass anything you've done.' 'Fine,' Dumas said, 'we thrive on competition. But tell me, have you a set of good characters?' The young man was ecstatic about his beautiful princess, his gallant prince, his evil baron, and his helpful priest. 'Great start, but have you an attractive setting?' Indeed yes! The chateaux along the Loire Valley and the back streets of Paris. 'A good plot?' Oh, yes! Twists and turns to delight the mind. And surprises too. 'And have you an overriding theme to hold attention?' Good versus evil, innocence versus corruption. 'Young man,' said Dumas, 'you are in excellent shape. Now all you need are two hundred thousand words, and they had better be the right ones.' In the end it does come down to words, and if you cannot find the right ones, the novel fails.

What is your attitude toward the point of view from which the tale is told? I used to think this did not matter much and was happy with various solutions: the all-wise, uninvolved and unidentified narrator; the shifting point of view as the narration unfolded; the story told from the restricted viewpoint of a principal character; and four different points of view derived from four characters intimately involved in the story. As a result of this experimentation, I have concluded that Henry James may have had the best solution: a sensitive observer informed, and concerned, and familiar with the main characters but not overly intrusive in their lives. Some splendid novels have resulted from this sophisticated approach, but ones just as good have resulted from the first approach, the all-wise, unidentified narrator who has the power to look into the lives of all his or her characters as each takes center stage.

How can I learn to write better dialogue? While working as an editor I was taught that a novel consisted of two almost distinct types of writing: *carry*, in which the forward movement of the novel is revealed in bold strokes, and *scene*, which reveals the character involved in a specific action at a specific site. 'So, as the armies began to gather in the early summer of 1939, Henri and Karl each faced perplexing problems' would be a beginning for an extended passage that set the stage for the action that was to follow. It carries the body of the novel forward. A representative opening sentence for a scene could be: 'When Paula entered the room clutching the paper, he could see that she had read the damaging report and was prepared to defend her husband.' A sentence like that demands that we be allowed to hear what she is about to say and by what steps she proposes to protect her husband. The art of narrative, it seems to me, is the judicious balancing of carry and scene, while the art of the novel as a whole is the revelation of character. But to achieve either, the writer must learn to write good dialogue. How to do this? Study John O'Hara to learn the devices of a master of American spoken language. Read Jane Austen to see how low-keyed, nonhysterical conversation can rivet attention. Reading the printed version of plays from all periods is also instructive, and listening carefully to good motion pictures can teach one how to use minimum words to maximum effect. Heavy dependence on regional dialect is enticing but, I fear, almost always self-defeating, because it drags the book away from the mainstream. Marvelously effective in the short tales of Hardy and Dickens, it can become tedious in larger doses. Yes, a writer can learn to use dialogue effectively, and when she or he does, it can become a scintillating technique. One learns to write carry almost automatically as one masters the rhythms of cultivated language; one has to work to master good scene, since it depends so inescapably on effective dialogue.

You seem to stress fiction at the expense of nonfiction. If true, I've been sadly misguided, because in today's market it seems easier and more profitable to break into the nonfiction field. What may prove to be the best book I've written was nonfiction, *Iberia*, a philosophical travel book on Spain, and I know that often a fine nonfiction book will outsell all the novels. Almost everything I've said about the effective writing of fiction also applies to nonfiction. Remember that nonfiction has one immense advantage: clever editors, their fingers on the pulse of the nation, often suggest titles to their nonfiction writers; this means that when the manuscript arrives, the editor is predisposed to like it and rush it into print. I heard one estimate that 60 percent of the best nonfiction books start in the mind of an editor, not a writer. But I have heard of no major fiction success that was first conceived by an editor and then farmed out to a novelist. (The sequel to *Gone With the Wind* may prove the exception.) Finally, more than half my published books were nonfiction, a fact that few realize.

What role should theme play in a book? Very differently in fiction and nonfiction. The received wisdom is: 'Any novel about a subject is sure to be a bad novel.' Stressing theme too obviously produces mechanical plotting, stereotypical characters, and tedious reading, so the thematic novel is to be avoided. On the other hand, a compelling theme is the lifeblood of the nonfiction book, and none can be so bizarre as to be ineligible for publication; self-help books, diet books, cat books, perceptive analyses of educational problems, acid-etched biographies, tracts for and against warfare, all have been used as the bases for highly successful books. And I would suppose that a high proportion of proposals submitted through the mail to publishers deal with such nonfiction brainstorms, for it is easier to describe effectively the sharply focused theme for a nonfiction book than the outline of a nebulous novel. Theme has been of extreme importance to me, for I have contradicted the advice just given about novelists avoiding thematic approaches. Early in my career I elected to write about far places in turmoil, men at war, new nations emerging, and that decision has served me well—even though I realize that there may have been a better approach that relied less on setting and more on character. If I were a beginning writer today, I would choose as my basic theme for fiction the revolutionized relationships between women and men, especially the difficult new patterns of courtship, marriage, and family life. If I were writing nonfiction I'm sure I would concentrate on recombinant DNA technology, in which the secrets of the forty-six chromosomes are being revealed with such astounding possibilities for the management of our heredity. Any young writer with imagination will be able to identify similar themes that ought to be addressed.

Should I take a job on a newspaper while trying to get started as a writer of books? If I were struggling to establish myself, I would accept almost any writing job that was available, save only the writing of pornography, (it tarnishes a reputation and doesn't even pay well). But handling public relations for a corporation, writing manuals to accompany a manufacturer's machines, managing publicity for a government agency, being staffer on a magazine—I would grab at any of them while I strove to hone my skills. But I would avoid, if I could, the newspaper, for it is an insidious master; since you see yourself in print every day, especially if you have a signed column, the danger is that you come to think of yourself as already being a writer, and the inner fire that is required to drive writers of books is dissipated. The years pass and you do not write your books. But you can console yourself reciting the names of newspaper people who have become fine writers: the Nobel Prize winners for literature Sinclair Lewis, Ernest Hemingway, and Henryk Sienkiewicz. The sportswriters Ring Lardner and Paul Gallico also made the jump, so it can be done. But I think the best collateral job for a would-be writer is working in the token clerk's booth of a New York City subway. You leave work after eight hours with your unused mind eager to tackle something of importance.

Are correspondence courses that promise to teach you how to write any good? None that I have heard of. And some were so rapacious without teaching anything that the law closed them down, to protect foolish subscribers from their own folly.

How about free-lance editors and agents who advertise that they'll help you get your manuscript in shape for submission to publishers? I am instinctively suspicious of such offers. I have never heard of an instance in which such supposed helpers have assisted anyone, but I have heard numerous complaints from would-be writers who were defrauded. Publishers pay their editors good salaries to help writers; agents do take 10 percent of your royalties, but only if they sell the manuscript, and reputable agents take nothing in advance. The prudent rule seems to be: 'Pay nothing to anyone in advance.' Of course, tuition fees to responsible colleges and universities that conduct organized seminars could be an honorable exception to this rule, but only if you pick one that teaches something.

What handbooks have been helpful? I use three dictionaries almost every day: a small book that gives only the spelling of 25,000 words; any one of the fine college dictionaries defining at least 200,000 words; and as big a master dictionary as I can afford, but one providing at least 315,000 entries. At two different desks I use one speller with 25,000 words, another with 35,000, and obviously the latter is some three times more helpful than the first, because most of the difficult words I need are in that additional 10,000. When I locate a speller with 40,000, I'll use it. When selecting either the collegiate-size dictionary (and that is adequate for most writers) or the unabridged, be sure it contains one invaluable feature: the date when the word came into the language, either into English generally or into American usage. For example, *graft* meaning the act of inserting a scion from one plant into the trunk of another was known in A.D. 1350, but *graft* meaning the American habit of collecting money dishonestly, dates only from 1855. Such help is invaluable to a writer of historical material, and by historical I mean dating back even twenty years. The amount of knowledge assembled in one of the big dictionaries is formidable, and writers should occasionally read one of the pages to remind themselves of the rich snippets of information that are available. Every writer needs a thesaurus, and the premier one is Rodale's *The Synonym Finder,* 1,361 pages of no-nonsense listing of words in alphabetical order, each with its four or six or a dozen different meanings, and each of them accompanied by several synonyms. I use my Rodale constantly, but never do I use any of the fancy synonyms that it provides in abundance, such as *nim, defalcate* or *deerjack,* for the word *steal,* but Rodale does remind me of words I already know but could not remember, such as *purloin, filch, mulct, commandeer,* or *plagiarize.* If you expect to spend your life writing, get a Rodale now. *Webster's New Biographical Dictionary* is a treasure for a writer like me; you may not need it as frequently as I do, but its amazing thirty thousand succinct biographies from all over the world is a rich resource, and Bartlett's *Familiar Quotations* has been in print so long and been reedited so many times by brilliant scholars that its plethora of footnotes indicating who first uttered an idea made famous by some who repeated it later are refreshing. For example, the great Swedish naturalist Linnaeus (1707–1778) said: 'Mingle your joys sometimes with your earnest occupation.' But roughly the same had been said by Menander (342–292 B.C.), Horace (65–8 B.C.) and Montaigne (1533–1592) but none better than Horace: 'It is sweet to let the mind unbend on occasion.' Because of my constant reference to geography I must have a big atlas, and the one published by the London *Times,* with those wonderful maps by the Scottish cartographer Bartholomew, is superb, but I have also used with satisfaction the *National Geographic Atlas of the World.* I want to recommend a specialized publication that has traveled with me for half a century, the 1915 version of the German scholar Karl Ploetz's *Epitome of History.* Quickly it went through twenty editions, but I came to know it only in 1940 in the American edition edited by William Langer assisted by a body of mainly Harvard scholars. It summarizes world history, and if a revised edition appears, buy it. I also carry with me a King James Bible containing the most complete concordance that space will permit. I need it weekly.

I love these books, none more than the twenty-nine massive volumes of the eleventh edition of the *Encyclopaedia Britannica* (1911), which I carry from place to place in a truck. The experience I enjoyed most came when I served as usage adviser to Houghton Mifflin's excellent dictionary and read in the material I was vetting: 'An adult English speaker knows that *tlip* is not an English word, and he does not have to go to the dictionary to discover that fact; no English word can begin with *tl-*.' Interestingly, I had just finished writing a book about the Tlingit Indians, among whom I had been living for three years. The word originated in Alaska and appears in dictionaries as a legitimate English word.

What is your final word to aspiring writers?
Remember that most successful writers compose their first three manuscripts at four o'clock in the morning prior to a full day's work in some office. If you can't discipline yourself to do that, you'll never be a writer. Of course, it could just as effectively be after eleven o'clock at night.

ABOUT THE AUTHOR

JAMES A. MICHENER graduated from Swarthmore College and continued his studies at many institutions at home and abroad. After teaching for many years and working as an editor at the Macmillan Publishing Company, at the age of forty he published his first book, *Tales of the South Pacific,* which won a Pulitzer Prize. In the course of the next forty-five years Mr. Michener has written such monumental bestsellers as *Sayonara, The Bridges at Toko-Ri, Hawaii, The Source, Iberia, The Covenant, Centennial, Chesapeake, Space, Texas, Alaska, Poland,* and *Caribbean*. He has taught writing courses and funded writing programs throughout the nation. He is the recipient of honorary doctorates in five fields from thirty leading universities. Decorated with the Presidential Medal of Freedom, America's highest civilian award, he has also been recognized by the President's Committee on the Arts and Humanities for his continuing commitment to the arts in America.

ABOUT THE TYPE

This book was set in Bodoni, a typeface designed by Giambattista Bodoni (1740–1813), the renowned Italian printer and type designer. Bodoni originally based his letter forms on those of the Frenchman Fournier, and created his type to have beautiful contrasts between light and dark.